D0906453

Baseball's Most Notorious Personalities

A Gallery of Rogues

Jonathan Weeks

THE SCARECROW PRESS, INC.
Lanham • Toronto • Plymouth, UK
2013

Published by Scarecrow Press, Inc.
A wholly owned subsidiary of The Rowman & Littlefield Publishing Group, Inc.
4501 Forbes Boulevard, Suite 200, Lanham, Maryland 20706
www.rowman.com

10 Thornbury Road, Plymouth PL6 7PP, United Kingdom

British Library Cataloguing in Publication Information Available

Library of Congress Cataloging-in-Publication Data
Weeks, Jonathan.
  Baseball's most notorious personalities : a gallery of rogues / Jonathan Weeks.
    pages cm
  Includes bibliographical references and index.
  ISBN 978-0-8108-9072-5 (cloth : alk. paper) — ISBN 978-0-8108-9073-2 (ebook) 1.
Baseball players—Biography. 2. Baseball players—Anecdotes. I. Title.
  GV865.A1W4195 2013
  796.3570922—dc23
  [B]
                                                                          2012047692

♾™ The paper used in this publication meets the minimum requirements of American National Standard for Information Sciences—Permanence of Paper for Printed Library Materials, ANSI/NISO Z39.48-1992. Printed in the United States of America.

~

Contents

Acknowledgments

Special thanks to my editor at Scarecrow Press, Christen Karniski, for endorsing my work and for promptly providing answers to my numerous questions. I would also like to extend my gratitude to several fellow SABR members: Jacob Pomrenke, who helped me better understand the White Sox scandal of 1919; Tara Krieger, who helped make the Johnny Allen piece stronger; Jan Finkel, who assisted with the Johnny Mostil bio; and Charlie Pall, who provided inside information about his great-uncle Johnny (Mostil).

Finally, I want to thank my father for promoting my first book and for inspiring so many of my passionate interests (one of which happens to be the greatest game ever invented). You've always been my hero, Dad.

~

Introduction

Of the 17,000-plus players who have worn major-league uniforms over the years, not all were particularly nice or ethical. The activities of a handful were so heinous, in fact, that they left an indelible mark on the sport. Boston Beaneaters catcher Marty Bergen murdered his family in cold blood. Brooklyn Dodgers' outfielder Len Koenecke attacked the pilot of a flight he had chartered in a maniacal attempt to crash the plane.

But baseball, like most human endeavors, has benefited from its dichotomous makeup over the years. Some of the sport's most unsavory characters inadvertently altered the game in a positive way (though I am not suggesting they be commended for their actions). Such was the case with eight members of the 1919 White Sox, who conspired to throw the World Series. In response to the devious scheme, baseball streamlined its power structure and made a concerted effort to eliminate the pervasive influence of gamblers. Likewise, the actions of Carl Mays, who killed an opponent with a brushback pitch, necessitated rule and equipment changes that were long overdue.

Not all of baseball's so-called bad guys were particularly nasty. Some were greatly misunderstood or unfairly stigmatized. Others were highly reputable individuals who committed a single unforgivable act. Roberto Alomar was a model of propriety before he spit in the face of an umpire. Jim Bouton penned one of the most important sports books in baseball history only to be ostracized by peers and rejected by the establishment.

Just as we need heroes to inspire us, we need villains to show us how *not* to behave. *Baseball's Most Notorious Personalities* explores the flip side of fame and glory. Where there are heroes, there are also scoundrels, misfits, and scapegoats.

Welcome to the gallery!
Jonathan Weeks

~

CHAPTER ONE

The Mysterious and the Macabre

Marty Bergen

The biography of Marty Bergen is more unsettling than a well-crafted horror novel. He had almost everything a man could ask for—natural talent, a handsome salary, and a supportive family. But he was mentally unbalanced. Tormented by paranoid delusions, he brutally murdered his wife and children as they slumbered in his New England farmhouse. He ended the rampage with his own grisly suicide.

Born to immigrant Irish parents in North Brookfield, Massachusetts, Bergen got his start in organized ball with a local club known as the Brookfields. Hailing from the same community, Connie Mack was also a member of the team. Bergen's eccentricities were apparent early on as he was known to sulk and stalk off the field if he felt he wasn't receiving adequate fan support. He squabbled with peers often, and in 1891, he engaged in a nasty fistfight with a teammate.

Bergen met his wife, a millworker named Harriet Gaines, the following season. The two were married in July of 1893. By that time, the volatile catcher had established himself as a hot prospect with an independent Northampton team. He joined the Eastern League briefly and ended up being drafted by the Pirates.

When Bergen's contract with Pittsburgh was unexpectedly nullified, the Kansas City Blues acquired his services. Not only did he play stellar defense for the Blues, but also his .372 batting average landed him among the top hitters in the Western League. Still, he was considered a detriment to the

club by president Jimmy Manning, who grew tired of Bergen's incessant griping and foul disposition. The exasperated executive was more than happy
to transfer Bergen's contract to the Boston Beaneaters (later known as the
Braves) in 1896.

Bergen spent four seasons in the big leagues—all of them with Boston. A
lifetime .265-hitter, he enjoyed his finest offensive year in 1898, when he
played in 120 games and established career-high marks with a .280 batting
average, 60 RBIs, and 24 extra-base hits. He also gunned down a total of 96
would-be base stealers while accruing a range factor (average putouts and
assists per game) of 5.17—third best in the National League.

Boston won two pennants with Bergen behind the plate, and sportswriters were soon singing his praises. One contemporary referred to him as "the
greatest catcher who ever looked through a mask." His impact would be lasting as Yankee manager Miller Huggins later ranked him among the top three
catchers of all time, behind Roger Bresnahan and Johnny Kling. Huggins
knew a thing or two about greatness, having piloted three world championship squads in the Bronx.

Off the field, Bergen is said to have had an amiable relationship with his
three children, Martin, Joseph, and Florence. He was sometimes spotted by
neighbors playing with them contentedly on the family's North Brookfield
property. But on the diamond, Bergen was at war with the entire league.
By May of 1896, the troubled star was already having problems with Boston teammates. A reporter described him as "a sullen, sarcastic chap" who
avoided peers and was perpetually discontent.

In a long series of unpleasant incidents, Bergen slapped future Hall of
Famer Vic Willis in the face after the hurler innocently seated himself
at Bergen's table in the dining room of a St. Louis hotel. He would later
threaten the entire club after a scuffle in the dugout. As could only be expected, he was a tremendous detriment to team morale. He was one of the
club's highest paid players, making more than twice the average American
salary at the peak of his brief career.

Injured while sliding into home at the end of the 1898 campaign, Bergen
underwent surgery for a hip abscess. He was put under anesthesia for several
hours, and sources close to him reported that he never fully recovered his
faculties afterward. His mental health suffered another serious blow in April
of 1899 when his eldest son, Martin, died of diphtheria. During a June road
trip, Bergen hopped off a train carrying players to Cincinnati and returned
to his home without permission.

When *Boston Globe* reporter Tim Murnane showed up at Bergen's farmhouse to investigate, the anguished catcher made numerous paranoid claims,

charging that his teammates were rooting against him. He also expressed outrage at the $300 fine levied by owner Arthur Soden for his desertion. Though he would return to the club after a brief absence, he would pull the same stunt in September, claiming a hand injury. In all, he sat out 80 games during the '99 slate.

At the end of the season, Bergen voiced concern to his doctor about his deteriorating mental state. He admitted that he sometimes had "strange ideas" and felt as if people were out to get him. The physician—a man named Dionne—prescribed medicine, but Bergen refused to take it unless he mixed it himself. It certainly didn't improve his condition.

In the early morning hours of January 19, 1900, Bergen suffered a final psychotic break. He grabbed an axe and used the blunt side to bludgeon his wife to death in their bedroom. From there, he proceeded to his son's chambers, where he used the sharpened blade to deliver a single fatal blow. After mauling his daughter in the same fashion as his wife, he grabbed a razor and sliced his own throat, nearly severing his head in the process. An article in the *Morning Herald* stated candidly that Bergen's "idiosyncrasies on the baseball field were only equaled by his peculiar dealings with the Boston club." Owner Arthur Soden expressed deep regrets and confessed that he had suspected for quite a while that Bergen "was not of sane mind."

At the time of the murder/suicide, Bergen's brother was working his way up through the minors. Marty had spent a great deal of time teaching his younger sibling the finer points of catching. In 1901, those efforts came to fruition as Bill Bergen joined the major-league ranks and remained there for 11 years, earning wide acclaim for sparkling defensive play. Interestingly, Bill failed to learn anything about hitting from his homicidal brother, posting the lowest career average of any player with a minimum of 2,000 plate appearances (.170). At least he managed to get along with teammates throughout his career.

Johnny Mostil

The story of Johnny Mostil is a curious one indeed. Among the top center fielders in the American League (AL), he showed no overt signs of mental instability prior to his graphic suicide attempt during spring training of 1927. Questioned about his motives, he failed to provide a satisfactory explanation. The episode remains one of baseball's most intriguing mysteries.

Mostil grew up in Chicago. As a boy, he enjoyed the thrill of sneaking into big-league ballparks, reportedly tearing his First Communion clothes climbing the fence at the Cubs' West Side Grounds. On another occasion, he was personally reprimanded by Charles Comiskey for entering White Sox Park without permission. He had no idea at the time that he would play for the iconic executive several years later.

According to some reports, a Chicago cabdriver who had spent time in the minors spotted Mostil playing second base on a sandlot in 1918 and drove him to Comiskey Park, where a tryout was arranged. Mostil performed well enough to be offered a contract. An opportunity surfaced when Eddie Collins joined the Marines and Mostil was briefly installed as a second baseman. He hit .273 during a 10-game trial but was demoted to Milwaukee of the American Association. In hindsight, the club was actually doing him a favor since he would avoid being implicated in the 1919 World Series scandal.

Demonstrating superior speed, Mostil was converted to a center fielder. He had a breakout year in 1920 with 45 extra-base hits and a .318 batting average for the Brewers. On the strength of those numbers, he landed himself a permanent roster spot with the White Sox the following year. By 1921, most of Chicago's top players had been banned from baseball for conspiring to throw the World Series. The effects were disastrous as the Sox would finish in the second division for nearly two decades. Disgusted with the entire affair, many fans turned their attentions elsewhere. Mostil gave loyal patrons something to cheer for.

A patient batsman with a keen eye, Mostil cracked the .300 mark four times between 1921 and 1926. He was fearless at the plate, getting hit by more pitches than any of his AL peers on three occasions. In his first few seasons, he was often used as a fifth- or sixth-slot hitter. When he later emerged as a threat on the base paths, he was moved to the top of the batting order. He would lead the league in stolen bases twice as a leadoff man. Mostil was far too modest about his abilities, commenting to a writer in 1960: "If it hadn't been for my fielding, I'd have trouble holding my job. You see, a .300-hitter in those days would be something like a .240-hitter today."

It's true that some of Mostil's finest moments occurred while patrolling the outfield. Hall of Fame pitcher Ted Lyons remarked that it was "like turning a rabbit loose" whenever the ball was hit in Mostil's direction. One popular anecdote alleges that he was the only center fielder in history to catch a foul ball. The play in question reportedly occurred during a 1925 spring training game at Nashville. According to numerous accounts, Mostil actually beat left fielder Bibb Falk to the ball. Mostil's superb defense preserved a perfect game for Charlie Robertson in 1922 and a no-hitter for Ted Lyons four years later.

Robertson's gem was just the fifth perfect game in history. He was so dominant against the Tigers that afternoon, both Ty Cobb and Harry Heilmann halted play to accuse the right-hander of doctoring the baseball. In a rare left field appearance, Mostil bailed Robertson out of trouble in the second inning with a diving foul-line catch on a liner by Johnny Bassler to end the game. During Lyons's magnum opus, Mostil made a shoestring grab on a hard smash by Boston's Baby Doll Jacobson. He then made an accurate throw to first base, catching Jack Tobin off the bag to end the first inning. During the course of his stellar defensive career, Mostil posted the highest range factor (average putouts and assists per game) among AL center fielders on four occasions. He ranks third of all time in that category behind Taylor Douthit and Richie Ashburn.

The wide-ranging Chicago ball hawk reached the peak of his career in 1926, when his productive bat and slick glove landed him second in MVP voting to George Burns of the Indians. He reached career-high marks in hits (197) and doubles (41) while accruing a .328 batting average. It was all downhill from there. By 1927, Mostil's health had taken a downward turn. He was suffering from a recurring dental condition and also from neuritis, an inflammation of nerves that caused him chronic pain. Reporters had insinuated that he was a hypochondriac. When he arrived at the White Sox spring training facility in Shreveport before the '27 slate, he was pretty rundown.

Checking into the Hotel Youree, Mostil was treated by one of the team's trainers for dental issues. During his first round of batting practice, he was hit in the chest with a ball. A doctor later looked him over and reported to teammate Ray Schalk that Mostil was in "bad shape."

The next day, practice was cancelled due to rain. After spending a portion of his idle time napping at the team's hotel, Mostil reportedly paid a visit to Red and Irene Faber. When that conversation was concluded, the ailing center fielder stopped by the room of Pat Prouty—an avid White Sox supporter who often traveled with the team. Prouty didn't answer the door, so Mostil let himself in.

A ghastly scene awaited Prouty when he returned to his room a bit later. Mostil lay sprawled on the bathroom floor in a pool of his own blood. According to newspaper accounts, the troubled star had used a pocketknife and razor to inflict 13 separate wounds to his neck, legs, wrist, and chest. Several teammates, among them Ray Schalk and Willie Kamm, administered first aid while an ambulance was en route. The wounds were so severe that Mostil was not initially expected to survive.

Members of Mostil's family were shocked by the sudden turn of events. His mother, Barbara, reportedly collapsed when she heard the news. Questioned by the press, all were at a loss to explain his actions. Defying a fatal prognosis, the resilient fly chaser left the hospital on March 28. He predicted a speedy return to the club but was listed as voluntarily retired in late May.

At that point, he still had not provided a viable public explanation for his impetuous behavior.

Several theories still exist, including the proposition that Mostil was distressed over financial matters. It has also been suggested that the outfielder was having an affair with Red Faber's wife, which led to a dramatic confrontation between the two. The first hypothesis can be summarily dismissed since Mostil had just signed a lucrative contract. The second assumption has been supported by the accounts of Bob O'Farrell, a teammate of Mostil's, and Johnny Dickshot, a former player and friend of Faber's. Without the testimony of Faber and Mostil, however, those claims cannot be substantiated. Faber remained married to his wife until the time of her death in 1943 and maintained an affable attitude toward Mostil in later years—facts that have led some researchers to consider other explanations.

One hypothesis that has grown in popularity involves a combination of factors. For certain, Mostil's painful neurological condition played a major role in his actions. But Mostil may also have been distraught over the loss of his longtime girlfriend, Margaret Carroll, to teammate Bill Barrett. Mostil reportedly began dating Carroll in 1924, and the relationship grew serious enough to include discussion of marriage at some point. Carroll and Barrett did end up together (they were wed in 1929), though the timeline of their romance cannot be firmly established. Carroll was not at spring training in 1927. She could indeed have been having an affair with Barrett at the time, but she could also have started the relationship *after* Mostil's suicide attempt. Mostil later confided to family members that his actions were irrational. He kept the details of his relationship with Carroll to himself.

Making a remarkable recovery, Mostil returned to the White Sox in September of '27. Signs of rust were evident as he misplayed the only ball hit to him in his first defensive assignment. He got into a total of 13 games that year and managed just 2 hits in 16 at-bats. He returned to full-time duty in '28 but had clearly lost a step on the bases, swiping just 23 bags in 43 attempts. In May of '29, he tripped over home plate executing a double steal and broke his ankle. He was out for the rest of the season and would never return to major-league play.

Mostil played and managed in the White Sox farm system into the 1950s, guiding his teams to a handful of playoff appearances and one league championship. He also served as a Chicago scout for nearly two decades. He retired from baseball at the age of 73. At the time of his death in 1970, he was living in a nursing home in Midlothian, Illinois. He was posthumously elected to the Hammond Sports Hall of Fame.

Eddie Waitkus

Eddie Waitkus didn't live long enough to see director Barry Levinson's 1984 classic *The Natural*, but he would almost certainly have been pleased to see himself portrayed on the big screen by the rakish Robert Redford. The film, which depicts a rising young baseball star shot by a mysterious woman on a train, was based on Waitkus's actual experience. In 1949, the Philly infielder fought for his life after being gunned down by a stalker in a Chicago hotel room. The slug entered the right side of his chest and settled precariously in the back of his lung. Numerous surgeries were required to repair the damage. At the root of this sordid drama was a mentally unstable teenager named Ruth Steinhagen.

Described by her mother as a "nervous" sort, Steinhagen had grown up in a lower-middle-class Chicago neighborhood. A bright pupil, she skipped a grade in high school before moving on to business college. Upon finishing her studies, she landed a job as a typist and moved into a local rooming house. Things appeared to be looking up. But somewhere along the line, she developed an unhealthy obsession that would eventually drive her to homicide. The obsession was Eddie Waitkus.

Waitkus was born in Cambridge, Massachusetts. He was a precocious student, fluent in four different languages. After his high school graduation, he played for Boston College briefly and then joined a semi-pro team based in Lisbon Falls, Maine. Moving up the ladder, he logged time in the Three-I and Texas Leagues before making a brief appearance with the Chicago Cubs in 1941. He failed the audition and was sent to Los Angeles of the Pacific Coast League. He played splendidly there, accruing a .336 average with 40 doubles in 1942. Invited to spring training with the Cubs again the following year, he was drafted into the army.

As a member of the 4th Engineer Special Brigade, Waitkus saw fierce combat overseas while taking part in amphibious landings in the Dutch East Indies and the Philippines. He was wounded in action and earned several battle stars. Honorably discharged in 1945, he was finally granted an elusive roster spot with Chicago.

The left-swinging first baseman made quite an impression in his first full season, hitting .304 while playing solid defense. Known as a reliable glove man throughout his career, he would finish among the top five in fielding percentage seven times between 1946 and 1954. At the plate, Waitkus had little power but hit for average, maintaining a mark of at least .283 in eight of his 11 big-league campaigns. After three full seasons in the Windy City, he was traded along with fading right-hander Hank Borowy to the Phillies in exchange for Monk Dubiel (a pitcher of little note) and Dutch Leonard, a valuable knuckleballer who would anchor the Chicago bull pen. No one was more aware of this transaction than Waitkus's number one fan, Ruth Steinhagen.

While living with her parents, Steinhagen was known to spread out pictures of Waitkus and stare longingly at them for hours on end. She once confided to her mother that she had nearly fainted at Wrigley Field one afternoon when Waitkus had walked past her in close proximity. Later still, she announced her intention of shooting the marquee first-sacker. Edith Steinhagen failed to take this threat seriously at the time, but when Ruth became distraught over the Waitkus trade—quitting her office job and acting more fanatical than usual—Edith convinced her daughter to meet with a psychiatrist.

Waitkus was off to a hot start with Philadelphia in 1949, hitting .307 through 53 games on his way to earning his second All-Star selection. Back in Chicago, Steinhagen was setting the stage for one of the most bizarre and frightening encounters in baseball history. At some point during the month of May, she purchased a rifle from a pawnshop and requested a full tutorial on how to load, fire, and disassemble it. She then consulted the Phillies' schedule to determine when they would be playing a series of games in Chicago. After obtaining a ticket for a June 14 matchup between the two clubs, she booked a room at the Edgewater Beach Hotel on Lake Shore Drive under a false identity—Ruth Ann Burns of Boston.

The police sergeant who took Steinhagen into custody referred to the psychotic 19-year-old as a "pathological liar" who seemed to "enjoy playing the role of a thrill-killer." Waitkus commented after the fact that she had "the coldest-looking face" he had ever seen. Her actions certainly contradicted the presence of a conscience. Hours before her confrontation with Waitkus, she attended a game at Wrigley Field that ended in a convincing 9–2 Philadelphia victory. Waitkus had a good day offensively, scoring twice in five plate appearances while running his on-base percentage up to .403. Steinhagen later described her experience at the park as "wonderful."

Returning to the hotel, she ate dinner and had several alcoholic beverages delivered to her room. She then composed two notes: one to her parents and one to Waitkus. In the latter memo, she gave Waitkus her false identity and room number and then asked him to see her "as soon as possible" to "discuss something of importance." Waitkus took the bait, phoning her room promptly. When Steinhagen insisted that she couldn't discuss matters over the phone, the unsuspecting infielder actually showed up at her door.

Steinhagen had originally intended to stab Waitkus with a paring knife. She placed the rifle, a .22 caliber Remington, in a nearby closet as backup. When Waitkus entered the room, Steinhagen was concealing the blade, but she opted for plan B after he unexpectedly sat down. Removing the rifle from the closet and aiming it at the stunned ballplayer, she told him: "For two years you've been bothering me. Now I've got a surprise for you. You're going to die" (several versions of the statement exist). With that, she shot him in the chest, narrowly missing his heart.

As Waitkus lay in a semi-conscious state, Steinhagen phoned the hotel operator to inform them of her crime. She then sat idly waiting for the police to show up. The crime scene was a study in madness. The rifle lay discarded on the floor near Waitkus's inert form. A framed action photo of Waitkus was situated on a nearby table. A scorecard was recovered with the words "Eddie Waitkus is a schmoe" scrawled upon it. Dozens of other baseball items were found in Steinhagen's suitcase, revealing the depth of her infatuation— statistics, armbands, Cubs' pennants, and ticket stubs from numerous games she had attended in Chicago.

Hospital personnel reported that the wound would have killed anyone in poor physical condition. As Waitkus fought to hang on, Steinhagen was taken to a Cook County jail. She was cooperative and chatty, going on about her compulsion to kill someone famous. She also explained that the All-Star first baseman had caused her great "anguish" because he bore a striking re-semblance to her father.

Waitkus's condition gradually improved, and Steinhagen was taken to his bedside at the hospital to be identified. She avoided eye contact when she was implicated as his assailant and refused to answer when questioned about her motives by police escorts. While incarcerated, she was seen frequently by Doctor William Haines of the county behavioral clinic to assess her mental status. Waitkus maintained a bitter attitude, telling reporters that he would prosecute her himself if she was found to be sane. After extensive interviews, Doctor Haines decided this was not the case, and Steinhagen was transferred to Kankakee State Hospital for treatment. She would remain there until she was 22 years old.

Inspired by his near-death experience, Waitkus battled his way back into major-league action. His finest hour was 1950 as he reached career-best totals in hits (182), doubles (32), and runs scored (102). He also led the league in putouts while posting a .993 fielding percentage—second best in the circuit. The Phillies were heavily laden with youthful talent that year, knocking off the powerful Dodgers on their way to a World Series berth. Waitkus played in all four games against Casey Stengel's Yankees. He reached base six times but failed to score or collect an RBI in the New Yorkers' efficient sweep. He would play steady ball through the 1953 slate before another trade moved him to Baltimore. Interestingly, an insurance claim on Waitkus's behalf was denied by the state workman's compensation board since he was not at work at the time of the shooting. He retired from the majors after the '55 slate and, in later years, worked as an instructor at the Ted Williams baseball camp.

In 1952, Steinhagen was declared sane and absolved of any legal charges in the unfortunate incident. Upon her release, she told reporters she hoped to work at Kankakee State Hospital as an occupational therapist. That same year, Bernard Malamud released his novel *The Natural*, in which one of the central antagonists is loosely based on Steinhagen. The mysterious and dark character, Harriet Bird, was played by Barbara Hershey in the 1984 film.

Don Wilson

Baseball has seen its fair share of tragic deaths, many of which fall into the realm of the suspicious and unexplained. Few such cases rival the story of Astros' pitcher Don Wilson, who was found dead in his garage in January of 1975. Though officials could find no verifiable evidence of murder or suicide, many questions still remain.

Wilson was born in Louisiana, but moved to Compton, California, where he grew up. He played Little League ball with future All-Stars Reggie Smith and Roy White. He later attended Centennial High School, which produced a gaggle of noteworthy players over the years, among them Lonnie Smith, Al Cowens, and Hubie Brooks. By the time Wilson entered 11th grade, hordes of scouts were in attendance every time he took the hill. Interest quickly waned after he suffered an arm injury during his senior year. An Angels' representative told him he would never pitch in the majors.

Refusing to accept that prognosis, he got back into playing shape at Compton Junior College. He effectively mastered a fastball/slider combination and was signed by the Colt .45s (known as the Astros after the '64 slate). In his first three professional seasons, he compiled a 29–16 record at various minor-league levels. He made his big-league debut at the end of the '66 campaign, tossing six strong innings in a relief win against the Reds, a team he would dominate throughout his career.

Pegged as a future staff ace, expectations were quite high during spring training of '67. Wilson got off to a slow start that year, losing three of his first four decisions. Briefly removed from the rotation after tearing an arm muscle, he eventually found his groove with a no-hitter against the Braves and a 13-strikeout effort versus the Giants. He also set a team record with 25 consecutive scoreless innings at one point.

Wilson's fastball had dramatic movement. He claimed that he could aim it at an opponent's belt and watch it rise to shoulder level by the time it reached the plate. Though he attained most of his strikeouts with the hard stuff, he later became a more complete player when he added a breaking ball and off-speed pitch to his repertoire.

There were plenty of other talented youngsters on the Houston roster during the late 1960s, among them second baseman Joe Morgan, center fielder Jim Wynn, and right fielder Rusty Staub. The pitching was relatively sparse, however, and the Astros placed fourth or lower in seven of Wilson's eight full campaigns. Between 1967 and 1974, the hard-throwing right-hander won at least 10 games every year. He reached a personal-best mark of 16 victories twice and tied a single-game major-league record for strikeouts (18—since broken) during the '68 campaign. He added a second no-hitter to his resume the following year.

Racial tensions were running pretty high in those days, and Wilson inadvertently drew some unwanted attention when he began rooming with first baseman Curt Blefary on road trips. Though baseball was integrated at that point, it was still an uncommon practice for Wilson to share his living space with a white player. An even bigger controversy arose in 1972, when Joe Morgan publicly accused manager Harry Walker of being a racist. Walker vehemently denied the charge as the media storm eventually subsided.

In '73, Wilson had his own problems with management. By that time, Walker had been replaced by the fiery Leo Durocher. Wilson was experiencing a frustrating season on the hill, having set a lofty personal goal of 25 wins for himself. In July, he was fined $300 and threatened with suspension when he called Durocher a crude name on the team bus. Durocher wanted to make sure he had heard Wilson correctly and asked the hurler to repeat himself. Wilson gladly accommodated him—several times.

In one of the most exasperating highlights from Wilson's career, he came within three outs of joining an elite group of pitchers with three no-hitters. It happened in a '74 game against Cincinnati. Through eight innings, Wilson had walked five and hit a batter, but had still not yielded a base hit. Despite this commanding performance, the Reds were leading, 2–1, thanks to a costly error by shortstop Roger Metzger. With Wilson slated to lead off the bottom of the eighth, manager Preston Gomez lifted him in favor of a pinch hitter. The no-hitter was lost by reliever Mike Cosgrove in the ninth when Tony Perez singled. The Astros failed to score in the bottom of the frame, making the game just another loss for Wilson. Though the exasperated hurler initially avoided reporters, he later commented affably to the media that he had "nothing but admiration" for Gomez.

Wilson was quite busy during the off-season of '74. He worked for the Astros' Speakers Bureau, an organization that booked public engagements for players. He also agreed to instruct at a youth baseball clinic along with pitcher Tom Griffin. Just days before his death, he served as a line judge for an ABC-TV competition called "Women's Superstars," which took place at the Astrodome. An unexpected debate arose when he failed to call an infraction on golfer Jane Blalock after she stepped over the line during a softball throw event. Responding to an official protest, Wilson was confronted by organizers Billie Jean King and Donna de Varona.

Controversy of a more serious nature would arise when Wilson was found dead at his Texas home. His body was discovered on the passenger side of the family vehicle in a garage adjoining the house. His son Alexander was also found dead in an upstairs bedroom. There was carbon monoxide gas throughout the building, and early reports categorized the fatalities as accidental. On further inspection, some of the details didn't add up.

Wilson's nine-year-old daughter, Denise, was found in her bedroom in a coma (from which she would later recover). His wife, Bernice, had somehow sustained a fractured jaw. Both were transported to a nearby hospital. Questioned by police, Bernice Wilson said she had been awoken by the sound of the car running. She decided to check on the children when she suspected she heard them "crying in their sleep." Unable to wake them, she reportedly carried young Alexander to the master bedroom and closed the door to Denise's room. Kept awake by the car's engine, she went downstairs to inspect the garage. Upon finding her husband's body, she allegedly called a friend— a registered nurse—who told her to check for a pulse. Initially, she had no recollection of how she had sustained the jaw injury.

In the days that followed, the plot thickened. An autopsy revealed that Wilson's blood alcohol level had been well over the legal limit. When police had arrived on the scene, the passenger side door of the vehicle, a '72 Thunderbird, was open along with the garage doors. The ignition was on and the car was out of gas. As near as investigators could figure, Wilson had arrived home around 1:00 a.m. His body was not discovered until more than 12 hours later.

While various media sources speculated about the possibility of a suicide, Bernice Wilson offered no further insight into the nature of her injuries. She initially said she might have been hit and then claimed she had fallen against a wall days prior to her husband's death. A family doctor later released an official statement that she was suffering from an "infected salivary gland." At that point, police were unable to classify the deaths as "accidental" due to numerous unanswered questions.

Less than two weeks into the investigation, Bernice began addressing all inquiries through her lawyer. It was an established fact that the Wilsons' marriage had been less than blissful. At least one journalist hypothesized that the death had come on the heels of a domestic disturbance. In the end, there was no sustainable evidence of foul play, however, and the case was closed on February 5. Despite an official ruling of "accidental death," the medical examiner noted that Bernice Wilson never adequately explained what her husband was doing in the car. The detective assigned to the case reported that she was "claiming amnesia" for the entire chain of events.

Wilson's uniform number (40) was retired by the Astros. Teammates wore black patches on their sleeves to honor him during the '75 campaign. Today, lingering doubts still exist regarding the circumstances of his demise. Even a superficial examination of the facts invites questions. What transpired during the 12 hours after Wilson arrived home? What happened to Bernice's jaw, and why did she hide behind her lawyer after altering her testimony? The answers will likely never be known.

Chick Stahl

In the annals of Red Sox history, the story of Chick Stahl is among the more puzzling and tragic. A key contributor to Boston's first World Series victory, he would firmly establish himself as one of the top outfielders in the game. But personal strife would drive him to suicide in the prime of his career. More than a hundred years later, his death remains shrouded in mystery.

Born in Avila, Indiana, to devout German Catholic parents, Stahl had enough siblings to form two baseball teams. He was one of 24 children. He grew up in Fort Wayne and got his first big break with the Roanoke Magicians of the Virginia State League in 1895. He doubled as a pitcher but ultimately became a full-time outfielder after accruing a .311 batting average with 49 extra-base hits. Signed by the Buffalo Bisons of the Eastern League the following year, he led the circuit in triples and runs scored.

The Boston Beaneaters acquired his contract in 1897. Though manager Frank Selee intended to use him as a stopgap in the outfield, Stahl quickly earned a full-time position with his reliable bat and smooth fielding. By the end of the year, he had established a franchise record for rookies with an impressive .354 batting average. The Beaneaters won the pennant in '97 and '98 as Stahl played marvelously both years.

After the 1900 slate, teammate Jimmy Collins landed a contract to play and manage for a different Boston squad in the newly formed American League. He convinced Stahl to follow him. In the early days, the Red Sox wore blue stockings and were referred to by various names, the most popular being "Americans." Stahl put up sturdy numbers for the fledgling ball club in 1901, finishing among the league leaders in numerous statistical categories. He also drew unneeded attention when a peculiar scene unfolded during the off-season.

Stahl was walking up the street in his home town of Fort Wayne when a woman named Louise Ortman pulled a gun from the folds of her dress and tried to shoot him. A local police superintendent had received a tip that "Lulu," a 22-year-old stenographer, was stalking the unwary outfielder. Somehow, the officer showed up in the nick of time to disarm and apprehend the troubled woman. She later claimed that she had been having an affair with Stahl and was feeling jilted. Stahl dropped the charges, declining comment. It would not be the last time he was associated with a scandal.

A leg injury in 1903 limited Stahl to 77 games, but he recovered sufficiently to appear in baseball's first official World Series. The marquee outfielder played in all eight games against Pittsburgh, collecting 10 hits—4 of them for extra bases—in a Boston win. The following season, he led the league with 19 triples, helping the Americans to another pennant. There would be no Series that year as Giants' owner John T. Brush boycotted the affair, claiming that it would damage the credibility of his club to participate in a showdown against an inferior team. It would be the only year without a World Series until the strike-shortened season of 1994.

Inexplicably, the entire Boston club fell into a slump in 1905. Catcher Lou Criger hit .198 while four other regulars failed to surpass the .250 mark. Stahl ended up nearly 50 points below his career average as the Americans dropped to fourth place with a mediocre 78–74 record. Stahl got back on track the following year, but the club played abysmally. Even the great Cy Young posted a substandard 13–21 record on the mound. With the team floundering in last place during late August, Manger Jimmy Collins took an unauthorized vacation and was suspended. Stahl was named active manager. He was even less successful than his predecessor, guiding the club to a pitiful 9–21 September record. In what would prove to be the last game of his career, he homered off New York Highlanders' pitcher Tom Hughes.

In November of '06, Stahl married Julia Harmon, whom he had met at a church function. He also accepted the manager's position for '07 at the urging of owner John Taylor. Even with the endorsement of his good friend Jimmy Collins, he took the job with reluctance. Well liked by teammates,

Stahl's kindhearted personality made him ill suited to run a baseball club. Before the team had even finished spring training, he resigned from his post, explaining that the release of players (a frequent occurrence that time of year) made him "sick at heart." He agreed to serve as temporary acting manager until a replacement was secured.

Stahl sent a telegram to his wife, telling her he felt good about his decision. He added that, with managerial distractions aside, he could now go out and play to the best of his abilities. But it was not to be. According to some sources, he developed a wound that was slow to heal at some point during the spring and was given carbolic acid—a widely used antiseptic—to clean it with. On March 28, he ate breakfast, checked the state of the practice field, and returned to his hotel suite, which he shared with Jimmy Collins. Collins witnessed Stahl disappear into an adjacent room and then stagger back toward his bed shortly afterward. Having consumed a lethal dose of carbolic acid, he collapsed in a heap.

Several accounts of Stahl's final words exist. The most widely accepted is as follows: "I couldn't help it. I did it, Jim. It was killing me and I couldn't stand it. . . ." Stahl writhed in agony and died within 15 minutes of ingesting the poison. Since his death was listed as a suicide, he was denied a Catholic burial. His funeral was attended by thousands, nevertheless, with the eulogy being delivered by Congressman James Robinson.

The reasons for Stahl's suicide and the nature of his dying words would be debated for many years. A reputable source claimed that Stahl had a "dark secret," but it was never revealed to the public. Several notable historians believe that, in March of 1907, Stahl was threatened with blackmail by a woman who claimed to be carrying his child. The impending scandal theoretically drove him to suicide.

Valuable insight was provided in a news story published shortly after Stahl's death. In it, several close associates confided that the popular star had been suffering from depression and suicidal thoughts for years. Predisposed to feelings of hopelessness, the stress of managing a slumping major-league club must have been quite difficult to bear.

In a racy theory based on circumstantial evidence, it has also been suggested that Stahl was having a homosexual affair with a man named David Murphy, a railroad engineer. Murphy, described as an "intimate friend" of Stahl's, took his own life with carbolic acid and left a note requesting that he be buried next to the fallen ballplayer. Some researchers believe that this may have been Stahl's previously mentioned "dark secret."

Murphy's suicide was the second associated with Stahl. The day after Stahl's passing, the *New York Times* reported that a shoemaker named

Stanley Kennison had taken his own life in Lynn, Massachusetts. Upon drinking a lethal dose of carbolic acid, he told his associates at the Ward 6 Democratic Club: "I've done what Chick Stahl did." Kennison had no direct association with the deceased ballplayer.

In Stahl's absence, four different men managed the Boston club in 1907, including Cy Young. The impact of Stahl's death was immense and proved to be a major distraction all year as the team finished in seventh place with a 59–90 record. In June, an exhibition game was played in Providence to raise money for Stahl's widow, Julia.

Completing the epic tragedy, Julia Stahl's body was found in the doorway of a Boston tenement house in November of 1908, an apparent victim of a robbery/murder. Elaborate rumors circulated that Mrs. Stahl had been drugged in a bar by a man who intended to steal the jewelry she was wearing. Four people were held for questioning but were cleared of wrongdoing when all of Julia's trinkets were eventually accounted for.

Len Koenecke

Life can be full of bitter disappointments. It's how we adapt to them that defines our character. Faced with losing his roster spot in Brooklyn during the 1935 campaign, Len Koenecke came completely unhinged. His senseless death is among the most bizarre chapters in baseball history.

Born in Baraboo, Wisconsin, Koenecke took a job with the Chicago and Northwestern Railroad upon finishing school. He was assigned the duties of a fireman, a grueling job that involved feeding the firebox with fuel. Several sources agree that Koenecke developed an impressive physique while employed in this capacity.

When not riding the rails, Koenecke played amateur ball in Wisconsin and Michigan, landing his first professional contract in 1927 with the Moline Plowboys of the Mississippi Valley League. In 117 games, he topped the circuit with 20 homers while hitting at a brisk .343 pace. Over the next four seasons, he would appear with four different minor-league clubs before earning a roster spot with the New York Giants in April of '32. Enthralled with Koenecke's talents, the Giants traded $75,000 worth of players to obtain his contract. He hit .255 in 42 games, failing to impress manager John McGraw. Demoted to the International League, the media referred to him as "the $75,000 Bust."

Koenecke continued his path to the majors undaunted, reaching the 200-hit threshold with the Buffalo Bisons in 1933. This caught the attention of Casey Stengel, who summoned him to Brooklyn the following year. The '34

Dodgers were a middling squad in need of help. The offense was driven by first baseman Sam Leslie and second-sacker Tony Cuccinello. In the throes of chronic alcoholism, Hall of Famer Hack Wilson was of minimal use to the club. The 30-year-old Koenecke was a standout in his first full major-league season, setting a new record for outfielders with an impressive .994 fielding percentage (later broken). Additionally, he finished second on the club with a .320 batting average while tying for the team lead in homers. Overall, his Brooklyn debut was a smashing success.

With success comes great expectations, however, and Koenecke failed to live up to his billing the following year. Through 99 games, he carried a fair .284 batting average with a meager total of 27 RBIs. Summoned to pinch-hit at a critical juncture in a September 15 contest, he failed to deliver. At the game's conclusion, Casey Stengel informed him that he was being cut from the roster along with pitchers Les Munns and Bob Barr. A strange and tragic scene unfolded during the trip home.

Upon boarding a plane in Chicago, Koenecke was spotted by a stewardess drinking from a bottle of alcohol he had brought along. About 25 minutes into the flight, he left his seat and got into a verbal altercation with another passenger. When the stewardess tried to settle the dispute, Koenecke knocked her to the floor. The unruly center fielder was eventually coaxed back to his seat by the copilot with the help of Munns and Barr. Koenecke was kicked off the plane at Detroit Airport.

Even in his distressed state, Koenecke was permitted to charter his own flight to Buffalo. Trouble began about midway to that destination when the jittery outfielder began harassing the plane's pilot, Joseph Mulqueeney. He was asked to switch places with flight assistant Irwin Davis, who was situated in the backseat. Koenecke complied with the request and was calm for a spell before assaulting Mulqueeney. Davis rushed to the pilot's aid and a struggle ensued.

According to initial testimony, Koenecke and Davis grappled for more than 10 minutes. At some point, Koenecke bit Davis on the arm, tearing through two layers of clothing and drawing blood. The plane was rocking dangerously at that point and veering off course. When Koenecke made another run at Mulqueeney, Davis hit him with a fire extinguisher. The implement was knocked from Davis's hands and retrieved by the pilot, who used it to fend off Koenecke. Several blows were necessary to subdue the out-of-control ballplayer.

As Koenecke lay unconscious on the floor, Mulqueeney struggled to get his bearings. He had no idea in which direction the plane was headed until he spotted the lights of Toronto. In search of a landing field, he circled and touched down at the Long Branch Race Track, which was used for thoroughbred horse competition. The plane was damaged in the process. Upon exiting the craft, Mulqueeney and Davis were greeted by growling security dogs. Mulqueeney told reporters that, in his disoriented state, he thought he was being "attacked by wolves." Both men were left unharmed. Koenecke was not so lucky, dying of a cerebral hemorrhage.

Mulqueeney and Davis were held on charges of manslaughter but were later released. At the trial, the pilot expressed his opinion that Koenecke's actions were indicative of a suicide attempt. The jury concurred and acquitted both men.

Koenecke was well liked by teammates, and when informed of the unfortunate developments, several wept openly. According to newspaper reports, first baseman Sam Leslie was the most visibly affected. Players wore black arm bands in honor of their fallen teammate. Koenecke left behind a wife and three-year-old daughter.

Donnie Moore

Ted Williams once remarked that failure was an acceptable aspect of baseball. Right-hander Donnie Moore should have internalized that philosophy. In 1986, he coughed up a decisive homer to Red Sox outfielder Dave Henderson in a playoff game. Instead of bouncing back from the experience, he allowed it to eat away at his psyche. In a final act of despondency, he shot himself and his wife in the presence of their children.

Moore's career came to be defined by a single moment. It was October 12, 1986—Game 5 of the American League Championship Series. The Angels held a 3–1 Series lead over the Red Sox, who were trailing 5–4 in the top of the ninth. When Moore entered the game, his club stood within three strikes of earning the first World Series berth in franchise history. On a 2–2 count, the veteran forkballer delivered a fat pitch to Dave Henderson, who crushed it for a two-run homer. California rallied in the bottom of the frame to send the game into extra innings, but Boston scratched out the winning run off Moore in the 11th. Completely deflated by the loss, the Angels dropped the next two games by a wide margin. Moore's life, already marred by habitual alcohol consumption and domestic discord, would continue on a downward spiral.

Before the disparaging Game 5 defeat, Moore was among the top relief men in the game. He had made a name for himself at Monterey High School in Lubbock, Texas, where he played well enough to capture the attention of Red Sox scouts in 1972. Instead of accepting a conditional offer that required him to become an outfielder, he opted to pitch for Ranger College—a small two-year school located west of Fort Worth. He led the team to a national championship in '73. That same year, he married his childhood sweetheart, Tonya Martin, whom he had fathered a child with.

Moore's professional career began with the Gulf Coast League Cubs. He would pitch at a variety of farm levels before making his major-league debut in 1975. A regular in Chicago from 1977 through '79, he was traded to the Cardinals for infielder Mike Tyson. The change of scenery didn't suit him at all as his ERA ballooned to 6.23 in 1980, earning him a demotion to the minors. By 1984, he had emerged as a top-flight reliever with the Braves, converting 16 of 21 save opportunities while accruing a serviceable 2.94 ERA. Shipped to California the following year, he would earn his first and only All-Star selection. He tossed two perfect frames in the '85 Midsummer Classic as the American League lost, 6–1. He finished the season with 31 saves and a career-best 1.92 earned run average. Not only did he receive Cy Young consideration, but also he also inked a three-year, $3 million deal with the Angels.

A shoulder injury kept him out of action for more than a month at the beginning of the '86 slate, but he returned to record 21 saves (fifth in the AL) while holding opponents to an average of less than three runs per nine innings. By the end of the season, his shoulder was bothering him again, and he began receiving cortisone shots. He also suffered from back trouble. Moore, himself, was surprised that he was called upon by manager Gene Mauch to pitch in the ill-fated ALCS.

Moore commented after the fact that he had made a "bad pitch" and assumed responsibility for the demoralizing loss. Given time to process the event, he described his feelings as "numb" and admitted: "This one's going to follow me around for a while." The press wouldn't let him forget it as he was widely blamed for the Angels' failure to appear in the World Series for the 25th consecutive year. He would never shake his negative association with Dave Henderson.

Injuries derailed Moore's season again in '87. He got into just 14 games and failed to convert nearly half of his save opportunities. Though his ERA held at a respectable 2.70, hometown fans began booing him every time he appeared on the mound. His frustration showed during a particularly tough loss in May when he raised his fist at the crowd. He openly vented his bitterness to the media, blaming injuries for his mediocre performance and stating he was "sick and tired" of the derision from fans. General manager Mike Port was unreceptive to Moore's plight, griping that the club wasn't getting their money's worth out of him.

More misery came in 1988 for the dispirited hurler as he underwent back surgery to remove a bone spur from the vicinity of his spinal column. He never fully recovered, staking the opposition to a healthy .343 batting average in 27 appearances that year. He could no longer be relied upon in save situations. Convinced that he had outlived his usefulness, the Angels released him in August. He finished the campaign in the California League.

Moore signed with Kansas City in '89 but ended up with the club's Omaha affiliate when he began the season on the disabled list. He pitched ineffectively in seven games and was released. He returned to his posh Anaheim Hills estate (which he could no longer afford) to find his wife and children gone. Possessive and controlling, Moore had been sporadically beating his wife for more than a decade, especially when he was in a drunken state. Upon his release from Omaha, Tonya Moore had packed up and left, later telling reporters that she "feared for her safety."

During a subsequent discussion over finances, Moore pulled out a .45 caliber handgun and shot his estranged wife three times. Incredibly, she survived as their 17-year-old daughter rushed her to the hospital. The couple's two sons, aged 8 and 10, remained with their father as Tonya sought emergency medical treatment. Ronnie, the younger of the two boys, was in the room when Moore turned the gun around on himself.

Moore's blown save in the '86 ALCS has been widely cited as the sole reason for his suicide. His agent, Dave Pinter, told reporters that Moore talked about it all the time—so frequently, in fact, that Pinter had encouraged him to seek psychiatric counseling. But a variety of factors must have weighed heavily on Moore's mind before he pulled the trigger, not the least of which being the loss of his marriage and the impending end of his pitching career. Teammate Brian Downing stated that, in the wake of the '86 postseason disaster, Moore had never been treated fairly by the fans or press. Angels' manager Gene Mauch remembered Moore for having "a lot of courage and a lot of heart."

CHAPTER TWO

~

Momentary Lapses of Reason

Lee Elia

Oh, to be a Cubs fan . . .

Entering the 2013 season, they were the longest suffering franchise in major-league baseball, having gone without a World Series title since the era of Joe Tinker, Johnny Evers, and Frank Chance—the proficient double-play tandem that inspired Franklin Pierce Adams's antiquated poem "Baseball's Sad Lexicon." Beginning in 1906, Chicago made three consecutive Fall Classic appearances, emerging victorious twice. The next four decades would bring a plethora of missed opportunities and a dreadful 9–28 postseason record.

A host of able-bodied men attempted to reverse the team's fortunes after World War II without success. Some of the failures were exasperating. At the All-Star break in 1969, the Cubs were sitting pretty with a five-game lead over the second-place Mets. Even with four Hall of Famers on the roster—Ron Santo, Billy Williams, Ernie Banks, and Fergie Jenkins—they managed to lose 11 of 12 games during a pitiful September swoon, handing the NL East crown to the surging New Yorkers. The following year, the same cast of characters would hang on to first place for more than two full months before an inexplicable 12-game skid left them fighting to get back on top for the rest of the season. They ended up five games behind the Pirates. By the time Lee Elia assumed managerial responsibilities in 1982, the team had become synonymous with failure.

Elia attended college at the University of Delaware. He played portions of two seasons in the majors, breaking in with the White Sox during the 1966 slate. After a shaky .205 showing at the plate, he was demoted to Indianapolis of the Pacific Coast League. In '67, his contract was sold to the other Chicago club. He was granted a short trial with the Cubs in '68 but was an offensive liability, failing to break the .200 mark. He played in the Yankee farm system briefly without earning a promotion.

Elia received his first managerial assignment with the Spartanburg Phillies in 1975, guiding the team to the best record in the Western Carolinas League. He logged time in the American Association and the Eastern League before joining the Cubs' coaching staff in 1980. During the strike-shortened '81 season, Joey Amalfitano piloted Chicago to a lackluster 38–65 record. Elia took his place the following year.

The '82 Cubs were a mediocre crew overall with a handful of standouts. Bill Buckner was a more than capable first baseman. Shortstop Larry Bowa had two Gold Gloves and five All-Star selections to his credit. Fergie Jenkins was an occasionally dominant presence on the mound at 39 years of age while infielder Ryne Sandberg and reliever Lee Smith, both in their early 20s, provided hope for the future. Beyond that, the talent was thin as Chicago mustered an uninspiring 73–89 record in Elia's debut.

Attempting to strengthen the infield, third baseman Ron Cey was added to the roster in '83. Cey had been a permanent fixture at the hot corner in Los Angeles for over 10 years before signing a blockbuster contract during the off-season. To accommodate him, Sandberg was moved to second base, where he would fashion a Hall of Fame career. There was no immediate remedy for the club's troubles given the state of the pitching staff. None of Elia's most frequently used starters gave him 200 innings of work. None posted an ERA below 4.00. As a collective unit, Chicago hurlers gave up more hits and runs than any National League staff while posting the highest WHIP average (walks and hits per nine innings) in the circuit.

The Cubs staggered out of the gate with a six-game losing streak, dropping each contest by at least three runs. Just two weeks into the season, they were already six games out of first place. Before a now infamous April 29 matinee against the Dodgers at Wrigley Field, pressure was mounting for the club to turn things around.

On that date, 9,391 people turned out to see Chicago blow a 3–1 lead in the top of the sixth when starter Paul Moskau walked Steve Sax and then surrendered a two-run homer to Ken Landreaux. Further spoiling the Cubs' afternoon, Landreaux doubled off reliever Bill Campbell in the eighth and then scored the go-ahead run on a wild pitch by closer Lee Smith. Peppered with boos from disgruntled fans, the hometown crew went quietly in the eighth and ninth, dropping a tough 4–3 decision. On the way to the club-house, Keith Moreland, Larry Bowa, and Ron Cey were heckled by unruly patrons. All three were showered with beer. When Lee Elia got wind of the incident, he went absolutely ballistic.

At the game's conclusion, most reporters shuffled off to the Dodger club-house for interviews. It was just as well since the comments offered by Elia were unfit to print. In one of the most profane and oddly amusing tirades in baseball history, the frustrated Chicago skipper gave a small gathering of press members a piece of his mind.

In essence, Elia defended his players, petitioning the fans and media to show them a little more respect. It wasn't so much what he said but how he said it. In a three-minute span, he used the "F-word" more than 30 times while resorting to miscellaneous vulgarity on numerous other occasions. Referring to fans as "mother f-ers," "c-suckers," and "nickel-dime people," he urged them all to find jobs instead of hanging out at the ballpark, which he labeled their "playground." After that, he turned on the press, slamming them for stigmatizing his club with "cheap sh-t" editorials. He described the practice as "sickening" and invited reporters to pick on him in place of his players.

With that, he stormed off, leaving reporters from the *Chicago Tribune*, *Chicago Sun-Times*, and *Daily Herald* speechless. He apologized afterward, but the damage had been done. A headline in the *Los Angeles Times* the next day read: "The Bleeps Hit the Fans as Cubs Lose." The entire performance was recorded by a local radio station—WLS 890 AM. Today, it is still easily accessible through several Internet sources.

Elia was eventually fired but not on account of what he'd said. The club struggled to reach the .500 mark all year, and by August, general manager Dallas Green had seen enough. Green's special assistant Charlie Fox was in-stalled as interim manager. The following season, Jim Frey would lead Cubs to their first playoff appearance in nearly 40 years. The displaced Elia would manage the Phillies for portions of two seasons in '87 and '88 before being dismissed. He later coached for several major-league teams, including the Yankees and Orioles. Later still, he worked in the Braves' front office.

Roberto Alomar

Upon receiving the news that he had been elected to the Hall of Fame, Roberto Alomar must have been tremendously relieved to know that his entire career had not been defined by one unfortunate incident. In 1996, the gifted second baseman tarnished his reputation when he spit in the face of umpire John Hirschbeck. He spent the rest of his playing days trying to live it down.

Hailing from Puerto Rico, baseball was in Alomar's blood. Three of his uncles played minor-league ball. His father, Sandy (also a second baseman), lasted 15 years in the majors with six different teams. His brother, Sandy Jr., would accrue 20 years of big-league experience as a catcher, hitting .273 overall while earning six All-Star selections.

Roberto was the most talented of the bunch, getting his professional start with Charleston of the South Atlantic League in 1985. Playing alongside his brother, he led the club in hits and runs scored. He compiled a handsome .346 average at Reno the following year, earning a promotion to the Double-A level. After stops in Wichita and Las Vegas, he was added to the San Diego Padres' roster in 1988. He proved his value to the club with a serviceable .266 average and a range factor that ranked second in the American League.

Over the next several seasons, numerous accolades would follow, including 10 Gold Gloves and four Silver Slugger Awards. Alomar played on the All-Star team every year from 1990 through 2001 and was MVP of the Midsummer Classic in '98. While helping Toronto to a pair of World Series victories, he accrued a lifetime .313 batting average in postseason play. Polishing off a highly attractive resume, he stole 50 bases in a season twice and retired with 474 thefts. But he lived in the shadow of one reckless act for many years.

On September 27, 1996, during a tightly contested American League wild-card race, Alomar, then with the Orioles, was arguing a third strike call with umpire John Hirschbeck. Many believed that Hirschbeck had missed the call, but debate was rendered pointless when Alomar lost his composure and spit on the arbiter. Making a bad situation worse, Alomar initially showed little remorse for the despicable act, attacking Hirschbeck's character in a postgame interview.

Hirschbeck had suffered a personal tragedy in 1993, losing his eight-year-old son, John, to adrenoleukodystrophy. At the time of the spitting incident, Hirschbeck's other son, Michael, was afflicted with the same rare disorder. Also known as Addison-Schilder's disease or ALD (in its abbreviated form), the illness is an inherited neurological condition that leads to progressive brain damage, paralysis, seizures, and ultimately death. There is currently no cure. Perhaps that's why the public outcry was so great when Alomar insensitively told reporters that Hirschbeck had become "bitter" due to "a problem with his family."

Informed of Alomar's comments, Hirschbeck had to be physically restrained and was forced to sit out the game he was scheduled to officiate.

Taking a somewhat lenient stance, American League president Gene Budig handed Alomar a light five-game suspension to be enacted at the beginning of the '97 slate. Alomar promptly appealed the ruling and then went out and played the same day, blasting a 10th inning homer that clinched a wild-card berth for Baltimore.

In support of their comrade, umpires threatened a postseason strike unless Alomar's suspension was served immediately. By then, the Orioles' star had realized the error of his ways, drafting an apology note to Hirschbeck and offering to donate $50,000 to the Kennedy Krieger Institute at Johns Hopkins University to help find a cure for ALD. The Union of Umpires urged the institute to reject Alomar's money, but Hirschbeck was somewhat moved by the gesture, giving it his support. A U.S. District Court judge ruled that the umpires would be in violation of a collective bargaining agreement if they walked out on the playoffs, and in the end, they decided against the gesture.

Making further amends, Alomar withdrew his appeal of the suspension. He took his lumps in the postseason, getting treated to all kinds of verbal abuse whenever Baltimore played on the road. Some fans got fairly creative, holding up targets inviting Alomar to spit at them. The heckling would go on for years.

In April of 1997, Hirschbeck proved he was ready to bury the hatchet when he accepted Alomar's public apology and shook hands with the in-fielder while standing at home plate before a game at Camden Yards. The two remained friendly toward one another from that point on. When Alomar became eligible for Hall of Fame election in 2010, Hirschbeck stated for the record that he hoped baseball writers were able to look past the incident. He said he would "feel awful" if the infielder was denied access to the Hall on his account.

For whatever reason, Alomar was not enshrined at Cooperstown in his first year of eligibility. The second time was a charm, however, as he received 90 percent of the vote and was inducted along with former strikeout artist, Bert Blyleven, who had been waiting more than a decade for his big day. Alomar was only the third player of Puerto Rican origin to be enshrined.

The spitting incident was not the first in the history of professional sports, nor would it be the last. In 1991, basketball's preeminent bad boy, Charles Barkley, spit in the direction of a heckler and hit an eight-year-old girl instead. A year after Alomar showered Hirschbeck, linebacker Bill Romanowski of the Broncos hawked a wet one in the face of 49ers' wide receiver J. J. Stokes. In 2010, Romania's Victor Hănescu walked off the court during a Wimbledon match against Daniel Brands and spit at the crowd when a small group of disorderly fans began harassing him. All were forced to pay stiff fines for their actions.

César Cedeño

Few public figures are as idealized as professional athletes. In particular, baseball players have been worshipped as virtual demigods in our culture for more than a century. Enamored with their accomplishments on the diamond, we often forget that our hardball heroes are vulnerable and flawed like everyone else. In the case of César Cedeño, those flaws became more evident as his career progressed.

When Cedeño was growing up in the Dominican Republic, his father didn't think much of baseball. Diogene Cedeño wanted his son to spend more time around the family's small store and also to help his mother out at home. If not for the encouragement of Mrs. Cedeño, who secretly bought her son a glove and a pair of cleats while periodically allowing him to skip out on chores, César might never have been discovered by Astros' scouts in 1967. When Pat Gillick and Tony Pacheco saw the lanky 16-year-old play at Santo Domingo, they were impressed by his raw talent. Cedeño's father had already balked at a $1,000 offer from the Cardinals, insisting that César finish school. When Gillick and Pacheco sweetened the signing bonus to $3,000, Diogene Cedeño gave his consent.

Cedeño began his professional career with two A-level teams in 1968, hitting .305 for the year. He slumped a bit in '69 but tore up the American Association the following season with a .373 average and 37 extra-base hits in just 54 games. The Astros decided he was too good for the farm and promoted him. Making his big-league debut on June 20, 1970, he rapped out a pair of hits against the Braves. More than 2,000 safeties would follow.

In 1971, the 20-year-old Cedeño led the National League in doubles but struck out far too often—102 times to be exact. His batting average dropped more than 40 points from the previous year. In '72, he began fulfilling his potential, winning the first of five consecutive Gold Glove awards while finishing sixth in MVP voting. With explosive speed on the bases, Cedeño stole at least 50 bags every year from 1972 through 1977. In that span, he collected 30 or more doubles four times and slammed a minimum of 22 homers on three occasions—no small feat given the spacious dimensions of the Astrodome.

By the time he celebrated his 21st birthday, the versatile center fielder was already drawing comparisons to the all-time greats, such as Clemente, Aaron, and Mays. His personal flaws began to show in December of 1973, however, when an ugly scene unfolded in a Dominican hotel room. While wintering in Santo Domingo, Cedeño met his mistress, Alta, at a seedy lodge in one of the city's disreputable neighborhoods. After consuming alcohol and other illicit substances, Alta began playing with the pistol Cedeño had brought for protection. Cedeño tried to get it back from her, and during a brief struggle, a single bullet was discharged, killing Alta. Instead of calling an ambulance, Cedeño panicked and fled the scene. He waited several hours before turning himself in to authorities.

Because Cedeño was a famous ballplayer who invoked a sense of national pride, he was given a lenient sentence. Held in jail for 20 days, including Christmas, he was fined a measly 100 pesos. Not a word of the incident was mentioned to the press by Astros' representatives. It was business as usual when spring training began in 1974.

Baseball does not exist in a vacuum. A sizeable group of fans had gotten wind of the scandal. Some began turning out at games to heckle Cedeño—shouting epithets such as "killer" and demanding to know who he was going to shoot next. Cedeño tolerated the abuse for years until one fateful night in Atlanta when he finally snapped.

On September 8, 1981, Cedeño jumped into the stands at Fulton County Stadium and assaulted a fan who had allegedly been heckling him for two straight evenings. Several of Cedeño's teammates followed him into the seats, restraining him before anyone was seriously hurt. The reckless act couldn't have happened at a worse time. During the strike-shortened '81 season, pennant contenders were decided by pitting the first-half winners against the second-half victors in a divisional showdown. At the time of Cedeño's meltdown, the Astros were vying for the second-half title, which they would ultimately clinch. Following Cedeño's ejection, Houston blew a 3–2 lead in the bottom of the ninth, losing the game, 4–3.

After reading umpire reports and viewing game footage, National League president Chub Feeney suspended Cedeño indefinitely. The outfielder appealed the ruling through the Players Association and, once again, ended up with a light slap on the wrist. He was fined $5,000 and allowed to return to action. Cedeño commented that he wouldn't have acted so rashly if his wife had not been in attendance. She was allegedly driven to the verge of tears by the insensitive taunting. On an interesting side note, Reggie Smith and Pete Rose were both penalized for similar actions less than three weeks later. The Dodgers' Smith was fined and suspended for attacking a fan in San Francisco while Rose (then with the Phillies) received a summons for disturbing the peace when he confronted hecklers at Busch Stadium by slamming a bat on the dugout roof.

In the 1981 Divisional Series, the Astros were edged by the Dodgers, who rallied for three straight wins after dropping the first two games. Cedeño was an offensive no-show, managing just three hits and two walks in 16 plate appearances. He failed to score or collect an RBI. The rest of his career was a gradual descent into mediocrity.

Cedeño's ugly side would resurface several times during the 1980s. In 1985, he ran his Mercedes into a tree after a heated argument with his girlfriend. Detained by police, he refused a breathalyzer test and tried to kick out the back windows of the squad car. In '86, his last major-league season, alcohol consumption was at the root of another unfortunate scene when Cedeño got into a bar fight and was subsequently charged with assault and resisting arrest. Two years later, he was in the news again, battering his latest girlfriend and then driving off with their four-month-old child in tow. He was again charged with assault and resisting arrest.

Though Cedeño proved he was unworthy of hero worship off the field, he did put together a fine career on the diamond. In the *New Historical Baseball Abstract* (published in 2003), he received an all-time ranking of 21 from statistical wizard Bill James. That grade placed him among the greatest center fielders in history behind Hall of Famers Hack Wilson and Hugh Duffy. According to sabermetric assessments, however, he is not likely to join Wilson and Duffy at Cooperstown.

Juan Marichal

You have to give Juan Marichal credit—when he fell from grace, he did it in spectacular fashion. A native of the Dominican Republic, the right-handed strikeout specialist was revered by his fellow countrymen, who affectionately referred to him as "the Dominican Dandy." He grew quite popular in the States, as well, with his sizzling fastball and dramatic leg kick. But his name would forever be associated with nastiness after he viciously assaulted an opponent during a 1965 game at Candlestick Park.

Marichal had three devastating pitches in his arsenal: a fastball, a late-breaking slider, and a screwball that was particularly tough on left-handed hitters. He delivered these in a number of ways: overhand, sidearm, and submarine-style, depending on the batter and the situation. His windup was equally baffling with an incredibly high leg kick almost vertical to his body in the tradition of Warren Spahn.

He used these weapons to win 243 games during a 16-year career, striking out no fewer than 166 batters per season from 1963 through 1969. He made the All-Star team nine times while leading the National League in victories, complete games, and shutouts (twice apiece). Despite these accomplishments, he never won a Cy Young Award thanks to Sandy Koufax, Don Drysdale, and Bob Gibson, who monopolized the honor throughout Marichal's era of dominance. By his own account, Marichal had mastered a curveball by the age of 10 and was already working on a screwball by age 15. He quit school in the 11th grade to pursue baseball as a full-time profession. Recruited by the Giants in 1957, he posted a 50–26 record with a miserly 2.36 ERA over portions of three minor-league seasons before earning a call to San Francisco. In his auspicious Giants debut, he allowed just one hit in a complete game shutout over the Phillies. He would remain at the major-league level until 1975.

The Giants were top contenders through most of Marichal's career. In the decade of the '60s, they made one World Series appearance while finishing in third place or higher eight times. The offense was driven by a trio of Hall of Famers: Willie Mays, Willie McCovey, and Orlando Cepeda. The pitching staff was anchored by Marichal, who would be joined by another future Cooperstown inductee, Gaylord Perry, in 1962. Even with a plethora of talent, the Giants were frequent runners-up to the powerful Dodgers.

The Dodger-Giant rivalry extended all the way back to the late-19th century, when the two teams had battled for supremacy of New York. In 1959, they exported their long-standing feud to the West Coast. By then, the clubs were pretty evenly balanced, both having won at least 10 pennants. The Giants actually owned an edge with five world championships to the Dodgers' two.

In 1965, the perennial rivalry was in full swing. Los Angeles would maintain sole possession of first place from early May into July before other contenders, such as Cincinnati and Milwaukee, fought their way into the mix. San Francisco remained on the periphery until mid-August, when they crept within striking of the division lead. On August 19, the Dodgers and Giants began a four-game series at Candlestick Park that would prove quite memorable.

The trouble began in the second game (won by the Giants, 5–1), when Los Angeles's shortstop, Maury Wills, made contact with the glove of catcher Tom Haller on a backswing. In the next inning, San Francisco's Matty Alou clipped the glove of John Roseboro, leading the veteran backstop to believe that the act was intentional. The vindictive tone carried over into the series finale on August 22.

Both clubs sent their aces to the hill that day—Koufax for the Dodgers and Marichal for the Giants. The largest crowd of the season (42,807) turned out to see the action. On three days' rest, Marichal didn't have his best stuff.

Maury Wills led off with a bunt single and then advanced to second on a groundout. An RBI-double by Ron Fairly put Los Angeles ahead, 1–0.

In the second inning, the Dodgers scored another run on a double by Wes Parker and a single by catcher John Roseboro. When Maury Wills made his second plate appearance, he was promptly flattened by a high, inside fastball. Ron Fairly got the same treatment when he faced Marichal in the top of the third. The game soon took an ugly turn.

Marichal was due to lead off for the Giants in the bottom of the frame, and Roseboro wanted payback. Since Koufax was too ethical to deliver a brushback pitch, Roseboro took matters into his own hands, grazing Marichal's ear with a well-placed return throw to the mound. Startled and angry, Marichal demanded an explanation. When the stocky backstop took a menacing step in Marichal's direction, the flustered hurler clubbed Roseboro over the head with his bat, opening up a gash that would require medical attention. Koufax immediately rushed to help his battery mate while Giants' third-base coach Charlie Fox was among the first to arrive on the scene for San Francisco. Blood streamed down Roseboro's face as both benches emptied. Willie Mays took charge of the situation, restraining Roseboro (a close personal friend) and issuing a sincere apology. Dodger outfielder Lou Johnson gave Mays credit for defusing a near riot.

The game was delayed for about 15 minutes. When play resumed, a rattled Koufax surrendered a three-run clout to Willie Mays that would stand as the game-winning hit. Mays's clutch homer was, of course, overshadowed by accounts of the melee. In one infamous newspaper photo, Giants' infielder Tito Fuentes is seen in the middle of the fray holding a bat, though he never actually used it.

The following day, Marichal issued a public apology, explaining that he thought Roseboro was going to hit him with his mask. The right-hander was suspended for eight games and fined $1,750. Roseboro was back in the Dodger lineup within three days. He sued Marichal for $110,000 in damages and then settled for far less when the case was finally decided several years later.

For the two combatants, time was a great healer. After Marichal was denied access to the Hall of Fame in his first two years of eligibility, Roseboro publicly campaigned for baseball writers to put any biases against the hurler aside. His petitions did not go unnoticed as Marichal was inducted to Cooperstown the next time around. Proving there was no bad blood between them, Roseboro and Marichal turned up at memorabilia shows to jointly autograph photos of their notorious brawl. In 1990, Marichal described his friendship with Roseboro as "very good."

Randall Simon

The 19th-century writer and poet Oscar Wilde once remarked that "the only thing worse than being talked about is not being talked about." That statement is relevant to the career of first baseman Randall Simon, whose mediocre performance on the diamond was far from inspiring. If not for his involvement in an embarrassing on-field incident in 2003, only a handful of American fans would even know who he was.

Simon was highly regarded in his native Curacao, a Dutch protectorate in the Caribbean. He grew up in the same town as center fielder Andruw Jones. At just 17 years of age, Simon was signed as an amateur free agent by the Braves. His minor-league career began in 1993, when he hit .254 in 61 games for Danville of the Appalachian League. It would take him four years to earn a September call-up from Atlanta.

In '97, the Braves were in the midst of a long stretch of consecutive playoff appearances, and the first-base job was occupied by slugger Fred McGriff, who would come up just shy of 500 homers during his distinguished 19-year career. No one was terribly impressed when Simon went 6 for 14 at the plate and fielded his position without an error. He was given another brief trial the following year but failed to contribute offensively. In '99, he played behind Ryan Klesko and, despite a promising .317 effort in 90 games, he was again demoted to the farm.

Simon was dropped by three major-league organizations during the 2000 slate. He would finally land a full-time position with the struggling Tigers. He enjoyed his most productive season in 2002, establishing career highs in hits (145), homers (19), and RBIs (82). Even after he was named team MVP, he couldn't hang on to his job. Detroit was a team in constant flux, and Simon was used as trade bait for two pitchers from the Pittsburgh farm system.

While wearing a Pirates uniform, the nomadic infielder became embroiled in a major controversy that would briefly make him a media sensation. The embarrassing incident happened during the ever-popular sausage race at Miller Park, a tradition dating back to the 1990s. The race is held during the sixth inning of every home game as a promotion for the Klement's Sausage Company of Wisconsin. During the event, employees dressed in seven-foot foam costumes engage in a footrace that begins along the third baseline and ends beyond the home team's dugout.

The event would draw far more attention than usual in early July of 2003. As the costumed contestants passed by the Pittsburgh dugout, Simon inexplicably reached out and hit the Italian sausage character with his bat. The halfhearted swing was just enough to send 19-year-old Mandy Block stumbling into 21-year-old Veronica Piech, who was wearing a Hot Dog suit. Both girls tumbled to the ground. Their injuries were very minor, but the repercussions were not.

After the game, Simon was arrested and booked for misdemeanor battery. Mobbed by reporters, he referred to himself as a "fun" player and explained that the gesture had been intended as a joke. Mandy Block held no grudges, openly expressing her amusement while requesting an autographed bat for her troubles. Veronica Piech was not so jocular. A volleyball player for Harding University in Arkansas, she already had a metal rod in her leg from a previous injury. She expressed bitterness over the fact that her sports career could have been ended and stated that she was "disgusted" with Simon.

Video footage of the incident appeared all over television and the Internet for weeks. The affair was mockingly labeled "Sausagegate" as Simon was made to look like a bully and a fool. Brewers' executive vice president Rick Schlesinger commented that the ill-advised act was among the most "outrageous" things he had ever seen on or off the diamond. Attempting a bit of damage control, the Pirates condemned Simon's actions and issued a formal apology.

In the end, the journeyman first-sacker did his penance, paying a $432 fine for disorderly conduct. He was also penalized $2,000 by league officials and suspended for three games. Trying to set things right, he apologized to both women and offered each an autographed bat. Mandy Block later received a complimentary trip to Curacao courtesy of the country's board of tourism.

Simon was traded to the Cubs a month after the fiasco. In his next appearance at Miller Park, he further atoned for his transgression by purchasing Italian sausages for an entire section of fans. It may have improved his standing with a handful of the Milwaukee populace, but it hardly revived his baseball career. In 2004, he signed as a free agent with the Pirates and was released in August after posting an anemic .194 batting average through 61 games. The following year, he exported his modest talents to the Mexican League. He later played for the Orix Buffaloes of the Japanese Pacific League and represented the Netherlands in the 2006 World Baseball Classic. An interesting side note: he was knighted by Queen Beatrix of the Netherlands less than a month after the sausage fiasco.

Pedro Martínez

Pedro Martínez was among the best of his generation—a big-game pitcher and a fierce competitor. Because he was such an overpowering presence on the mound, he often brought out the worst in opponents. When 72-year-old

Yankee bench coach Don Zimmer angrily rushed at him during a playoff game, Martínez was faced with two options: avoid the conflict or tangle with a man more than twice his age and in questionable health. Most people agree he made the wrong decision.

Martínez was born in Manoguayabo of the Dominican Republic. He grew up in the shadow of his older sibling, Ramon, a highly regarded right-hander who would enjoy several winning seasons with the Dodgers. Rail-thin at six-foot-four, 165 pounds, Ramon failed to demonstrate consistent durability during his fourteen-year tour of the majors. The somewhat sturdier Pedro (5 feet 11 inches, 170 pounds) would surpass his brother in nearly every facet of the game.

Also a product of the Dodger system, Pedro began his professional career in 1990 with Great Falls of the Pioneer League. Within two years, he was ranked among the top 10 prospects by *Baseball America*. Primarily a starter in the minors, Martínez appeared almost exclusively in relief during his first full major-league season. He took the hill 65 times in '93, posting a 10–5 record with a 2.61 ERA. The performance captured the attention of the Expos, who traded second baseman Delino DeShields to acquire Pedro's contract.

Martínez returned to a familiar starter's role in Montreal. Obviously feeling he had something to prove, he hit 11 batters, engaged in 3 fistfights, and earned 12 ejections during the '94 slate. Though he would gradually learn to control his temper, he would never completely discard the image as an agitator and a headhunter.

Pedro's breakthrough season was 1997. He captured the National League Cy Young Award with a 17–8 record, 1.90 earned run average, and 305 strikeouts. Always salary conscious, the small-market Expos decided they couldn't afford the marquee hurler anymore, trading him to Boston. It was there that Martínez became an integral part of baseball's most intense rivalry.

The "Babe Ruth curse" is a well-weathered tale. All superstitions aside, the Red Sox have been smothered by the Yankees since the 1920s. When Martínez came to the Hub in '98, New York had 23 world championships to Boston's five. Even more frustrating, the Sox would finish second to the Bombers in the AL East every year from 1998 through 2005—often by a slender margin. Any resentment on the part of players and fans is highly understandable.

Martínez did little to cool the bad blood between the two teams. Asked about the "curse," he once growled at reporters: "Wake up the Bambino. I'll drill him in the ass." As Joe Torre's troops consistently found ways to beat him over the years, the fiery hurler eventually conceded that the Yankees were his "daddy." Fans in the bleacher sections of Yankee Stadium never let him forget this colorful comment, chanting, "Who's your daddy?" every time Pedro took the mound in the Bronx.

By no means did Martínez perform poorly against the Yankees, but he did look a bit more human, losing 11 of 22 lifetime decisions while posting an ERA 27 points above his career mark. The intensity of the rivalry is reflected in Pedro's hit-by-pitch totals as he plunked 17 Yankee batters over the years—more than any other club by far. He once hit Gary Sheffield with a pitch after the right fielder had called for time. At the very least, Sheffield and Martínez were roughly the same age. When Pedro threw septuagenarian Don Zimmer to the turf during Game 3 of the 2003 AL Championship Series, many fans on both sides of the rivalry agreed he had finally gone too far.

Boston spent most of the 2003 slate chasing the Yankees as usual. Hope surfaced in September when the Sox moved within three games of the division lead on the eve of a three-game series in the Bronx. The Hub Men throttled the Bombers in the first two games by a combined score of 20–3, but they couldn't solve southpaw David Wells in the finale, losing a close one, 3–1. The pennant race was never terribly close after that, as the Bean Town crew settled for yet another wild-card berth.

Boston rallied for three straight wins against Oakland in the AL Division Series, earning the right to face the Yankees for the pennant. After splitting the first two games at Yankee Stadium, the Red Sox stood within three wins of earning their first World Series appearance in 17 years. Enthusiasm in Boston had reached a fever pitch. Decades of hard feelings between the two clubs spilled out onto the field.

The pitching matchup for Game 3 featured the American League's premier right-handers, Pedro Martínez versus Roger Clemens. Boston jumped out to a quick 2–0 lead in the first, but New York knotted the score in the third. An inning later, Pedro got into a serious jam when Jorge Posada walked and Nick Johnson singled. With runners on the corners, Hideki Matsui hit a ground rule double that gave the Yanks a 3–2 lead.

In retaliation, Martínez aimed a pitch at Karim García's head. García ducked out of the way as the ball grazed his back. Pumped up on adrenaline, he later slid into second with unnecessary force on a double-play ball hit by Alfonso Soriano. As he swaggered back to the dugout, he taunted Pedro: "F—k you, punk. That was for you." Angry words were exchanged between several players. With the crowd chanting wildly ("Yankees suck!"), umpire Tim McClelland was forced to issue a warning to both benches that the next close call would result in ejections. The inning ended without further incident.

In the bottom of the fourth, Roger Clemens threw a high pitch to Manny Ramirez, which in no way resembled a brushback. Ramirez began pointing and shouting, nevertheless. The benches cleared, and it looked as if cooler heads would prevail before an unimaginable event transpired. In a blind rage, Yankee bench coach Don Zimmer came lumbering out of the Yankee dugout headed straight for Pedro Martínez.

Zimmer's playing career had begun during the 1940s. After it ended in '67, he collected more than three decades of experience as a manager and coach. He still carried four metal plugs in his skull from a serious beaning that had left him in a coma for two weeks during the 1953 slate. Even in his agitated state, Zimmer posed no serious threat to the 32-year-old Martínez, who was in peak physical condition.

Martínez encountered Zimmer in front of the Red Sox dugout. Instead of sidestepping his elderly assailant, he grabbed Zimmer's face with both hands and shoved him roughly to the ground. The highly respected baseball guru (known affectionately as "Popeye" in some circles) landed face-first and then rolled into Ramirez's discarded bat. He was eventually helped to his feet by trainer Gene Monahan as blood trickled from a cut on his head. Fortunately, he was not seriously hurt.

Taking the fall for the incident, Zimmer later issued a tearful public apology, accepting a $5,000 fine for his part in the fracas. Additional fines were imposed upon Martínez ($50K), Manny Ramirez ($25K), and Karim Garcia ($10K). Martínez expressed regret but ultimately defended his actions. The Yankees won the game in question, 4–3, and the series by the same margin on a dramatic 11th inning walk-off homer by Aaron Boone in Game 7. The Sox would have their revenge the following year, taking down the Yanks in an ALCS rematch and then ending an 86-year championship drought with a World Series sweep over the Cardinals.

Pedro's last season in Boston was 2004. He spent the next four years with the Mets nursing nagging injuries a good deal of the time. In '09, he was traded to the Phillies and returned to World Series play against his archrivals, the Yankees. They proved they were still his "daddy," saddling him with an 0–2 record and 6.30 ERA in two starts. With more than 200 career victories and one of the highest winning percentages of all time, Martínez is a prime candidate for enshrinement at Cooperstown.

Ben Christensen

Brushback pitches in baseball have been a source of ethical debate for many years. No pitcher has ever met with long-term success by allowing batters to get too comfortable at the plate. But at what point does throwing at hitters become unsportsmanlike? Right-hander Ben Christensen defined that boundary very clearly when he beaned Anthony Molina in the on-deck circle.

Christensen was selected by the Orioles in the fortieth round of the '96 amateur draft. He enrolled at Wichita State University and worked his way up to a ranking of 37 among major-league prospects. With a crackling 90-plus mile-per-hour fastball and a career record of 21–1, he was at one time considered the top pitcher in the NCAA. But his reputation would be irrevocably blemished during his senior year.

Anthony Molina was a star infielder for Evansville University. He was described by one writer as "scrappy" and "tough"—the kind of player who grated on opponents' nerves. On April 23, 1999, Molina was situated in the on-deck circle preparing to face the toughest collegiate hurler in the nation. According to Wichita State coach Brent Kemnitz, the pesky Evansville leadoff man appeared to be timing Christensen's warm-up tosses. Kemnitz was strongly against this practice and had instructed his pitchers to issue brushbacks whenever it occurred. Instead of waiting for Molina to step into the batter's box (which would have been the sporting thing to do), Christensen unleashed a 90-mile-per-hour fastball that struck the unsuspecting Molina squarely in the left eye. The reckless throw was more than 20 feet off the plate.

Though Molina was not as highly regarded as Christensen, he had a very good shot at being drafted and playing professionally. In an instant, all his hopes were destroyed. The impact of the pitch broke three orbital bones and opened a cut requiring 23 stitches. Three surgeries would follow—one to relieve the pressure in his eye, one to insert a new lens, and one to repair his damaged retina. Despite the best efforts of doctors, he was left with a permanent blind spot, poor peripheral vision, and virtually no depth perception.

The incident made national headlines. Christensen's agent described the hurler as "inconsolable" for hours after the occurrence. He was suspended for the remainder of the '99 slate along with Coach Kemnitz. Initially charged with battery, the indictment was later dropped in favor of a civil suit. The case would be litigated in the Kansas court system for over three years.

Incredibly, Christensen was drafted by the Cubs two months after the outrageous occurrence. A reward for appalling behavior, he signed a million-dollar contract and immediately started at the Rookie level. Karma would catch up to him eventually as he developed tendinitis in his shoulder and required surgery to repair it. After accruing a 12–19 record over portions of six minor-league campaigns for Chicago, he was sold to Seattle. He managed a bloated 9.35 ERA in five Texas League games before earning his release in 2004. On the 10-year anniversary of the incident, he refused all interview requests, even from his hometown newspaper.

Molina, whose vision deteriorated from 20/10 to 20/400, returned to the Evansville squad for his senior season in 2000. No longer considered a major-league candidate, he accrued a fair .266 batting average. He never talked to Christensen after the incident and told reporters he had no desire to do so. When the civil case was finally settled in 2002, Molina reportedly received a cash award of $400,000 (apparently the going rate for a human eye). Sadly, he told reporters that giving up on his dream of playing big-league ball has haunted him every day of his life.

~

CHAPTER THREE

Liars, Cheats,
and Tattletales

Jose Canseco

With his rugged good looks, chiseled physique, and mammoth home-run power, Jose Canseco was almost too cartoonish to be a real-life character. He once hit a ball into the fifth level at Toronto's Sky Dome, a moon shot estimated to be roughly 484 feet from home plate. While his superhuman feats on the diamond drew admiration from many fans, his activities off the field did not. A rampant steroid abuser, he would leave the majors in 2001, never to return.

Born in La Habana, Cuba, Canseco considered himself a mediocre athlete and stated that he had no motivation to be a star until he made a promise to his dying mother. He followed through with that pledge in 1986 when he captured American League Rookie of the Year honors. Proving his performance was no fluke, he became the first member of the 40/40 club in '88 with a league-leading 42 homers and 40 stolen bases. He was a unanimous choice for MVP that year.

Canseco and teammate Mark McGwire, referred to as the "Bash Brothers" by an admiring media, helped put the Athletics back on the map after more than a decade of mediocrity. McGwire had a pretty fair rookie season himself in '87, clubbing a total of 49 long balls, a record for a freshman. It was the best and the worst of times to be a baseball fan as the sport became infiltrated by performance-enhancing drugs.

Rumors of Canseco's steroid use surfaced in his MVP season. He denied such allegations throughout his big-league career, but his private life painted a different picture. Steroids promote aggressive behavior in some users—a phenomenon commonly referred to as "roid rage." Canseco certainly matched the profile, as he compiled a prolific arrest record over the years. In 1989, he was arrested for reckless driving after leading an officer on a high-speed chase. Two months later, he was cited for carrying a loaded semi-automatic pistol in his car. In '92, he was charged with aggravated battery after running his Porsche into his wife's BMW. Five years later, he was arrested for assaulting his second wife. Later still, he engaged in a brawl at a Miami Beach nightclub, breaking one patron's nose while leaving another with 20 stitches in his lip.

The volatile slugger was injured often during his 17-year career, appearing in 150 or more games just five times. Because he commanded a large salary and was such a high-risk commodity, he changed uniforms fairly often. After 1994, he played for six different clubs and was involved in numerous transactions. He appeared in his last major-league game during the 2001 slate, and although he expressed interest in returning to the Big Show many times, there were no serious suitors.

In 2003, the district attorney of Northern California began investigating BALCO after an anonymous call connected the sports nutrition center to a non-detectable steroid used by ballplayers. Agents from the IRS, FDA, and a federal narcotics task force raided the BALCO facility and found evidence of steroid distribution along with customer lists. The register included athletes from multiple sports, including football, boxing, and various track and field events. Several high-profile baseball players were also implicated, among them Barry Bonds, Jeremy Giambi, and Benito Santiago. A new testing process was created to detect the presence of the drug in question, tetrahydrogestrinone—a.k.a. "the clear."

In 2005, Canseco attempted to blow the lid off the entire affair, releasing a tell-all book entitled *Juiced: Wild Times, Rampant 'Roids, Smash Hits, and How Baseball Got Big*. In it, he candidly admitted to injecting himself with anabolic steroids and claimed that roughly 85 percent of all major-league players used them. He specifically identified former teammates Mark McGwire, Rafael Palmeiro, and Jason Giambi (among others) as fellow users. Embarking on an extensive book tour, he repeated the allegations on *Hardball* with Chris Matthews, the *Today Show* with Matt Lauer, and *60 Minutes* with Mike Wallace.

Not only was the book panned for lack of literary merit by numerous sources, but also the reaction from peers was scathing. Jason Giambi called the manuscript "delusional and far-fetched." Tony La Russa said he was "embarrassed" to have managed Canseco in Oakland. Mark McGwire commented that he felt sorry for the disgraced slugger.

If the point of *Juiced* was to get the establishment to address the problem, the book failed miserably. Sandy Alderson, chief assistant to Commissioner Bud Selig, refused to investigate Canseco's claims, stating that a stronger drug policy was already in the process of being implemented. The indifference of league officials surprised *Chicago Tribune* reporter Bob Verdi, who pondered in his column why "the minions within Selig's management structure" would not at least "go through the motions" since Canseco had named several players who were still active.

Though Canseco would be regarded as a liar and a traitor in most baseball circles, he would have his comeuppance soon afterward. In March of 2006, Selig entrusted Senate majority leader George Mitchell to investigate the use of performance-enhancing drugs within the sport. The inquiry took place in response to the book, *Game of Shadows*, penned by *San Francisco Chronicle* reporters Lance Williams and Mark Fainaru-Wada. The best-selling work, which deals extensively with the BALCO scandal, inspired several members of Congress to make disparaging remarks about the ineffectiveness of Selig's drug-testing policies.

After pursuing the matter for over a year and a half, Mitchell released a 409-page document referred to as "the Mitchell Report." In it, he described the Major League Baseball Players Association as being "largely uncooperative" and alleged that Toronto Blue Jays' slugger Frank Thomas was the only player who willingly submitted to questioning. Chief witnesses in the report were Brian McNamee, a personal trainer employed by several marquee players, and Kirk Radomski, a clubhouse employee for the Mets. In all, 89 names were placed on the table, among them Roger Clemens, Andy Pettitte, Miguel Tejada, and Barry Bonds.

Bud Selig referred to the report as "a call to action" and finally elected to do something about it. Drug testing became far more stringent, as all players were required to undergo screenings twice a year. The tests themselves became more expansive, checking for numerous kinds of stimulants and steroids. Before the Mitchell Report, players could test positive up to four times before receiving a moderate one-year suspension. After Selig's call to arms, a third infraction merited a lifetime suspension from the sport.

In the midst of the scandal, Jose Canseco released his second book, *Vindicated: Big Names, Big Liars, and the Battle to Save Baseball*. Originally slated to be carried by Berkley Books, the publisher (an imprint of the Penguin Group) backed out at the last minute, worrying that Canseco didn't have enough solid evidence to support his charges. The CBS-affiliated Gallery Books put his work on the shelves in March of 2008—just three months after the release of Mitchell's infamous report.

In *Vindicated*, Canseco took a bitter, I-told-you-so attitude and alleged that he was forced into retirement through blacklisting. He claimed that passages implicating Roger Clemens had been purged from *Juiced* by the publisher. He also added two big names to the list of drug users: Alex Rodriguez and Magglio Ordóñez. Backing his charges, he underwent two lie-detector tests, one of which was administered by a former FBI affiliate. At the very least, the results proved that he believed his own story.

Divorced twice, Canseco lost his Encino, California, home in 2008, claiming that the two settlements had cost him a total of $15 million. That same year, he was arrested by immigration officials trying to bring a contraband fertility drug across the border from Mexico. He stated that it was for use in hormone-replacement therapy necessitated by his steroid abuse. He pled guilty in federal court and received 12 months of unsupervised probation. In 2012, he joined the Quintana Roo Tigers of the Mexican League but was banned for using testosterone. Shortly afterward, the Worcester Tornadoes of the Canadian American Association signed him to a one-year contract at the age of 47. For a period of time, his activities could be followed by the public on Twitter. Not surprisingly, several of his "tweets" were aimed at provoking fights with others.

The 1919 White Sox

The story of the White Sox scandal has captivated fans for generations, not just because it nearly ruined the sport but also because it created an intriguing "what if" scenario. Several of the eight culprits were bona fide superstars, and when lifetime suspensions were handed to them by Commissioner Mountain Landis, their careers would forever be left in limbo. Junk-baller Eddie Cicotte had accumulated 209 victories and a 2.38 ERA. "Shoeless" Joe Jackson was a lifetime .356 hitter. Lefty Williams, a 27-year-old southpaw, was just entering the prime of his career, having notched 45 wins over the previous two campaigns. Barring unforeseen injuries, all of the named parties would have had several seasons ahead of them. Whether their career paths would ultimately have guided them to Cooperstown will never be known.

Despite exhaustive research, pieces of the story remain shrouded in mystery, since most of the participants refused to divulge intimate details. In reconstructing events, one needs to be extremely cautious in sorting out the truth. For many years, Eliot Asinof's *Eight Men Out* was considered to be the definitive tome on the subject. But Asinof later admitted that he sought to paint players in a sympathetic light. In doing so, he left behind a number of enduring misconceptions.

A common error among many contemporary baseball writers is the paint-ing of White Sox owner Charles Comiskey as a tightfisted villain who drove his negligently underpaid players to commit the crime of the century. Much has been made of his miserly practices—how he forced players to pay for their own laundry bills and delivered a case of stale champagne as a "bonus" for winning the 1917 World Series. Though the first charge is true, the sec-ond is an outright fabrication.

Comiskey was owner of the White Sox from 1900 to 1931. A competent baseball man, he served as both a pitcher and infielder during his playing days. In 1894, he purchased the Sioux City club of the Western League, later moving it to St. Paul. When the Western circuit became the American League, Comiskey's troops migrated again to Chicago, where they became known as the White Sox.

Despite various claims to the contrary, Comiskey was actually fairly gen-erous in some respects. After financing the construction of Comiskey Park in 1910, he allowed various Chicago organizations to use the facility free of charge. He also handed out free grandstand tickets to thousands of school-boys every year. During World War I, he donated 10 percent of his income to the Red Cross. And yes, despite what has been said about him, he paid his players relatively well in comparison to other clubs.

The White Sox opening-day payroll in 1919 was rivaled only by the Red Sox and Yankees. Eddie Cicotte, among the chief conspirators, was the second-highest-paid pitcher in the majors behind Walter Johnson. Among third basemen, Buck Weaver's salary was second only to Frank "Home Run" Baker. Chick Gandil, self-acknowledged ringleader of the fix, was making more money than all but three AL first-sackers. Shortstop Swede Risberg was adequately paid considering the fact that he lost the starting job several times during his tenure with the White Sox due to substandard offensive produc-tion. Joe Jackson certainly could have been paid a little more given his vast talents, but his $6,000 salary would have made him the second-highest player on the Tigers, Indians, Browns, and Senators. Had he played for the A's, he would have been top dog.

So why did they do it? No one knows for sure. Gambling was an intrinsic element of baseball culture at the time. Players like Hal Chase (who will be discussed in great detail a bit later in this chapter) had been getting away with throwing games for years. Jacob Pomrenke, who chairs the SABR's 1919 Black Sox Scandal Research Committee, believes the "Eight Men Out" were looking for an easy payday. In regard to Comiskey's role in the scandal, Pom-renke asserts that the owner's treatment of his players "was not so historically unjust nor out of line with how other major-league owners were treating their players as to give the White Sox players extra motivation to throw the World Series." Of course, Comiskey was disliked by many of his employees. That is the natural order of things in any line of work. As the old saying goes, it's lonely at the top.

Though the motivation of players remains a source of endless debate, many of the basic facts have become universally accepted. By his own admission, Chick Gandil was the one who approached gamblers with the idea of fixing the Series. At the time, the club was divided into two separate social cliques with tension existing between the groups. The educated players gravitated to second baseman Eddie Collins (an Ivy League graduate) and the others to Gandil. A former boxer, Gandil embodied the tough-guy persona and made no attempt to hide his contempt for upper management. Swede Risberg served as Gandil's right-hand man, helping him refine the scheme and recruit others to carry it out. Poorly educated, Risberg pulled a boneheaded move when he telegrammed his friend Joe Gedeon (an infielder for the Browns) before the Series and told him to bet on the Reds. Gedeon later blew the whistle on Risberg, hoping to collect a $20,000 reward offered by Comiskey for information regarding the fix.

Though there were some harrowing moments in early July, the 1919 pennant race was fairly anticlimactic as the Sox maintained a healthy lead through August and September. By the time the World Series got under way on October 1, Gandil and Risberg had added six players to their scheme while securing the involvement of several gamblers. According to multiple accounts, Boston-based bookmaker Sport Sullivan convinced Jewish mafia kingpin Arnold Rothstein to bankroll the plot. Others involved included "Sleepy Bill" Burns (a former pitcher) and Abe Attell (at one time a featherweight boxing champion). Both were associates of Rothstein's.

Chicago's opponents, the Cincinnati Reds, were no slouches, having lost just 22 games from July through September. The offense was propelled by speedy center fielder Edd Roush (a future Hall of Famer), while the pitching staff, anchored by 19-game winner Dutch Ruether, accrued an impressive 2.23 collective ERA. In an attempt to increase revenue and popularity, Major League Baseball tried a best-of-nine World Series format that year.

The Series opener took place at Cincinnati's Redland Field. Unbeknownst to Chicago manager Kid Gleason, the only innocents in his starting lineup that day were second baseman Eddie Collins, catcher Ray Schalk, and right fielder Shano Collins. Around the diamond, the conspirators were represented by Cicotte, Gandil, Risberg, and third baseman Buck Weaver. Happy Felsch started in center field while the somewhat reluctant Joe Jackson was stationed in left. On the bench, Lefty Williams was slated to pitch the following afternoon while utility man Fred McMullin was available as a defensive replacement or pinch hitter.

To indicate he was prepared to throw the match, Eddie Cicotte executed the prearranged signal by hitting Cincinnati's leadoff man, Morrie Rath, with a pitch. He could have been far more convincing in his role that afternoon as he allowed a barrage of hits in the fourth inning, staking the Reds to a 6–1 lead. Southpaw Dutch Ruether allowed just six hits and went the distance in a 9–1 Cincinnati victory.

Lefty Williams was more subtle the following day, tossing three scoreless frames before yielding three tallies in the bottom of the fourth. He coughed up another run in the sixth, but surrendered just four hits overall. Conspirators Buck Weaver and Joe Jackson made themselves look good with a combined 5-for-8 showing at the plate. It was little more than window dressing as the Sox lost, 4–2.

During the early going of Game 3, dissention may or may not have broken out among the ranks. Gandil's crew disliked starter Dickey Kerr and had initially planned to throw the game, but Gandil delivered a key two-run single in the bottom of the second. Kerr ended up spinning a three-hitter, and the Sox triumphed, 3–0.

The fix continued in Game 4, with Cicotte resorting to ham-acting on the hill. With one out in the fifth, he threw wildly to first on a slow roller by Pat Duncan for a two-base error. After giving up a single to Larry Knopf, he cut off Joe Jackson's throw to the plate and then bobbled the ball, allowing Duncan to score. The crowd reportedly groaned at his inexcusable gaffe. Greasy Neale then raked Cicotte for a double, scoring Knopf. It was all the offense Cincinnati would need as Jimmy Ring held the White Sox to just three hits all afternoon.

After a Game 5 loss, the Sox made a show of it in Cincinnati, battling back from a four-run deficit to send Game 6 into extra innings. In the 10th, Buck Weaver doubled and then moved to third on a bunt single by Joe Jackson. Chick Gandil came through with another clutch hit, chasing Weaver across the plate. Dickey Kerr closed out a hard-fought 5–4 victory for the Sox.

Cicotte pitched a gem in the seventh contest, yielding just one run on seven hits through nine frames. Chicago was aided by four Cincinnati errors in the 4–1 win. In a story popularized by Asinof in *Eight Men Out*, Arnold Rothstein was allegedly so distressed by this turn of events, he sent one of his associates to speak to Lefty Williams, who was slated to start Game 8. Rothstein's thug reportedly told the left-hander to throw the game early or risk grave consequences for him and his wife. Though anecdotal evidence of the incident does exist, Asinof admitted that he concocted portions of his account. Regardless of what transpired before the eighth contest, Williams turned in his worst performance of the Series. After retiring Morrie Rath on a harmless pop-up, he gave up two singles and a pair of doubles in succession. He never made it out of the first inning as the Reds converted an early 4–0 lead into a 10–5, Series-clinching triumph. It was the first championship in franchise history.

Of all the conspirators, Cicotte and Williams carried the lion's share of the dirty work, combining for a 1–5 record. Collectively, they gave up 19 earned runs on 31 hits and 13 walks in 38 innings of work. Risberg managed a miserable .080 batting average while Felsch was only slightly better at .192. Fred McMullin was paid mostly for keeping his mouth shut, getting into just two games and going 1-for-2 at the plate. Burdened by a guilty conscience, Jackson played hard most of the Series, gathering 12 hits. Buck Weaver did little to hurt the club offensively with a .324 average while Gandil collected five RBIs, two of which were game winners.

Newspaper stories circulated widely suggesting that the games had been fixed. Chicago owners suspected but would not admit it publicly. Seeking counsel as to what he should do with the money he had received, Joe Jackson tried to arrange a meeting with Comiskey. His efforts were ignored.

The fix was ill timed, as a postwar depression was gripping America. People were disenchanted, and racial tensions were running high. When the story finally broke, it was like a slap in the face. In September of 1920, the White Sox were in a tight pennant race with the Indians. A Cook County jury in Chicago was investigating reports that the Cubs had thrown a three-game series to the Phillies. When the probe was extended to include the 1919 World Series, a legion of skeletons were discovered in the White Sox closet. Baseball dissolved its National Commission, a three-man governing body, and installed Judge Kenesaw Mountain Landis as the first commissioner. He was given unlimited power.

Eight players, along with several gamblers, were indicted for conspiracy to defraud the public. Rothstein was not among those implicated. Sport Sullivan, charged with multiple counts of conspiracy, was supposedly paid by Rothstein to flee the country to avoid testifying. The final decision was surprising as all of the conspirators were acquitted. They scarcely had time to celebrate before Landis acted, banning them all from the sport for life. In a famous statement, he declared soberly that: "Regardless of the verdict of juries, no player who throws a ball game, no player that undertakes or promises to throw a ball game, no player that sits in conference with a bunch of crooked players and gamblers where the ways and means of throwing a game are discussed and does not promptly tell his club about it, will ever play professional baseball."

The Chicago players who did not participate in the throwing of games each received a bonus from Comiskey in the fall of 1920. The troubled owner tried diligently to rebuild a winner, but his club would finish in the second division for 15 straight seasons. The Sox would not return to World Series play until 1959. By then, Comiskey was nearly three decades in his grave.

Baseball survived the debacle as Landis remained committed to cleaning up the sport, abolishing the use of spitballs and various deceptive pitching deliveries. Umpires were encouraged to put fresh balls into play more often as a new cork center was introduced by the Spalding Company. The result was an offensive outburst unrivaled in the game's history to that point. With the advent of the so-called Lively Ball Era, the game would flourish until the Great Depression took its toll.

Jim Bouton

Years ago, baseball insiders had a code of ethics equivalent to the popular slogan "What happens in Vegas, stays in Vegas." When Jim Bouton violated that code in 1970 with his tell-all book *Ball Four*, the rewards were as vast as the consequences. His work became one of the most celebrated tomes in all of sports, but he was ostracized by associates at every level of the game.

Born in Newark, New Jersey, Bouton grew up as a Giants fan and attended many games at the Polo Grounds in New York. His family later moved to Chicago Heights, Illinois, where he attended high school. He was not a standout on the baseball team until his senior year, when he tossed a no-hitter. He had a variety of pitches in his repertoire, including a knuckleball, which would later save his professional career.

At the University of Michigan, Bouton had a successful freshman year and earned a scholarship for the following season. He caught the attention of scouts while competing in a Chicago amateur-league tournament during the summer of 1958. When the Yankees put $30,000 on the table, the young hurler promptly signed his first professional contract.

In those days, the ace of the New York staff was Hall of Famer Whitey Ford, who still had several productive seasons ahead of him. Ralph Terry was also a mainstay, but several members of the old guard—Don Larsen, Bobby Shantz, and Bob Turley—were soon to be traded or seldom used. Bouton's big break came in 1962, when he made the team out of spring training. Manager Ralph Houk used him in the role of a swingman as he started 16 games and relieved in 20. It was a promising debut overall as he compiled a 7–7 record with two saves and a perfect fielding percentage. In one of his finest outings of the year, he yielded just seven hits to the Senators in a complete game shutout. The Yankees won the World Series that year, though Bouton saw no postseason action.

In '63, the aspiring right-hander became a full-fledged star. He started the year out of the bull pen but soon earned a regular slot in the rotation. Bouton's pitching style was kinetic. He lunged toward the plate after every pitch with his arms and legs whirling. The violent motion often sent his cap flying right off his head. By the close of the regular season, he had compiled a 21–7 record with a stellar 2.53 ERA. In addition to making his first and only All-Star appearance, he pitched Game 3 of the World Series, losing a tough 1–0 decision to the Dodgers.

Despite being warned against the practice, Bouton gravitated toward sportswriters, especially the greener ones he felt an affiliation to. His salary disputes became an annual occurrence, and he openly disclosed details of the negotiations to the press. He also liked to discuss topical issues, such as politics and war, a policy strongly discouraged by the baseball establishment. Perceived as a wise guy, he began to fall out of favor with certain teammates. After another promising performance in '64 (18–13, 3.02 ERA), he fell on hard times.

Bouton reported to spring training in '65 with a sore bicep. He tried to pitch through it, but the condition never fully improved. His brief reign as a superstar was over as he accrued a 4–15 record with a bloated 4.82 earned run average. By 1967, he began bouncing up and down from the majors to the minors. Unable to regain his velocity, he began polishing his knuckleball.

Bouton was sold to the Seattle Pilots before the expansion draft of 1968. He began taking notes on his comeback experience, dashing to the bull pen bathroom to record incidents that struck him as humorous. He also spoke into a tape recorder nearly every day. His comical and insightful musings eventually became one of the most beloved baseball books of all time.

Released in June of 1970, *Ball Four* met with glowing reviews from a host of reputable literary sources. Those who offered praise marveled at how the book transcended the sport. Pulitzer Prize winner David Halberstam called it "a book deep in the American vein." Roger Angell of *New Yorker* magazine applauded Bouton's "ironic" and "courageous" mind. Others were not so enamored with the work.

Though *Ball Four* was not the first book of its kind (pitcher Jim Brosnan had chronicled his baseball exploits in *The Long Season* and *Pennant Race*), it was by far the most frank and revealing. A host of dirty secrets were aired to the public, among them the rampant use of amphetamines by players. Mickey Mantle's heavy drinking was also brought up in detail—a side of "the Mick" that had been largely kept out of the press over the years. In Bouton's world, players frequently used foul language and resorted to boorish behavior, such as looking up the skirts of women. In one comical incident, a hole was actually drilled into the back of a dugout wall for that purpose. Managers and coaches were often portrayed in a favorable light, though their tendency to be trivial and demeaning did not go unmentioned.

The reaction from people within the sport was scathing. Commissioner Bowie Kuhn called the book "detrimental to baseball." *New York Post* columnist Dick Young referred to Bouton and his editor as "social lepers." The Yankees weighed in on the topic as well, unofficially banning the articulate hurler from Old-Timer's Games at Yankee Stadium.

Midway through the 1970 campaign, Bouton was again demoted to the minors. He became a sports anchor for *Eyewitness News* on WABC-TV and dabbled at television acting. The TV series based on his book was cancelled after a few episodes in 1976. In '77, he was signed to a minor-league contract by the White Sox and progressed to the Double-A level but failed to win a game in 10 appearances for Knoxville. His perpetual comeback attempt ended the following year when he finally earned a September call-up from the Atlanta Braves. He was strapped with a 1–3 record and 4.97 ERA.

Bouton added several chapters to his enduring manuscript over the years. He also penned a handful of other books: *I'm Glad You Didn't Take It Personally*, *Strike Zone*, and *Foul Ball*. In 1996, *Ball Four* was included among the New York Public Library's "Books of the Century." It was the only sports book to make the list.

Following the tragic death of Bouton's daughter Laurie in 1997, his son Michael wrote a touching letter asking George Steinbrenner to lift the unofficial ban on Bouton from Old-Timer's Games at Yankee Stadium. It was published by the *New York Times* on Father's Day. Several weeks later, Bouton was allowed to step onto the field with some of his old teammates, among them Moose Skowron and Hank Bauer. He received a standing ovation and later likened the experience to "walking in a dream." As of 2012, he was working as a motivational speaker and earning up to $10,000 per appearance.

Hal Chase

A contemporary once commented that Hal Chase "was completely and congenitally amoral." Among the most gifted first basemen of his generation, he indeed seemed to be lacking a moral compass as his almost pathological habit of throwing games led to his eventual blacklisting from the majors in 1919. He died penniless and disgraced, groveling to clear his tarnished name.

Chase was born in Los Gatos, California. He was the youngest of six siblings. Growing up around his father's sawmill, he was regularly exposed to rough, burly characters. Disenchanted with school, he quit in the 10th grade to devote more time to playing semi-pro ball in the Santa Cruz Mountains and Santa Clara Valley. He later enrolled at the University of Santa Clara with vague aspirations of becoming an engineer. His academic records have been lost to posterity. A left-hander who batted from the right side, he was installed as a second baseman on the university team (an unusual position for a southpaw). He played well enough to earn a line in his college yearbook: "Chase would be difficult to replace."

He first appeared in the majors with the Highlanders in 1905, quickly earning acclaim for his brilliant work around first base. Several colleagues, including Babe Ruth and Cy Young, later cited him as the best first-sacker they had ever seen. Given his ethical shortcomings, it seems fitting that Chase landed in New York, since the Highlanders were owned by Frank Farrell, proprietor of a well-known illegal casino, and Bill Devery, a notoriously corrupt police captain.

During Chase's eight-plus seasons in the Big Apple, the team went through six different managers and finished at the .500 mark just three times. In that span, Chase paced the circuit in errors on five occasions—a peculiar fact considering that he was so highly regarded at his position. He topped the circuit in putouts once during the 1911 campaign.

Chase was contentious and self-serving. He once referred to his infield mates as a bunch of "dopes." He argued with Farrell regularly over a variety of topics ranging from salary to managerial choices. After a stellar season in '06 (.323 BA, 76 RBIs), he asked for a significant raise. When his request was denied, he demanded a trade, but the reserve clause bound him to the Highlanders. In '07, he threatened to join the outlaw leagues if his salary demands were not met. In '08, he jumped the club briefly when Kid Elberfeld was named as a managerial replacement for Clark Griffith. With George Stallings at the helm, trouble of a more grave nature surfaced.

During the 1910 slate, the Highlanders were seriously contending for their first American League pennant. On the heels of a lackluster performance one afternoon, Stallings confronted Chase and accused him of throwing games. A heated argument ensued, and the two almost traded blows. Chase was relegated to the bench afterward. A full investigation was supposedly conducted by AL president Ban Johnson, but in reality, Johnson swiftly dismissed the claim because Chase was a major fan attraction. Likewise, the owners failed to act because they needed his bat in the lineup. Angry and insulted, Stallings resigned from his managerial post. In a laughable turn of events, he was replaced by none other than Hal Chase. The club ultimately finished a distant second to the Philadelphia A's.

According to pitcher Chet Hoff, Chase was well liked and genuinely seemed to understand his players. Regardless of this fact, he was not the greatest choice for manager. In 1911, he guided the Highlanders to a mediocre sixth-place finish. He was succeeded by Harry Wolverton the following year.

More drama unfolded in 1913 when Farrell and Devery installed former Cubs' standout Frank Chance as manager. Chance was allegedly so unpopular with players that they would sometimes lie down in practice just to irritate him. Mired in last place throughout the month of May, the so-called Peerless Leader told the press that Chase was dragging the team down. Chase had been saved by the owners once before, but that was during his most productive period in New York. Off to a slow start with a .212 batting average, the marquee infielder was traded to the White Sox. Neither of the two players acquired for Chase had a positive impact on the club as the Highlanders (by then known as the Yankees) finished 37 games below .500.

Chase began the 1914 slate with Chicago and then caused a major controversy when he abruptly jumped to the newly formed Federal League. In a standard baseball contract, clubs were required to give unwanted players 10 days' notice before their release. Chase boldly turned the "ten-day clause" around on the White Sox, angering league executives. The case was taken before a judge, who admonished AL leaders for "interfering with the personal freedom of the men they employed."

After scoring a personal victory in court, Chase hit .347 in 75 games for the Buffalo Buffeds. His follow-up performance was even better as he slammed 31 doubles, 10 triples, and a league-leading 17 homers for the sixth-place Buffalo franchise in 1915. Many players who defected to the Federal League had trouble finding work when the circuit folded after the '15 slate. Chase wrangled a contract with the Reds and was by far the most productive member of the club, claiming the National League batting title with a .339 mark.

"Prince Hal" was in trouble again during the 1918 campaign, getting suspended by manager Christy Mathewson for offering bribes to teammates and opponents. One such offer had reportedly been made to teammate Jimmy Ring in a game Chase had bet on against the Giants. A hearing was held in the postseason, presided over by NL president John Heydler. Despite the testimony of several players, Heydler could not substantiate the claims, and Chase escaped penalty.

Even with his name in ill repute, Chase was signed by the Giants shortly before the 1919 slate. Manager John McGraw commented affably: "I have found him a most agreeable chap and I am sure we will get along without a hitch." McGraw spoke too soon, as Chase and teammate Heinie Zimmerman made multiple attempts to corrupt teammates. According to historian Fred Lieb, Chase's career came to an end before the 1920 slate when President Heydler obtained a copy of a $500 check given to Chase by a gambler in 1918. With irrefutable evidence that Chase was crooked, Heydler informed Giants' owner Charles Stoneham that Chase was barred from participating in future games. In February of 1920, the *New York Times* officially reported that he would not be attending spring training.

The year 1920 brought a fresh round of allegations. Former Cincinnati teammate Lee Magee revealed that he had conspired with Chase to throw games in 1918. Additionally, Chase was accused of scheming with Pacific Coast League players, a charge that resulted in his banishment from baseball in the state of California. When the White Sox scandal broke, he was implicated and questioned by investigators. His role in the World Series fix could not be firmly established, however, and he avoided punishment. He later admitted to having prior knowledge of the scheme.

Life was not kind to Chase after his playing days were over. In 1926, his Achilles tendon was severed in a car accident. By 1933, he had become a "shambling derelict," according to one source. Forced to live in a small cabin on his sister's California ranch, he was interviewed twice by the *Sporting News*. Though he openly admitted to being "involved in all kinds of bets with players and gamblers" over the years, he insisted that he had never bet against his own team. He died in 1947 of a kidney ailment.

Pete Rose

Looking at a list of Pete Rose's career accomplishments, it's difficult to believe he's not in the Hall of Fame: 17 All-Star selections, 3 batting titles, 3 World Series rings—the list goes on. In addition to collecting more hits than any player in the history of the game (4,256), Rose holds several other records, including most singles, times on base, at-bats, and plate appearances. He is also the only player to have logged more than 500 games at 5 different positions. When A. Bartlett Giamatti banned him from the sport in 1989, it was undoubtedly the most controversial decision he ever had to make.

Born in Cincinnati, Rose was encouraged by his parents to play multiple sports. Prioritizing football over his studies, he ended up repeating 10th grade. In 1960, he joined the Dayton Amateur Baseball League, serving as a catcher, second baseman, and shortstop. Though he was not considered a major-league prospect, he compiled an almost superhuman batting average of

.626. Rose had connections—his uncle was a scout for the Reds—and after much haggling, he was offered his first professional contract.

A hard-nosed player with passion for the game, Rose once said that he would "walk through hell in a gasoline suit to keep playing baseball." In a spring training match against the Yankees in 1963, he drew a walk from Whitey Ford. When he sprinted to first base, the hurler sarcastically dubbed him "Charlie Hustle." The moniker stuck.

Known for his headfirst slides and aggressive baserunning, Rose's playing career was marked by a handful of unsavory on-field incidents. He is perhaps best remembered for delivering the winning run during the 1970 All-Star Game in uncompromising fashion. With the game tied in the 12th inning, Rose led off with a single and moved to second on another safety by the Dodgers' Billy Grabarkewitz. Cubs' outfielder Jim Hickman then dropped a hit in front of Kansas City's Amos Otis. Otis's throw eluded Indians' catcher Ray Fosse as Rose plowed into him at home plate, literally knocking him senseless. Fosse suffered a separated shoulder, which went undiagnosed and worsened when he tried to continue playing. He lost his power stroke and was never the same again, becoming a mediocre platoon player. Rose later commented that Fosse should be thankful since the infamous collision was his only claim to fame.

Another unpleasant scene involving Rose unfolded during the 1973 National League playoffs. The Series was tied at one game apiece, and the Mets had just dealt the Reds a humbling 5–0 setback in the second contest. Before Game 3, New York's light-hitting shortstop Bud Harrelson innocently quipped to reporters that the Reds resembled him at the plate (he was a lifetime .236-hitter). Cincinnati's Joe Morgan took offense to the comment and confronted Harrelson. The two resolved their differences, but Morgan warned him that Pete Rose was still angry and would be looking for a way to get at Harrelson on the base paths. After the Mets had jumped out to a commanding 9–2 lead, Rose did just that, knocking the pint-sized infielder flat while breaking up a double play. Rose was solidly built at 5-foot-11, 200 pounds. Harrelson had earned the nicknames "Twiggy" and "Mighty Mouse" for his diminutive 160-pound frame. When Rose scuffled with Harrelson at second base, causing both benches to empty, he cemented his image as a bully.

Rose would become player/manager of the Reds in 1984. He logged his last at-bat in '86 and then piloted the club for three more seasons. He was equally feisty in a manager's role, baiting umpires and engaging in periodic disputes. In April of 1988, he went a bit too far, pushing umpire Dave Pallone during a heated debate. Rose claimed that Pallone had scratched him in the face, provoking the aggressive act. His argument fell on deaf ears as he was suspended for 30 days—the longest penalty ever imposed on a manager for an on-field incident.

Rose's reputation suffered another serious blow the following spring when rumors surfaced that he had wagered on games he was involved in, a direct violation of baseball's Rule 21. Faced with the prospect of ineligibility, Rose remained upbeat, joking with reporters about it. He was far less jovial when trial attorney John Dowd compiled a 225-page report supported by the testimony of some of Rose's close associates. In it, baseball's all-time hits leader was accused of being a compulsive gambler and of betting on Reds games from 1985 to 1987. Though he adamantly denied the claim, Rose's personal records would later show that he bet more than a half million dollars on hundreds of games, some of which he took part in.

Rose sought to overturn the investigation in a common pleas court, but this tactic failed to produce results. The case was heard at the federal level. In August of 1989, he was declared "permanently ineligible" to play or manage in professional baseball. He signed an agreement to accept his banishment in return for the possibility of reinstatement.

In 1990, Rose's world continued to unravel as he pled guilty to felony counts of concealing income on tax returns. He served five months in jail and expressed regret over the mistakes he had made. Erasing any hopes that he might be enshrined at Cooperstown, the Hall of Fame adopted a rule in 1991 stating that "any player on baseball's ineligible list shall not be an eligible candidate."

A ray of light surfaced in 1999, when Rose was included on the roster of Major League Baseball's "All Century Team." The ban on Rose was temporarily lifted so he could participate in pregame introduction ceremonies before Game 2 of the World Series at Turner Field in Atlanta. He received the loudest ovation of all, but his shining moment was sullied when NBC's Jim Gray aggressively questioned him about his gambling. Many were angered by the interview, including Yankee outfielder Chad Curtis, who refused to speak to Gray after his game-winning homer in Game 3 of the Series.

Rose continued to lobby for reinstatement. In 2002, he met with Bud Selig to plead his case. Selig asked Rose point-blank if he had bet on baseball. Rose answered in the affirmative but insisted that he had never bet against his own team. The meeting was recounted in Rose's 2004 autobiography, My Prison without Bars.

Using the 322-page book as a pulpit for his restoration, Rose openly admitted to gambling on baseball, a charge he had denied for more than a decade. He also answered the long-standing question of why he had done it:

because he didn't think he'd get caught. Extensive passages of the manuscript were devoted to descriptions of his attention deficit disorder and oppositional defiant disorder, conditions theoretically resulting from a chemical deficiency in his brain. He attributed much of his compulsive and occasionally reckless behavior to these diagnoses. One reviewer referred to the work as "a fascinating study of denial."

By 2007, Rose had admitted to having wagered on the Reds every night. During an ESPN radio interview with Dan Patrick and Keith Olbermann, he affirmed that the Dowd Report was accurate. He also insisted that he should be reinstated because he was baseball's "best ambassador." Commissioner Bud Selig reconsidered the prospect in 2009 but, in the end, decided it would draw far too much controversy. Today, baseball's self-proclaimed "ambassador" still lies in wait.

Heinie Zimmerman

In the world of baseball, there are few things more disappointing than unfulfilled potential. According to numerous sources, Heinie Zimmerman had all the skills necessary to become one of the greatest infielders of the Deadball Era. But his questionable work ethic and lack of integrity led him on an inexorable path to career destruction.

Zimmerman's unfortunate nickname—vernacular for Henry—was fairly common in the early part of the 20th century. Born in the Bronx, he became a plumber's apprentice at the age of 14 to help his struggling family. He dominated the sandlots of New York City and moved his way up to the semi-pro level while still in his teens. In 1906, he made his minor-league debut, hitting just .186 for Wilkes-Barre of the New York State League. His follow-up was far more promising and earned him a September summons from the Chicago Cubs.

The Cubs were a powerful team in those days, capturing four pennants and two World Series between 1906 and 1910. A versatile infielder, Zimmerman's ascent to full-time status was blocked at nearly every position. When second baseman Johnny Evers succumbed to injuries in 1911, Zimmerman shined as a replacement, hitting .307 with 85 RBIs. Fate took another turn the following spring when Jim Doyle tragically died of appendicitis. The empty third-base job was handed to Zimmerman, who made the most of the opportunity by narrowly missing a Triple Crown with a .372 batting average and 14 homers. He fell short in the RBI department, gathering 99 to Honus Wagner's 102.

Described by one writer as having an "awkward loping gait" and a "perpetual sneer," Zimmerman developed a reputation as an inconsistent performer.

Teammates complained that he would play hard one day and then put in a lackadaisical effort the next. In 1911, he was pulled off the field and suspended by manager Frank Chance for "indifferent fielding." A few years later, he was benched by Joe Tinker for "laying down on the job." The *Sporting News* commented more than once that his vast talent was going to waste.

On a good day, Zimmerman was belligerent and ultra-competitive on the diamond. In 1913, he was ejected three times in a five-day span, prompting the *Chicago Tribune* to publish the following lines from a letter written by an anonymous fan: "He gets canned too often for fighting umpires. It ain't fair to those who pay their money to see Zim swat the pill." In reality, the so-called letter was an elaborate ruse cooked up by the *Tribune* staff. Hall of Fame umpire Bill Klem gave Zimmerman a fragment of a hundred-dollar bill on behalf of the mythical "fan" and promised that he would receive the other portion if he could avoid ejection for two straight weeks. Though it was quite a stretch, Zimmerman maintained his composure and earned the full $100. The *Tribune* later revealed that the entire scam had been concocted in an effort to curb the infielder's unpredictable temper.

Off the field, Zimmerman was affably eccentric with a taste for elaborate practical jokes. While Cubs' players were relaxing in the smoking room of their hotel one evening, Zimmerman and pitcher Lew Richie got into a verbal altercation that escalated into a round of fisticuffs. After being separated by teammates, both men stormed off, leaving those in attendance wondering what had caused such a row between them. Just before curfew that night, there was a tremendous disturbance coming from Richie and Zimmerman's suite. Several players looked in to find the two pranksters rehearsing their next phony bout, which was slated to take place the following afternoon.

Though Zimmerman never regained the levels of production he had set in 1912, he did display periods of brilliance. Traded to the Giants in late August of 1916, his appearance on the roster sparked the club to an unprecedented 26-game winning streak. Unfortunately, the New Yorkers had gotten off to such a poor start that they ended up in fourth place. "Zim" led the league with 83 ribbies and finished among the top 10 in runs scored, hits, doubles, and total bases. Even so, writers found cause to criticize his inconsistency.

In 1917, the enigmatic, hot corner guardian stepped up his game again, topping the circuit with 102 RBIs while helping the Giants claim the pennant by a wide margin. But a miserable performance in the postseason helped solidify his reputation as an erratic player. In a six-game Series loss to the White Sox, Zimmerman hit just .120 and was unfairly blamed for a glaring defensive lapse that proved costly.

With Game 6 scoreless in the top of the fourth, "Zim" made a poor throw on a ball hit by Eddie Collins for a two-base error. Outfielder Dave Robertson then muffed a routine fly by Joe Jackson, putting runners at second and third with no out. Happy Felsch followed with a ground ball right back to pitcher Rube Benton. Benton threw to Zimmerman at third, trapping Collins in a rundown. When Zimmerman relayed the ball to catcher Bill Rariden, Collins spryly eluded his pursuers and bolted for home. No one was stationed at the plate, so the lumbering Zimmerman had no choice but to engage Collins in a footrace. The results were predictable as Collins plated the first of three Chicago runs that inning. The Sox won, 4–2, clinching the Series.

Zimmerman was blasted by the press for a play that wasn't even his fault. Discouraged, he slumped mightily in 1918. In July of that year, he was benched by manager John McGraw for not hustling. The following season would bring more dishonor for the former batting champion. Many who followed his career suspected all along that he had been involved in the fixing of games. Any credible uncertainty was erased after the ethically bankrupt Hal Chase joined the club and recruited Zimmerman as a henchman. The two eluded the watchful eyes of McGraw until September 11, when "Zim" tried to coerce right-hander Fred Toney to ease up on the Cubs. Toney promptly asked to be removed from the game. That night, Chase and Cubs' infielder Buck Herzog approached Rube Benton and tried to talk him into throwing a game the next day. When Benton won the contest anyway, Zimmerman confronted the hurler, informing him that he had missed out on a $400 dividend. Less than a week later, Chase and Zimmerman were at it again, attempting to lure outfielder Benny Kauff into their fold. It would prove to be their undoing as several players finally blew the whistle on their misdeeds.

McGraw suspended Zimmerman, covering up the scandal by citing the infielder for breaking curfew. Soon afterward, Zimmerman confessed his indiscretions to McGraw and owner Charles Stoneham. In the wake of the White Sox scandal, his activities were reported to a grand jury assigned to investigate gambling within the sport. Zimmerman admitted that he had offered bribes to Toney, Benton, and Kauff. He was blacklisted, later returning to the plumbing trade. During prohibition, he operated a speakeasy frequented by notorious mobster Dutch Schultz. His brother-in-law became a top lieutenant in Schultz's order. Both were killed in gangland shootings, and Zimmerman returned to a life of manual labor. He died in 1969.

~

CHAPTER FOUR

Hostile Hurlers

Dolf Luque

At 5-foot-7, 160 pounds, Dolf Luque was among the smallest men ever to pitch in the majors. What Luque lacked in physical stature, he made up for with fire and fortitude. Among the most petulant moundsmen in history, he was described by a contemporary as "a snarling, vulgar, cursing, aggressive pug." While this certainly worked to his advantage at times, it also served to overshadow his on-field accomplishments.

Born and raised in Havana, Cuba, Luque was among the first Latino players to attain a large measure of success in the big leagues. Light-skinned with blue eyes, he slipped right through the color barrier in 1913, compiling a 22–5 record for Long Branch of the New York / New Jersey League. He was called up to the Braves in May of 1914 but didn't stick around long enough to see the club upset the heavily favored Philadelphia A's in the World Series that year. He would spend most of the next four seasons in the minors, finally earning a regular spot in the Reds' rotation at the end of the 1918 campaign.

In 1919, Luque served as a swingman in Cincinnati, beginning an impressive run of 10 consecutive seasons with double-digit victory totals. The Reds captured their first pennant of the 20th century that year, and Luque got into two October contests as a closer. He twirled five scoreless frames, but his numbers can hardly be taken seriously since most of the White Sox starters conspired to throw the Series. The diminutive hurler would return to the Fall Classic with the Giants 14 years later and ultimately end up tied for the lowest ERA in Series history. He allowed no runs and three hits while striking out 11 batters in 9.1 innings of postseason work overall.

Often referred to as "the Pride of Havana," Luque enjoyed his finest season in 1923, when he made a serious bid for a pitching Triple Crown. His 27 wins and 1.93 ERA paced the circuit while his 151 strikeouts landed him second to Brooklyn's Dazzy Vance. Aside from Luque and Vance, only three NL moundsmen reached the century mark in that department during the '23 slate. Luque would duplicate the feat just once more during his long career.

Since there were so few of his fellow countrymen serving in the majors, Luque dealt with a lot of racism in his day. The fact that he played in an era when bench jockeying was a conventional aspect of the game made matters quite difficult for him. Luque was sensitive about his ethnicity and seemed to perfectly fit the Latin American stereotype: quick to anger—eager to solve disputes with his fists.

By the time he retired from the sport in the 1950s, stories of his unbridled temper abounded. The most infamous episode took place at Redland Field in Cincinnati during the '22 slate. An overflow crowd that day forced teams out of their standard dugout areas closer to the field. The Giants spent a large portion of the game peppering Luque with taunts and ethnic slurs, which were rendered more audible due to their proximity. After several innings, the hot-blooded hurler lost his cool, charging the New York bench. He took a wild swing at outfielder Bill Cunningham but missed, clouting Casey Stengel (still in his playing days) squarely in the jaw. Numerous versions of the fracas exist. Most of them end with Luque having to be forcefully removed from the field by four policemen after threatening Giants' players with a bat.

Luque's anger was indiscriminate. He once threw an ice pick at a teammate who had made an ethnic remark to him. While playing for the Dodgers in the early '30s, he tangled with an ill-mannered fan. The patron in question kept shouting "Lucky Luque!" from his seat every time the right-hander retired a batter. At wit's end, Luque approached manager Wilbert Robinson and warned that he would personally shut the man up if the taunting persisted. Robinson was in the process of discouraging such retaliation when the fan began to poke fun at his rotund frame. "Okay, Dolf," the corpulent skipper conceded, "go ahead and clobber the jerk." Luque reportedly did as he was instructed.

Luque's explosive temper directly impacted the outcome of a game in May of 1921. Incensed by a safe call at the plate in the eighth inning of a contest at Forbes Field, he irritably fired the ball into his own dugout. Pirates' infielder Clyde Barnhart took off running on the play as the ball was retrieved in time to nail him at third base. Pittsburgh's manager George Gibson strenuously argued the call, insisting that the ball should have been ruled dead immediately upon entering the Cincinnati dugout. The argument fell on deaf ears. After the Reds won in extra innings, Gibson took his complaint to a higher authority. NL president John Heydler ordered the game replayed from the point it had been disrupted with the Reds leading 3–2. The Pirates won the replay, 4–3.

After leaving the majors in 1935, Luque went on to a long, fruitful career as a player and manager in the Cuban winter league. Only one Cuban hurler—Hall of Famer Martín Dihigo—surpassed Luque's cumulative win totals in winter ball. As a manager, Luque led several different squads to championships. Time did not mellow his high-spirited ways, however. A two-fisted drinker and notorious womanizer, Luque enjoyed wagering on cockfights, an activity forbidden in the States. Described by one writer as "a brash and often profane public figure," he endangered the lives of his players on more than one occasion.

In a possibly apocryphal story, Luque was arguing with pitcher Terris McDuffie during a playoff series. Luque wanted McDuffie to start on two days' rest, but McDuffie refused. Exasperated with the rebuttal, Luque called the moundsman into his office, where he allegedly pulled out a gun and said threateningly: "Now, motherf—r, are you going to pitch or not?" McDuffie took the assignment and spun a two-hitter.

Another frightening account of Luque's gun-toting behavior involved Negro League standout Ted "Double Duty" Radcliffe. Convinced that Radcliffe had been dogging it on the field, Luque tried to shoot him in the locker room. Radcliffe was supposedly saved by a hairsbreadth when teammate Rodolfo Fernandez brushed Luque's arm aside and persuaded him to put the weapon away.

Over the course of his life, Luque spent money frivolously and was nearly bankrupt when he died of a heart attack in 1957 at the age of 66. He was never a serious candidate for the Hall of Fame in Cooperstown, peaking at 5.6 percent of the vote in 1958. He was posthumously elected to the Mexican Hall of Fame in 1985 and the Latino Baseball Hall of Fame in 2011.

Early Wynn

No serious discussion of the most fearsome pitchers in history would be complete without mention of durable flamethrower Early Wynn. Mickey Mantle once groused that Wynn was so ornery, "he'd knock you down in the dugout." Ted Williams (not exactly a warm and fuzzy character himself) categorized Wynn as the toughest pitcher he ever faced. In the end, sportswriters decided the hard-nosed hurler was among the all-time greats, electing him to the Hall of Fame in 1972.

Wynn was born in a small Alabama town bordering the Florida Panhandle. His father was an auto mechanic and a semi-pro ballplayer. After breaking his leg playing football, Wynn decided to give baseball a try. According to a popular myth, Wynn was 17 when he showed up at a camp run by the Washington Senators in bare feet and coveralls. Scouts in attendance were impressed with the chunky 200-pounder, offering him a contract after seeing just a handful of pitches.

Wynn dropped out of high school and spent five seasons polishing his craft in the farm system prior to becoming a regular in the Washington rotation. He accrued a fair 66–55 record in minor-league play. When the big right-hander first appeared in the majors, he had little more than a fastball in his arsenal. But he had plenty of attitude. Cantankerous Cleveland outfielder Ben Chapman stopped by the Washington dugout one afternoon to find out who was pitching. When manager Bucky Harris pointed out Wynn, Chapman boasted arrogantly that he would get five hits. Wynn scowled at Chapman and allegedly retorted: "If you get five hits, the last three will be from a prone position."

After a mediocre performance in his first full campaign, Wynn won 18 games in 1943, helping Washington to a distant second-place finish. Before then, the club had wallowed in the second division for six straight seasons. He led the league with 17 losses the following year before joining the army and serving in World War II. The Senators finished in second place without him.

Upon returning to action, Wynn pitched inconsistently. His 17–15 effort in 1947 captured the attention of Indians' owner Bill Veeck, who made Clark Griffith a generous trade offer. The elderly Washington proprietor spurned the deal only to see his coveted fireballer go 8–19 with a career-worst 5.82 ERA the next year. Before the '49 campaign, Wynn was shipped to Cleveland along with first baseman Mickey Vernon for three players, one of whom was Griffith's son-in-law.

The Cleveland brass was well aware of Wynn's raw talent and untapped potential. In an effort to expand his repertoire, former mound master Mel Harder (who had won 223 games for the Indians during his 20-year career) was recruited to teach Wynn how to throw a curve and a slider. The results were dramatic as Wynn would reach the 20-win threshold five times during the 1950s. Along the way, he developed a reputation as one of the nastiest pitchers in the majors.

Researcher Lew Freedman described Wynn as "focused" and "intense, with the glower that made edgy batters nervous." Another source remarked that he "treated every ballgame as if it were a war." Wynn reveled in such descriptions and fueled the fire with a plethora of surly witticisms. "I've got a right to knock down anybody holding a bat," he once told a reporter. Offering advice to aspiring hurlers, he told another scribe that "a pitcher has to look at the hitter as his mortal enemy."

In his career, Wynn hit just 64 of the 19,408 batters he faced—a figure that doesn't even place him among the top 200 headhunters of all time. But there is no official statistic for brushbacks, which were the right-hander's stock and trade. Wynn was not afraid to throw at the greatest hitters of his time. Mickey Mantle was a favorite target. Ted Williams was also forced to duck and run on a regular basis. While playing for the White Sox in 1960, Wynn had a two-hitter going through five innings at Fenway Park. After yielding a single to Pete Runnels, the ultra-competitive hurler knocked Williams down with a carefully placed fastball. Not easily intimidated, "Teddy Ballgame" got back up and smashed a 450-foot homer—the 497th of his career.

Explaining his intensity on the mound, Wynn once remarked that "every fourth or fifth day of summer, I go into a Jekyll and Hyde act." He would occasionally feel guilty about what he had done and encourage an opponent to spend time with him off the field. Wynn once invited Ted Williams to go fishing in the Florida Everglades. When Williams declined (despite his great passion for fishing), Wynn playfully prompted the slugger to admit he was scared. Williams did just that, commenting that any hitter who entered the Glades with Wynn stood a chance of turning up missing.

Wynn was known to throw chairs and other items in the locker room after losing. He also despised being taken out of games, distrusting the bull pen to finish what he had started. One day, when Wynn was arguing with an umpire, White Sox manager Al Lopez came out to calm him down. Wynn assumed he was being replaced and threw the ball at Lopez, hitting him in the stomach. Though Lopez described it as more of a "flip/toss," the press had a field day with the incident.

Wynn took a stab at sportswriting himself in 1955, when he began publishing a regular column in the *Cleveland News* entitled "The Wynn Mill." Not surprisingly, his blunt commentary on various issues angered many. He particularly enjoyed griping about the management in Cleveland, a practice that put him at odds with general manager Hank Greenberg.

By 1961, Wynn was 41 years old and all but washed up. Unfortunately, he was 16 wins shy of the coveted 300 mark. He hung around the majors for three more seasons trying to reach the elusive threshold. On July 13, 1963, he was sent to the showers early after yielding four runs on six hits to the lowly Athletics. But Jerry Walker tossed four scoreless innings in relief, and the Indians tagged struggling Kansas City right-hander Moe Drabowsky for five runs of their own. Wynn emerged victorious for the 300th time in his career. He would never win another game in the majors.

The tenacious hurler waited nearly a decade to get into the Hall of Fame. When he was snubbed yet again in 1971, he reacted bitterly, attacking the election process. He referred to the prestigious Cooperstown shrine as "the Hall of Shame" and commented acidly that "the next thing you know, they'll be putting a vendor who sold a hell of a hot dog in next to Babe Ruth." When he finally got the call in '72, he grumbled: "I'm not as thrilled as I would have been if I had made it the first time." For those who had played against the testy hurler, the comments were not all that surprising.

Dizzy Dean

Jay Hannah Dean's star burned brightly for just a short time. Of all the pitchers in the Hall of Fame, he ranks near the bottom in most statistical categories. But for five seasons, he was a force to be reckoned with. A larger than life personality with pomp and swagger, he loved to bait and intimidate opponents. He was also prone to blatantly reckless behavior.

Dean was born in Logan County, Arkansas. His mother died of tuberculosis when he was only eight years old. Parental guidance was scarce since his father put in long hours as a tenant farmer and sawmill worker. As a result, Dean's school attendance was intermittent. He stopped going altogether in 1926 and joined the army. By his own admission, he acquired the equivalent of a fourth-grade education.

Dean allegedly picked up his nickname when an army sergeant saw him throwing peeled potatoes against a garbage can and called him a "dizzy son of a bitch." Upon leaving the service, he spent portions of two seasons in the Texas League before earning a promotion to the Cardinals. He enjoyed his prime years between 1932 and 1936, winning 120 games while leading the National League in numerous departments. During that span, he captured four consecutive strikeout titles and twirled 19 shutouts. In 1934, arguably his best season, he was named NL MVP on the strength of his 30–7 record and 2.66 ERA. In the postseason, he combined with his younger brother, Paul, to win all four games of the World Series for St. Louis. It was the club's last Fall Classic appearance of the decade.

Dean was among the most arrogant players ever to step onto a diamond. While playing in the Texas League, he once called up a rival manager before a start and announced that he would hold his opponents to "just two or three hits." In 1934, he predicted that he and his brother would win 45 games. He made good on both of those claims, later becoming famous for the statement: "It ain't braggin' if you can back it up."

Dean's tendency toward showboating often embarrassed adversaries. He once bet a teammate that he could strike out Vince DiMaggio four times in a game. DiMaggio went down on strikes three times and then hit a pop-up behind the plate in his fourth at-bat. Dean screamed at his catcher to drop the ball. After his teammate had obliged him, he proceeded to win the bet. In 1935, the cocky right-hander showed up Babe Ruth before a huge crowd in Boston. After giving Ruth nothing to hit in his first two plate appearances, Dean got two quick strikes on the iconic slugger. He then made quite a show of waving his outfielders back toward the fence. Grinning widely, he grooved a fastball straight down the center of the plate. Ruth, 40 years old and out of shape, swung right through it.

Though he was immensely popular with fans, Dean could be selfish, irresponsible, and mean. In 1934, he and his brother were fined by the Cardinals for skipping an exhibition game in Detroit. They balked at the punishment and refused to report. Paul gave in after a couple of days, but Dizzy held out, taking his case to Commissioner Mountain Landis. During the hurler's subsequent suspension, manager Frankie Frisch commented acerbically: "There are ten million people out of work in this country yet Dizzy Dean is willing to sacrifice the income of approximately $50 to fill the role of a playboy."

In June of the following year, Dean became irritated with what he believed to be sloppy fielding by teammates. He chastised them in the dugout before a sizable gathering of writers and fans. Rip Collins and Joe Medwick yelled back, and a fight nearly broke out. When he returned to the mound, Dean showed his disapproval by deliberately lobbing changeups at Pittsburgh hitters. The Pirates scored nine times before Frisch finally put an end to Dean's antics. It would not be the last time Frisch was forced to yank his star pitcher off the field.

In a spring training game against the Giants, Dean was tagged for seven runs in one inning. According to one account, he fussed and fumed on the mound, grumbling: "They're not going to hit the master that way!" In retaliation, he allegedly beaned seven straight New York hitters before Frisch finally screamed at the umpire to get the "maniac" off the hill. The arbiter agreed that things had gone too far and ejected the careless hurler.

Dean instigated a number of fights during his tumultuous career. In 1933, he tangled with Reds' pitcher Paul Derringer during batting practice. Three years later, he traded fists with former teammate Tex Carleton in a game against the Cubs. He reportedly lost both scrapes. In one of the most unpleasant incidents from his playing days, the impulsive moundsman initiated a full-scale brawl at Sportsman's Park in St. Louis during the '37 slate. After issuing a number of brushback pitches to the Giants, Dean knocked down outfielder Jimmy Ripple in the ninth. Ripple bunted toward Dean, but the ball rolled past him to second baseman Jimmy Brown. Dean plowed into Ripple anyway as the benches immediately emptied. Police assistance was required to clear the field. After the game, Dean refused to retract a series of disparaging remarks he had made in response to a balk call in the sixth inning. He was suspended by NL president Ford Frick.

Dean's meteoric career effectively ended during the 1937 All-Star Game, when he was hit by a line drive off the bat of Cleveland's Earl Averill. The ball fractured his toe, but Dean, who rarely followed advice, rushed back into action with an altered delivery. He hurt his arm in the process and lost his fastball. Realizing he was damaged goods, the Cards traded him to Chicago for three players and cash. The Cubs hung on to him for portions of four seasons, mostly for his ability to draw fans. He was let go in 1941.

When his playing days were over, Dean embarked on a successful broadcasting career, calling games for the Cardinals and Browns. His grammar was so bad, the St. Louis Board of Education complained that he was a bad influence on young listeners. "Let the teachers teach English and I will teach baseball," he responded. Asked by a detractor if he knew the King's English, he quipped: "Yes, sir, I do. And I know the Queen's English, too."

In an attempt to lure fans through the turnstiles of Sportsman's Park, Dean was recruited to pitch the final game of the 1947 campaign for the Browns. He held the White Sox to just three hits over four innings and singled in his only at-bat, but pulled a leg muscle and had to be removed. The game attracted nearly 16,000 spectators—far above the season average.

Despite his carefree ways and vindictive behavior, sportswriters recognized his contribution to the sport, electing him to the Hall of Fame in 1953. His induction speech contained at least one memorable sound bite as he thanked the Lord for giving him "a good right arm, a strong back, and a weak mind."

Carl Mays

Carl Mays had difficulty accepting his status as the most universally detested pitcher of his time. "I always have wondered why I have encountered this antipathy from so many people wherever I have been and I have never been able to explain it, even to myself," he once groused. Given his association with the ugliest incident in baseball history, hostility from fellow players should have come as no surprise.

The event in question happened on August 16, 1920, at the Polo Grounds in New York. Ray Chapman, a shortstop for the Cleveland Indians, stepped into the box against Mays on a damp, overcast day. The 29-year-old Chapman was primarily a gap-hitter with decent speed but little power. He was just coming into his prime offensively, having hit .300 in 1919 and carrying a .304 average into that August game against the Yankees.

Mays, a right-hander, used a quirky submarine delivery to keep hitters off balance. He had a good rising fastball and could make the ball sink or curve depending on his arm angle at the time of release. He was also notorious for throwing spitballs. Hitless in two trips to the dish, the right-handed Chapman crouched slightly and crowded the plate as Mays wound and fired. Camouflaged in a wet, hazy background, it's doubtful that Chapman even saw the pitch, which struck him squarely in the left temple. There was an audible crack.

Accounts of what happened next vary widely. According to a newspaper report, the ball bounced toward Mays, who picked it up and threw to Wally Pipp at first base. Pipp stepped on the bag, making the apparent out as Chapman staggered out of the box and then collapsed in a heap. At some point, the Cleveland infielder regained consciousness and was helped to his feet. He tried to walk but fell again before being transported to St. Lawrence Hospital. Eight hours later, he was dead. Having already established a reputation as one of the most disagreeable men in the majors, Mays became a pariah overnight.

Mays was born in Liberty, Kentucky—the son of a Methodist minister. His commitment to his faith would be evident later on as he refused to pitch on Sundays. His father died when he was 12 years old, and it has been said that the event left him with a contentious personality. He was described by a teammate as having the temperament of someone "with a permanent toothache."

Mays made his professional debut in 1912 for Boise of the Western Tri-State League, where he compiled a 22–9 record and 2.08 ERA. He was promoted to Portland the following season and then Providence in 1914. The Tigers were given one pick from the Providence roster that year but passed over Mays for pitcher Red Oldham. Oldham would average more than four runs per nine frames and retire with a winning percentage below .500. Mays would become one of the most dominant pitchers of his era.

Sold to the Red Sox before the 1915 slate, the irascible rookie sent a clear message to competitors: enter the batter's box at your own risk. In the heat of a tight September pennant race, Mays was given a mop-up assignment against the Tigers one afternoon. He threw at Ty Cobb repeatedly, eventually hitting him on the wrist. Cobb slung his bat at Mays in retaliation and was showered by the Fenway crowd with bottles when he took the field in the bottom of the frame. It would not be the last unsettling incident associated with Mays.

During the last game of a 1919 Decoration Day series, the A's rallied from a 2–0 deficit off Red Sox hurler Bill James. Philadelphia fans began pounding on the roof of the Boston dugout. Incensed by the crowd, Mays appeared on the dugout steps and rifled a fastball into the stands. The throw struck a fan named Bryan Hayes, who obtained a warrant for Mays's arrest. In order to avoid authorities, the foul-tempered moundsman would be forced to avoid appearances in Philadelphia for more than a year. He later apologized to Hayes in a meeting arranged by Philly manager Connie Mack. The charges against him were subsequently dropped.

Mays touched off a major controversy when he deserted the Red Sox in July of 1919. He had been bellyaching about various issues all season, including the poor run support provided by teammates during many of his starts. In a game against the first-place White Sox, he was hit in the head with a throw from catcher Wally Schang. Intensely frustrated, he walked off the field and refused to return to action that day.

Standing his ground, the ill-tempered hurler jumped a train back to Boston. He gruffly told reporters: "It will be impossible for me to preserve my confidence in myself as a ballplayer and stay with the Red Sox. . . . I do not care where I go." Red Sox owner Harry Frazee approved a deal for Mays to go to the Yankees, but American League president Ban Johnson declared the transaction void and suspended the hurler. Yankee owner Jacob Ruppert objected and eventually won contract rights in a New York Supreme Court ruling. From that point on, Johnson restricted Frazee's ability to barter with most American League clubs. Mays helped the New Yorkers to a respectable third-place finish that year with a 9–3 record in the second half.

In the wake of the gruesome Chapman incident in 1920, Mays tried to pin the blame on umpire Tommy Connolly, alleging that the official had allowed a badly blemished ball to be left in play. Fellow arbiters Billy Evans and Will Dinneen rushed to Connolly's defense, charging that no pitcher in the American League used more deception than Mays "in attempting to rough a ball to get a break on it." Mays endured a maelstrom of negative publicity as several teams clamored for his lifetime suspension. He remained out of action for a week after the tragic event.

Before his return to the mound on August 23, Mays received a menacing note from Ty Cobb accusing him of "arrogance, viciousness and greed." Ignoring the taunt, he pitched a 10–0 shutout and then pointed out to writers after the game that both Joe Bush and Howard Ehmke had hit more batters than he had that year. In the face of overwhelming adversity, he won 26 games and followed with his signature season. He compiled a 27–9 record with a league-leading seven saves during the '21 slate. Incredibly, teammate Bob Shawkey remembered Mays encouraging younger hurlers to throw at opponents even after Chapman's death.

Mays anchored the Yankee rotation until October of 1922, when he fizzled in the World Series against the Giants. Staked to a 2–0 lead in Game 4 at the Polo Grounds, he was virtually unhittable before allowing a sudden four-run outburst. He had lost twice in similar fashion during the '21 Fall Classic, and rumors surfaced that he was accepting bribes to throw games. One supporter of this claim was manager Miller Huggins, who benched Mays for most of the '23 campaign. In July of that year, the Yankee skipper deliberately left Mays on the mound to endure a 13–0 thrashing at the hands of the Indians. The embattled submariner coughed up 20 hits that afternoon and then later sat out the entire World Series as the Yankees finally beat their intra-city rivals.

Sold to the Reds after the '23 slate, Mays had a couple of good seasons left in him, winning 20 games in 1924 and 19 more two seasons later. According to sabermetric measurements, his lifetime statistics are roughly equivalent to Cooperstown inductees Stan Coveleski and Chief Bender. Despite his impressive .623 winning percentage, Mays appeared on just 2 percent of Hall of Fame ballots in 1958. "I won over 200 big league games," he reflected later in his life. "No one remembers that. When they think of me, I'm the guy that killed Ray Chapman."

Johnny Allen

Some pitchers are more intense than others. Master of the brushback, Bob Gibson was known to yell at batters and refuse mound conferences with catchers. Lefty Grove threw furniture in the clubhouse after tough losses. Among the sorest losers in history, Johnny Allen took his frustrations out on anyone who barred his path to victory.

Allen's temper was so notorious that even his 1959 obituary was unflattering. In it, an Associated Press writer recounted an unpleasant incident that followed a disappointing loss to the Red Sox. Allen had exchanged angry words with opposing pitcher Wes Ferrell during the game, and unable to contain his fury upon returning to the team's hotel, he grabbed a fire extinguisher and sprayed the corridor. That was after upending stools in the hotel bar and kicking over an ashtray full of sand. While Allen's intensity gave him an edge over batters, it also interfered with his prosperity at various points during his 13-year career.

Allen was born in September of 1904, a native of Lenoir, North Carolina, and the son of a police chief. When his father tragically died of appendicitis, his mother, Almyra, couldn't provide for Johnny and his three siblings. She shipped three of them off to the Thomasville Baptist Orphanage, where Johnny learned to play baseball. After attending Thomasville High School, Johnny landed a job in a Sanford, North Carolina, hotel. He met Yankee scout Paul Krichell while working there. Krichell was a former major-league catcher who had a keen eye for talent. In nearly 40 years of scouting the majors, he signed a slew of Cooperstown greats, among them Lou Gehrig and Tony Lazzeri. Allen told Krichell he was a pitcher, and a tryout was arranged. Krichell was impressed with the right-hander's talents and offered him a minor-league contract.

Allen's professional career began in 1928. He quickly moved his way up through the ranks in the Piedmont, East Carolina, and Georgia-Alabama circuits. In 1931, he posted a 21–9 record for Toronto and New Jersey of the International League. He earned a roster spot in the Bronx the following year.

In his auspicious major-league debut, Allen assembled a remarkable 17–4 record. With six Hall of Famers in the Yankee batting order (Ruth and Gehrig among them), his slightly inflated 3.70 ERA mattered little. The Bombers had plenty of punch to back him all year, including Game 4 of the 1932 World Series, when he staked the Cubs to a 4–1 first-inning lead. Allen retired just two batters that afternoon, but the New Yorkers tagged five Chicago hurlers for 13 runs on 19 hits, completing an efficient Series sweep.

Allen had a lively fastball and elusive curve. He threw from various arm angles. Frequent battery mate Bill Dickey was most impressed with Allen's sidearm heater, describing it as "the meanest delivery in the league for a right-handed hitter. You simply cannot get hold of it. He'll buzz it over the bat handle before you can see it." Allen's nasty fastball complemented his on-field persona.

Yankee trainer Earle "Doc" Painter took Allen under his wing, serving as an amateur psychologist of sorts. Explaining Allen's unpredictable temperament to a writer, Painter commented: "He expects to win every time he pitches and if he doesn't win, he may turn on anybody." The moody hurler disliked the way manager Joe McCarthy handled his pitching corps. McCarthy favored right-hander Johnny Broaca as a complement to the one-two punch of Red Ruffing and Lefty Gomez. Allen wanted more playing time and boasted to the press one day: "If I'm not a better pitcher than Broaca, I'll eat this shirt." Allen never reached the 200-inning threshold in New York. The Yankees grew tired of his frequent holdouts and sour attitude, shipping him off to Cleveland in December of 1935.

Allen notched 20 wins during the '36 slate, dropping a career-high 10 decisions in 243 innings. While facing the Browns early in the season, opposing manager Rogers Hornsby noted that Allen tended to lose focus in response to heckling. The secret quickly got out as other teams began turning their bench jockeys loose on him. Relentlessly razzed by the Tigers one afternoon, the tempestuous moundsman had to be restrained by umpires when he rushed angrily at Detroit coach Del Baker. Trying to ward off a major problem, the Indians petitioned AL president William Harridge to protect Allen from verbal harassment.

Allen had his finest campaign in 1937, jumping out to a 15–0 record despite being sidelined with appendicitis for several weeks. On the last day of the season, he had a chance to tie the American League record for consecutive wins held by Walter Johnson. He might have accomplished the feat if not for a miscue by third baseman Odell Hale. The play in question happened in the first inning after Allen had surrendered a double to Pete Fox. Hank Greenberg hit a grounder to Hale, who allowed the ball to pass through his legs, scoring Fox. It would prove to be Allen's undoing as southpaw Jake Wade held the Indians to just one hit. Allen, of course, blamed Hale for the 1–0 loss and went ballistic after the game. Manager Steve O'Neill had to restrain Allen twice when he tried to assault the error-prone third-sacker.

The following year, Allen was involved in one of the most renowned wardrobe controversies of all time. The ill-tempered twirler had cut the sleeves of one of his sweatshirts and worn it under his jersey during several of his starts in '38. He claimed the purpose of the alteration was let more air in, but the fluttering fabric served to distract hitters. When umpire Bill McGowan ordered him to either remove the sweatshirt or clip the tattered strips off of his sleeves during a game at Fenway Park in Boston, he refused and stormed off the field. In blatant defiance of manager Ossie Vitt, he declined to finish the game. The frayed sweatshirt was displayed in a Cleveland department store (with the proceeds of its sale going to Allen) and eventually found its way into the museum at the Baseball Hall of Fame.

During the '38 All-Star break, Allen suffered an injury of questionable origin. Accounts differ as to what exactly happened. Many sources agree that something snapped in his shoulder during his All-Star appearance, but it has also been proposed that he slipped on a bar of soap in the shower. Either way, he was never the same pitcher afterward. Off to a 12–1 start, he accrued a 2–7 record with a 6.29 ERA in the second half.

One thing that remained unchanged was Allen's penchant for causing trouble. In 1940, he took part in a plot to have Cleveland manager Ossie Vitt removed from his post. The Indians were in contention all season long before hitting a brief rough patch in June. Notoriously critical of his players, Vitt openly denigrated staff ace Bob Feller after a rough outing against the Red Sox. The following day, he pulled right-hander Mel Harder off the mound. Before taking the ball, he made a snotty remark about the hurler's salary. After the game, Allen, Feller, and Harder conspired to petition owner Alva Bradley for Vitt's dismissal along with several teammates. Their ruse failed to produce results, and when details of the scandal broke, the entire team was referred to as "Vitt's Crybabies."

The Browns purchased Allen's contract before the '41 campaign but waived him in July. The rapidly fading hurler spent portions of three seasons in Brooklyn, causing numerous headaches for management. In March of 1942, he was ordered out of uniform by club president Larry MacPhail for breaking training rules in Havana, Cuba. He was reinstated after manager Leo Durocher and chief scout Ted McGrew put in a good word for him. The following year, he completely lost his composure in a May contest at Forbes Field in Pittsburgh. Called upon in relief of Rube Melton, he failed to retire any of the four batters he faced. When umpire George Barr called a balk on him, Allen rushed at the arbiter like a wild man. It took several players to restrain him. An article in the *Pittsburgh Post Gazette* stated that the Brooklyn Press Corps admitted to never having seen "such an all-out physical attack by a player against an umpire." Allen was suspended for 30 days and fined.

Unable to deal with Allen's unstable temper, the Dodgers shipped him off to the Giants along with aging slugger Dolph Camilli in return for three players of little note. He was released in 1945. He played in nine minor-league games that year, racking up a 4–0 record and an impressive 1.31 ERA in the Carolina League. He was finished as a professional player after that.

Despite his numerous run-ins with officials over the years, Allen got to see what the game was like from the other side, serving as an umpire in the Carolina League. "It will be interesting to see what happens to the first manager who comes out of the dugout to protest a decision," a *Milwaukee Journal* writer commented shortly after Allen was hired, "The betting in most circles is that he will be met by a left hook to the jaw." By his own account, Allen managed to avoid major conflict as an arbiter, ascending to the level of umpire in chief before retiring in 1953. After leaving baseball behind, he entered the real-estate business in St. Petersburg, Florida. He left behind a wife (Mary Leta) and son (John Jr.) when he died from a heart ailment at the age of 54 in 1959.

Lefty Grove

In his later years, Hall of Famer Lefty Grove gave back to the community. He provided uniforms for Philadelphia sandlot players and even put two underprivileged youths through college. But those who knew him in the early days remembered him quite differently—a ruthless competitor with a vile disposition. The quick-tempered southpaw was known to tear apart a room on the heels of a defeat. Fortunately for those around him, he lost just 32 percent of his career decisions.

According to some sources, Robert Moses Grove was a descendant of Betsy Ross, who is universally given credit for creating the first American flag. The son of a Maryland coal miner, Grove toiled in the mines himself for a short spell but found the work disagreeable and quit. In 1919, he began playing amateur ball in the town of Midland. He ascended to the professional level in 1920, tossing six games for the Martinsburg Mountaineers of the Blue Ridge League. The team had recently upgraded their stadium, and seeking to pay off the debt, they sold Grove to the Baltimore Orioles (then a minor-league club). Grove later commented that he was the only player in history to be traded for a fence.

Grove had a blazing fastball and scant control. From 1921 through 1924, he averaged 156 walks per year while consistently collecting more than 200 strikeouts. In his five seasons with Baltimore, he won 108 games and guided the club to a pennant every year. When the Yankees and A's both expressed interest in the 24-year-old left-hander after the 1924 campaign, Orioles' owner Jack Dunn sold the hurler to his old friend Connie Mack for $100,600 (the Bombers had offered 100K).

When he first reached the majors, Grove had three pitches in his repertoire: fast, faster, and fastest. Teammate Doc Cramer once marveled that "everyone knew what they were going to hit at, but they still couldn't hit him." Grove's battery mate in Philadelphia was Mickey Cochrane, who was nicknamed "Black Mike" for a temper that nearly equaled Grove's. The gritty backstop commented that working with the erratic southpaw in his rookie season was like "catching bullets from a rifleman with bad aim." Manager Connie Mack decided that Grove was working too quickly on the mound and instructed him to count to 10 in between pitches. Batters could see the hurler's lips moving and began to step out of the box and ask for time to break his concentration. Grove posted a cumbersome 4.75 ERA in his rookie year, but led the league with a stellar 2.51 mark during his sophomore effort.

The ornery moundsman would soon evolve into one of the greatest pitchers in baseball history, winning back-to-back pitching Triple Crowns in '30 and '31. In addition to six All-Star selections, he led the league in strikeouts for seven consecutive seasons and accrued a 1.75 ERA in eight World Series games. The Athletics won the pennant every year from 1929 through 1931. Grove led the way with a remarkable 83–17 record (including postseason play) during that span.

The Maryland native was intense and menacing on the hill. Hall of Fame shortstop Joe Cronin commented of Grove: "Just to see that big guy glaring down at you from the mound was enough to frighten the daylights out of you." A close personal friend, infielder Jimmy Dykes, claimed that he was the only one allowed to approach Grove on the mound. "If I saw his blood pressure going up, I would get the ball and hold on to it for a while," Dykes said. According to Ted Williams, Grove's blood pressure was in the stratosphere quite often. "He was a tantrum thrower like me, but when he punched a locker or something, he always did it with his right hand," Williams recalled. "He was a careful tantrum thrower."

Grove's outbursts became the stuff of legend. Traded to the Red Sox in December of 1933, he developed a touchy relationship with manager Joe Cronin. One day, Cronin instructed Grove to walk Hank Greenberg of the Tigers with two outs, a man on and the Sox ahead by a 4–3 margin. Grove grudgingly complied and then surrendered the lead to Detroit after issuing three straight singles. On his way to the clubhouse, he threw his mitt into the stands, ripped off his shirt, and smashed one of Cronin's bats.

In Philadelphia, he tested the patience of the gentlemanly Connie Mack on a regular basis. Once, when Mack came out to remove him from a game, Grove allegedly told the elderly skipper to "go take a s—t ." Mack, who despised profanity, resorted to its usage on that rare occasion. As he took the ball from the insubordinate hurler, he countered: "You go take a s—t , Robert."

Grove's most notable outburst occurred in 1931, when he sought to break the AL record for consecutive wins set by Walter Johnson. He was brilliant that day as the Browns touched him up for just one run on a single and an error by utility outfielder Jimmy Moore. Moore was playing in place of Hall of Famer Al Simmons, who had sought medical attention for an infected ankle. When opposing pitcher Dick Coffman shut out the A's, Grove went into an uncontrollable rage, smashing furniture in the clubhouse, ripping his shirt to shreds, and throwing equipment. He held a grudge against Simmons for years.

In addition to ostracizing teammates, Grove avoided reporters like the plague. He cited an incident during spring training in which he had talked to a representative from a Philadelphia newspaper for nearly three hours only to have the man get all of the facts wrong. He also dodged photographers and fans. According to first baseman Tony Lupien, a young fan encountered Grove outside the Boston clubhouse on the heels of a defeat one day. When the kid asked for an autograph, Grove allegedly cuffed him in the face with a rolled up newspaper.

Even off the field, Grove's associates had reason to be wary of him. In November of 1928, the hurler was hunting in West Virginia when he accidentally shot a man named Roberdeau Annan. Annan, a friend of the pitcher's, was blinded as a result and sought legal compensation. In the spring of '31, a court found Grove not liable for the unfortunate mishap.

At the very least, Grove refrained from the use of knockdowns, plunking just 42 batters in close to 4,000 innings of work. "I never threw at a hitter," he once told a reporter. "If I ever hit a guy with my fastball, he'd be through. I was naturally wild enough to give them something to think about." Grove's memory may have been somewhat faulty. During a split-squad spring training game one year, he reportedly plugged Doc Cramer in the ribs after Cramer had raked him for a double.

The truculent moundsman retired after the 1941 slate with exactly 300 career victories. He suffered through two mediocre seasons to get the last few. Time changed him in a positive way. After his retirement, he was accommodating to writers and fans. He gave time and money to charity. Connie Mack was among the first to notice the difference, commenting to a press member: "I took more from Grove than I would from any man living. He said and did things, but he's changed. I've seen it year by year. He's got to be a great fellow."

Better late than never, or so the saying goes.

CHAPTER FIVE

~

Toxic Teammates

Kevin Mitchell

It's surprising that there has never been a made-for-TV movie produced about the life and times of Kevin Mitchell. The troubled slugger came of age in a violent neighborhood, later capturing National League MVP honors. Though it may sound like a feel-good story, it actually isn't. During his 13-year major-league career, Mitchell developed a nasty reputation as a malingerer and a toxic clubhouse presence. Aside from one great season in 1989, he never lived up to his full potential as a player.

Mitchell grew up in southeast San Diego in a neighborhood blighted by ramshackle housing and abandoned storefronts. He is believed to have been affiliated with a violent street gang known as the "Picrules." The lawless outfit was among the first to become heavily involved in drug trafficking, and Mitchell is said to have been shot more than once as an active member. He escaped the streets when he was signed by the Mets as an amateur free agent in 1980. He logged significant time in the minors with varying degrees of success before ascending to the Big Show for an uninterrupted nine-year run beginning in 1986.

Primarily an outfielder, Mitchell served as a third baseman for two full seasons. Despite his limited range and below-average defensive skills, he is still remembered for a spectacular barehanded grab he made in 1989 on a ball he misjudged off the bat of Ozzie Smith. The catch sent him crashing into the wall and through a door leading to an area beneath the stands at

Busch Stadium. It would prove to be the high point of his outfield career as he finished among the top five in errors on six occasions.

Mitchell made up for his ineffectiveness in the field with his powerful bat. He averaged 32 homers per year between 1988 and 1991—his most productive span. He authored his greatest season in '89, leading the league with 47 long balls, 125 RBIs, and a .635 slugging percentage. The ultimate sign of respect, he was intentionally walked 32 times that year. He was an obvious choice for MVP.

A poster child for behavioral problems, Mitchell was hardly worth his weight in awards. He would eventually become the subject of more than one urban legend. In Game 6 of the 1986 World Series, his Mets stood on the brink of elimination with two outs in the bottom of the 10th. Instead of watching from the edge of his dugout seat with teammates, he snuck off to the clubhouse to make travel arrangements. Meanwhile, back on the field, teammate Gary Carter singled to keep the game alive. Summoned to pinch-hit for pitcher Rick Aguilera, Mitchell pulled his uniform back on in a hurry and rushed to the plate to deliver a single without the benefit of his protective cup. The Mets would eventually win the game and the Series. Years later, Mitchell would attempt to refute the story in a radio interview, claiming he never wore a cup because he could not find one big enough to accommodate him.

An incident of a more disturbing nature was documented in Dwight Gooden's autobiography, *Heat*. The All-Star pitcher allegedly dropped by Mitchell's home unannounced one day accompanied by events promoter Mead Chasky. The two found Mitchell in a drunken state, arguing with his girlfriend and holding a 12-inch kitchen knife. Convinced that Gooden had brought the police with him, Mitchell irately ordered the hurler to barricade the doors. The two stunned visitors accommodated their host by blocking the front door with a couch. When Mitchell's girlfriend told him to stop "acting crazy," he reportedly grabbed the woman's cat and cut the animal's head clean off. He then allowed Gooden and Chasky to leave. At the ballpark the next day, he supposedly said to Gooden: "Yesterday never happened."

Interviewed for Jeff Pearlman's book, *The Bad Guys Won!*, Mitchell adamantly denied that the events had taken place and made reference to Gooden's notorious cocaine usage. In examining the facts, investigators from Snopes.com, a popular website that prides itself on debunking urban myths, could find no reason to condemn Gooden's claim though they could not confirm it either.

Mitchell would spend the majority of his career jumping from team to team and causing problems wherever he went. In 1991, he was arrested on suspicion of rape in Chula Vista, California. He escaped prosecution when the alleged victim refused to press charges. That same year, Mitchell's criminal past came back to haunt him when his friend, gang member Kyle Patrick Winters, was arrested in connection with the slaying of a 24-year-old police officer. At the time of the arrest, Winters was driving Mitchell's car, having just dropped the outfielder off at Candlestick Park before a game. Winters was charged with conspiracy to commit murder. Mitchell was not charged with a crime but would be traded by the Giants in the off-season.

The following year, Mitchell arrived at the Mariners' training camp 30 pounds overweight. His weight issues would be recurring along with various other maladies. Some of his injuries were so bizarre, he was suspected by managers and teammates of faking them to avoid playing. He was once benched after straining a stomach muscle vomiting. On another occasion, he skipped a start when he injured his mouth eating a frozen donut. The tooth he allegedly broke was replaced with a gold crown.

In 1994, Mitchell put up excellent numbers in the strike-shortened season for Cincinnati: 30 HRs, 77 RBIs, and a .326 batting average in 95 games. Looking for a change of venue, he signed with the Fukuoka Daiei Hawks of Japan. He became one of the highest paid players in Japanese history but angered management when he opted to defect back to the States in the middle of the '95 slate due to knee problems. In Japan, there is a strict code of conduct that requires players to remain active despite injuries. Mitchell had not been given permission to leave the team, and Hawks' executives were extremely unhappy.

In all, the former MVP played for eight teams during his major-league career. In '99, he jumped to the Mexican League and was arrested for assaulting his father during a domestic dispute. The following year, he was at it again, punching a rival in the face during an on-field brawl in a Western League game. He tried to clean up his act a decade later, donating time to a nonprofit organization known as "Athletes for Education," which served troubled inner-city youths. But violence crept into his life again two years later when he reportedly attacked a man on a Bonita, California, golf course. He was arrested for misdemeanor battery. In 2010, he was listed among the top delinquent tax payers in California with a debt of $5.2 million.

John Rocker

According to numerous sources, Abraham Lincoln once remarked that it was "better to remain silent and be thought a fool than to speak out and remove all doubt." He had no idea when he uttered those words how relevant they would be to the career of relief pitcher John Rocker. During his brief and turbulent major-league stint, Rocker may have set an unverifiable record for most fans offended by his social commentary. Stubbornly clinging to his divisive personal dogma, he continued to affront others long after his retirement.

In essence, Rocker was a flash in the pan. Selected by the Braves in the 18th round of the 1993 amateur draft, he was initially used as a starter. He had good velocity but poor control. He was also a bit eccentric. At Danville in '94, he was known to bite baseballs and allow throws from his catchers to hit him in the chest. He was not terribly impressive in the minors overall, posting a 23–32 record with a 4.39 ERA.

In 1998, the Braves discovered that he was far more effective as a reliever. He appeared in 47 games out of the bull pen that year, accruing a stellar 2.13 ERA. During the postseason, he was nearly unhittable, holding opponents scoreless in eight assignments. Despite his contribution, the Braves lost the NLCS to the Padres, four games to two.

In '99, Rocker became Atlanta's official closer. He was spectacular in the role, notching 38 saves while striking out 104 batters in 72.1 innings of work. For the second year in a row, he yielded no earned runs in 10 postseason games. There was every reason to believe that he might have a long and fruitful career in the majors. But then he started opening his mouth.

In December of '99, he allowed *Sports Illustrated* writer Jeff Pearlman to ride with him to a speaking engagement at the Lockhart Academy, a school for disabled children. During the relatively short trip, he committed career suicide by making numerous prejudiced remarks. Asked by Pearlman if he enjoyed speaking to children, he answered bluntly: "Not really." He then poured his derision upon the city of New York and its inhabitants.

Rocker's distaste for New Yorkers stemmed primarily from the harsh greetings he often received upon entering games at Shea Stadium. The prickly hurler was accused of spitting at fans and giving them the finger. One day, he allegedly threw a fastball straight at a net separating patrons from the field. He then called them "stupid" because they had jumped skittishly out of the way. During a series of postseason games in '99, Mets' fans pelted Rocker with garbage and dumped beer on his girlfriend. Instead of reacting in a dignified manner, Rocker showed his true colors.

Asked by Pearlman if he would ever consider playing in New York, Rocker asserted that he "would retire first." He compared the city to Beirut and complained that the subway was full of unsavory characters he would not want to ride with, such as homosexuals, ex-cons, and teenage mothers. He also stated that he was "not a very big fan of foreigners." Before Pearlman's interview was through, Rocker had additionally spit on a toll machine and charged that Asian women were among the worst drivers on the road. Pearl-man later referred to the bigoted moundsman as "a one man psycho circus."

The article caused a major stir as Rocker was ridiculed on the popular late night programs, *The Tonight Show with Jay Leno* and *Saturday Night Live*. Cautioned by Major League Baseball about tarnishing the image of the sport, he was forced to apologize publicly for his comments. He was also obligated to undergo drug testing and mandatory psychological counseling. A $20,000 fine was reduced to $500 on appeal. Likewise, his 28-game suspension was shortened to 14.

Having immersed the Braves in a media storm, Rocker's pitching began to suffer tremendously. After collecting just 24 saves in 2000, he was 5–9 with an awkward 4.32 ERA the following season. He was traded to Cleveland in June of '01 and then dished to Texas later that year. While playing for the Rangers, he generated negative headlines again when he made homophobic remarks about patrons in a Dallas restaurant he was eating in. The Rangers dumped him after the '02 slate, and Rocker wrapped up his big-league career with Tampa Bay in '03.

Though he may have been finished in the majors, the garrulous hurler was not done sharing his opinions with others. A few years after his retirement, he started a website intended to promote the use of English as a second-ary language among immigrants in America. In his mission statement, he praised past generations for changing their names to make them sound more Americanized and claimed that, in order to maintain a "strong, cohesive and united" nation, immigrants must assimilate the culture. The website was still up and running as of 2012, offering bumper stickers and T-shirts emblazoned with the words "Speak English."

In 2007, Rocker was implicated in a Mobile, Alabama, steroid ring. Asked by journalist Mike Silva in a 2011 interview if the charge was true, he said: "Yeah of course I was [using them]. Let's be honest, who wasn't?" That same year, he released his autobiography, entitled *Rocker: Scars and Strikes*. In it, he claims to have metaphorically died in December of '99, citing the infa-mous *Sports Illustrated* interview as the cause of his demise.

He refers to Jeff Pearlman as an "assassin" who resorted to "ambush style journalism." In trying to discredit Pearlman, he alludes to the writer's long history of character defamation. According to Rocker, Pearlman's victims were such upstanding individuals as David Wells (a self-proclaimed bad boy), Roger Clemens (at one time a suspected steroid user), and Barry Bonds (who is believed to have lied in front of a grand jury about his involvement in the BALCO steroid scandal). Pearlman labeled Rocker "an absolute, 100 percent liar" and stated that "his memories of the interview are comically off."

In *Scars and Strikes*, Rocker revisits the topic of immigration. To anyone who immigrated legally and demonstrated a "desire to become a productive member of American society," Rocker extends his best wishes. But to those he perceives as resistant to the "rules of our ancestors," he offers the following sentiment: "I sure as hell don't like you and have high hopes that at some point you will be forced to drag your freeloading, parasitic ass back to wherever you came from." In one damning review of the book, Internet journalist Matthew Callan compared Rocker to a schoolyard bully who would "run to the principal" if you "punched him back."

Presently, Rocker is not employed by U.S. Immigration and Customs Enforcement. Some would say: thank God for small favors.

Dave Kingman

Even as a boy, Dave Kingman had home run power. By his own report, he averaged about one dinger per game as a Little Leaguer in Hawthorne, California. He remembered driving several pitches into a drainage ditch located about 50 feet beyond the left field fence. As he came of age, his titanic blasts grew longer and longer.

Ralph Kiner once commented on Kingman's tendency to propel baseballs into the stratosphere: "He can hit them out of any park, including Yellowstone." In 1976, he hammered what has been estimated to be the longest shot in Wrigley Field history. The ball cleared a 30-foot screen above the ivy and crossed Waveland Avenue before bouncing off a neighbor's porch. Several years later, he launched a drive into the ceiling at the Metrodome in Minnesota. It entered a drainage hole in the roof and got stuck. Second baseman Tim Teufel commented after the game that "it was like a rocket going off."

Long before then, Kingman was a pitcher for Prospect High School in Illinois. He turned down contract offers from the Angels and Orioles to play for the University of Southern California. He posted impressive pitching stats, but his .353 batting average inspired Coach Rod Dedeaux to convert him to an outfielder. A towering presence at 6-foot-6, the prodigious slugger was the number one draft pick in 1970. He played in just 165 minor-league games before ascending to the majors.

At one time, Kingman's 442 homers were the most by any player excluded from the Hall of Fame. There were plenty of reasons to bar his access to Cooperstown. For starters, he hit just .236 for his career and struck out at least 100 times in 13 of his 16 seasons. He was also a subpar fielder, finishing among the top five in errors three times. In 1981, he led the league in miscues as a left fielder and also placed second as a first baseman—a dubious feat to say the least. One day, after Kingman had torn the webbing of his mitt and the trainer was summoned to fix it, Phillies' commentator Richie Ashburn quipped: "They should have called a welder."

Kingman was discontent nearly everywhere he went. *Chicago Sun-Times* columnist Brian Hewitt once described him as "an unquestionable slugging talent with a puzzling psyche marked 'fragile.'" Writing for the *Hardball Times* years after Kingman's retirement, correspondent Steve Treder was less charitable, commenting that Kingman's name was synonymous with "sluggishness, unpopularity and dysfunctionality." "Sky King" (as he came to be widely known) began his career with the Giants but eventually grew listless and requested a trade. Sold to the Mets in '75, he ignored all constructive advice and concentrated most of his energies on hitting tape-measure homers. He was highly undisciplined at the plate, drawing few walks and striking out often. Displeased with his situation in New York, he requested another trade. This itinerant lifestyle would continue throughout his career—especially in 1977, when he played for four different clubs.

Kingman enjoyed his finest offensive campaign with the Cubs in 1978, smashing 48 homers while driving in 115 runs. Despite a league-high 131 strikeouts, he compiled the highest batting average of his career at .288. That same year, he provoked the ire of Los Angeles manager Tom Lasorda when his three homers sank the Dodgers in a 15-inning affair. Asked by reporter Paul Olden after the game what he thought of Kingman's performance, Lasorda went into an obscene rant, dropping the "F-bomb" repeatedly. Kingman had a negative effect on some people. Mets' catcher John Stearns once compared Kingman's personality to a tree trunk, complaining that "when you talk to him, about all he does is grunt." According to one source, a fan at Shea Stadium held up a sign one day reading: "Kingman is the Worm of the Big Apple."

Over the years, Kingman had a contentious relationship with the press. Feeling that he was being misquoted by reporters while playing in Chicago, the inscrutable slugger began producing a ghostwritten column in the *Chicago Tribune*. Mike Royko of the *Chicago Sun-Times* mocked the column with a series of articles attributed to "Dave Ding Dong." In 1980, Kingman reportedly dumped ice water over a journalist's head. In 1983, he was reprimanded by the Mets for verbally abusing a female press member. An even uglier incident occurred while he was playing for Oakland.

Ditched by the Mets in January of '84 after a largely unsuccessful second stint with the club, Kingman signed with the A's. He would prove to be a fine addition to the roster, capturing Comeback Player of the Year honors as a designated hitter with 35 homers and 118 ribbies. He hit 30 more round trippers the following year and professed that he was "happy" in Oakland, which was somewhat out of character. Harassing members of the press was par for the course, however, and the sulky DH got himself into hot water in '86.

Kingman objected to female reporters in the clubhouse and clashed with Sue Fornoff of the *Sacramento Bee* on more than one occasion. In the first inning of a June contest between the A's and Royals, Kingman arranged to have a live rat delivered to Fornoff in a pink box. Attached to the rodent was a tag reading: "My name is Sue." He reportedly threw tissues at her after the fact and invited her to "go ahead and cry." Few people found the prank amusing, least of all the Oakland brass, who issued an apology to Fornoff and warned Kingman that he would be released if an incident of a similar nature occurred. He was fined $3,500 for the thoughtless gesture. Commenting on the events, *Sun Sentinel* scribe Steve Hummer wrote: "It can only be a matter of weeks before Kingman sends a king cobra to a woman sports writer with the note, 'kiss my asp.'"

Kingman hit 35 homers in '86 and then was granted free agency. The Giants signed him in '87 but declined to promote him when he hit just .203 in 20 games for the Phoenix Firebirds of the Pacific Coast League. He played for West Palm Beach of the Senior Professional Baseball Association in 1989 and hit 35 points above his career average. His 35 clouts in '86 were a record among players in their final season.

Vince Coleman

When most baseball fans think of stolen bases, they think of Rickey Henderson, Lou Brock, or Ty Cobb. Very rarely does Vince Coleman's name surface. Though the record books clearly show that Coleman is sixth on the all-time list behind Cobb and Tim Raines, Coleman's reprehensible behavior with the Mets from 1991 to 1993 overshadowed his considerable accomplishments on the field.

Coleman attended Florida Agricultural and Mechanical University, a school that also produced standouts Andre Dawson, Hal McRae, and Marquis Grissom. He was picked in the 10th round of the 1982 amateur draft by the St. Louis Cardinals and would spend portions of four seasons in the minors before earning a promotion to St. Louis. Nicknamed "Vincent Van Go" for his blinding speed on the base paths, the Cardinals gave him the green light nearly 700 times during his first six seasons. He led the league in stolen bases every year from 1985 through 1990, tying a major-league record set by

Maury Wills. In that span, he captured Rookie of the Year honors, played on two All-Star teams, and received MVP consideration twice. Additionally, he was the first player to swipe at least 100 bags in his first three campaigns.

As a hitter, Coleman was little more than competent. He compiled a .264 lifetime average with a high of 180 safeties in 1987. He liked to put the ball in play, never drawing more than 70 walks in a season. Likewise, he was a serviceable but not outstanding fielder. Despite his exceptional speed, he was assigned to left field, where he failed to capture a Gold Glove.

Coleman hit .221 in 17 postseason games with the Cardinals and is best remembered for a bizarre injury he sustained in the 1985 NLCS. With a light rain falling prior to the start of Game 4 in St. Louis, the grounds crew decided to cover the infield. Busch Stadium was equipped with an automatic tarp machine. Coleman, who was on the field at the time the device was activated, did not notice the mechanism in motion. It rolled over his leg, chipping a bone and badly bruising him. His replacement, Tito Landrum, hit .385 as the Cards took the NLCS, but lost the World Series to Kansas City.

Granted free agency after the 1990 slate, Coleman decided to test the market. When the Mets offered to boost his salary, he transferred his goods to New York. The four-year deal was reportedly worth $11.95 million and included a hefty signing bonus. It was the most lucrative contract he would ever sign as his career soon went into a tailspin.

Hamstring and rib injuries significantly curtailed Coleman's production in '91 and '92 as he had several stints on the disabled list. He sat out nearly 200 games during that span. Even so, he led the club in stolen bases both years. At the same time, he established himself as an incessant troublemaker.

Before arriving in the Big Apple, Coleman had played most of his career on artificial turf. He complained bitterly that the infield dirt at Shea Stadium was "keeping him out of the Hall of Fame." He also had more than one ugly run-in with management. In 1991, the temperamental outfielder engaged in a loud and profane argument at the batting cage with coach Mike Cubbage. The verbal sparring match, which was witnessed by members of the press, would later be cited as one of several pretenses for the firing of manager Bud Harrelson. In September of 1992, Coleman locked horns with Harrelson's replacement, Jeff Torborg. During a 4–1 loss to the Braves, Coleman was arguing a third strike call for the second time in three days. He poked his finger into umpire Gary Darling's chest, and when Torborg arrived on the scene to take charge, Coleman screamed at him and shoved his hand away. Their spat continued off the field, resulting in a two-game suspension for Coleman along with a considerable fine, which Coleman insisted was "undeserved."

Coleman's personal life came into question during spring training of '91, when a 31-year-old New York woman accused him of rape along with teammates Dwight Gooden and Daryl Boston. Preliminary DNA testing linked Gooden to the incident, which allegedly took place at the hurler's Port St. Lucie rental home. An investigation continued into April of 1992, when the charges were dropped due to lack of conclusive evidence.

The year 1993 brought a fresh round of unfortunate incidents. In April, Coleman injured Dwight Gooden's arm as he was carelessly swinging a golf club in the clubhouse. On July 24, Coleman was riding in a Jeep driven by Eric Davis of the Dodgers when he threw a lit firework into the Dodger Stadium parking lot. Three people were injured, among them a two-and-a-half-year-old girl named Amanda Santos. She suffered second degree burns and a lacerated cornea. The firework was believed to be of the M-100 variety—a powerful explosive used by the military to simulate grenades.

The repercussions of the incident were immense as Santos's parents pursued legal action. Coleman initially avoided reporters but issued an official statement three days after the occurrence. During a press conference, he portrayed himself as a "loving father" who never meant to hurt anyone. Coleman's teammate, third baseman Howard Johnson, commented: "It's embarrassing for the New York Mets. I hope this will teach some guys a lesson down the road."

After criminal charges were formally announced on August 3, Coleman was put on paid administrative leave. Mets' co-owner Fred Wilpon stated definitively that the outfielder was no longer welcome in New York. In November, Coleman pled guilty to a misdemeanor and negotiated an agreement that kept him out of jail. In addition to paying a $1,000 fine, he was sentenced to three years of probation with 200 hours of community service. It came as no surprise when the Mets traded him to the Royals for outfielder Kevin McReynolds in January of '94.

The years following the firework incident were relatively quiet ones. Coleman managed to cause no major problems for the clubs he played with after his departure from New York. He would wear four different uniforms between 1994 and 1997, swiping 40 or more bases twice in that span. During the '96 campaign, he lost the ability to hit, posting a weak .155 average in 33 games with Cincinnati. The Tigers tried him in six games the following year but released him when he went 1-for-14 at the plate.

Coleman finished his career with Memphis of the Pacific Coast League. Regardless of his past transgressions, he is still remembered fondly in St. Louis. In May of 2012, he was called upon to throw out the first pitch of a game at Busch Stadium. He spoke warmly of his days with the Cardinals and referred to the club of that era as "one of the greatest teams ever assembled."

Carl Everett

Carl Everett spent a lot of time reading the Bible, but there were several verses he might have skipped. A passage from Proverbs 29:22 warns that "a man of wrath stirs up strife, and one given to anger causes much transgression." During his 14 years in the majors, the power-hitting outfielder went from team to team doing exactly that. It would prove to be his ultimate downfall.

Born in Tampa, Florida, Everett attended Hillsborough High School several years after Dwight Gooden and Gary Sheffield had made names for themselves there. Everett was signed by the Yankees in the first round of the 1990 amateur draft and remained in their farm system until November of '92, when the Marlins acquired him in the expansion draft. At the time, he was ranked among the top 100 prospects according to *Baseball America.*

Everett plugged away in the minors through the '95 slate, earning a well-deserved reputation as a problem child. While playing for the Edmonton Trappers at the triple-A level, he was suspended for insubordination after a heated argument with manager Sal Rende. According to multiple sources, it took three coaches to restrain Everett during the dispute. Traded to the Mets after the '94 slate, he would cause friction in the Big Apple as well.

On the first day of training camp, Everett walked slowly to retrieve a ball while shagging flies. Feeling that he was loafing, manager Dallas Green categorized him as a "dog." Everett never got along well with Green and saw limited playing time until Green's dismissal in '96. "He wanted me to kiss his tail and I wouldn't," the outfielder told Tom Verducci of *Sports Illustrated.*

Everett joined the Venezuelan winter league in '96 but was kicked out after he went up into the stands to square off against several fans he claimed were dumping beer on him. He generated more negative publicity in August of '97, when he and his wife were charged with abusing their six-year-old daughter Shawna and five-year-old son, Carl IV. Though the charges were eventually dropped, a family court judge ruled that Linda Everett, Shawna's stepmother, resorted to "excessive use of corporal punishment." Shawna was placed in the care of her maternal grandmother while Carl and Linda retained custody of four other children.

Dropped by the Mets like a hot potato, Everett had a breakout season with the Astros in '98, hitting .296 with 15 homers and 76 RBIs. He was even better the following year, driving in 108 runs while compiling a career-best .325

batting average. But his tendency to self-destruct would send him packing yet again. Irritated about being left out of the lineup one day, he confronted manager Larry Dierker. Tearing the lineup card to shreds, Everett threw the pieces on Dierker's desk and demanded that he fill out a new one. Not surprisingly, it was Everett's last campaign with Houston.

In 2000, Everett prospered in the friendly confines of Fenway Park, joining a very small group of switch-hitters who have collected 100 RBIs in both leagues. Embraced warmly by Boston fans initially, he appeared to have found a home . . . and then he opted to share his religious beliefs.

A devout Apostolic Christian, Everett believed that the Bible should be interpreted literally. While being interviewed by a Boston beat writer, he refuted the existence of dinosaurs since they are not mentioned in scripture. Asked to explain the origin of fossils, Everett said they were man made. He would later be referred to as "Jurassic Carl" by *Boston Globe* writer Dan Shaughnessy.

While Everett's spiritual views were tolerable to some in Bean Town, his volcanic temper was not. In addition to a nasty shouting match with manager Joe Kerrigan (precipitated by his tardiness at a team workout) and a spat with teammate Darren Lewis that nearly escalated into a fistfight, Everett had a complete meltdown in an interleague game between the Red Sox and Mets. During the nationally televised contest, plate umpire Ron Kulpa contended that Everett's batting stance was illegal since his foot was crossing the inside line of the batter's box. When the arbiter drew a line in the dirt to indicate where a batter should stand, Everett lost his cool and head-butted Kulpa. Ejected from the game, he further disgraced himself by flailing at teammates, throwing a bat, and tipping over a watercooler. He was suspended for 10 games and fined. In the aftermath, Jeff Jacobs of the *Hartford Courant* commented that Everett was "clearly a five-tool player: selfish, unstable, obscene, odd and scary."

The next several years were marked by more episodes of bad behavior. In 2001, the controversial slugger was fined for grabbing his crotch and yelling at Mariners' pitcher Jamie Moyer after hitting a homer. While playing for the White Sox in 2005, Everett angered many when he shared his antigay beliefs with a writer from *Maxim* magazine. He boldly remarked that being gay is "wrong" since two women and two men can't produce offspring. Despite the resulting media circus, he hit .444 in Chicago's World Series sweep over the Astros.

Everett once commented that being hated gave him an edge. Maybe so, but it sure didn't help him stay in any one place for very long. After hitting .227 in 2006 for the Mariners—his eighth team in 14 years—he fell from the major-league ranks. He continued in the Atlantic League through 2010, driving in at least 80 runs and topping the .300 mark for three consecutive seasons.

So far, life after baseball has not been kind to Everett. In 2011, he was arrested twice for domestic violence. Police reported that Everett threatened his wife with a gun on April 25 of that year. When she attempted to call 911, he broke two of her phones. Five months later, he was arrested for assaulting a family member at his home in Colleyville, Texas.

Milton Bradley

Raw talent alone is not enough to be successful in the major leagues. In order to fashion a winning career, a player needs self-control and the ability to adapt to his environment. Milton Bradley was lacking in both respects, flaws that would ultimately prevent him from living up to his vast potential.

Bradley was born in Harbor City, California, and grew up under what has been described as "difficult circumstances." Raised by a single mother who reportedly had trouble providing for him, he cited this as a motivating factor to succeed as a ballplayer. Ultimately, he planned on rescuing his mother from a life of hardship. In the process, he encountered numerous troubles of his own.

It was evident early on that Bradley had difficulty getting along with others. One scout remembered him hitting a home run in a game for Polytechnic High School in Long Beach only to be snubbed by teammates as he crossed the plate. He was temporarily kicked off the squad during his sophomore season. Baseball writers would wax poetic about the switch-hitting outfielder's tiresome personality years later. *Seattle Times* columnist Jerry Brewer called Bradley "mercurial and tormented." Another scribe praised his "athletic virtues" while condemning his "me-first-and-only" mind-set.

Selected in the second round of the 1996 amateur draft by the Expos, Bradley was considered a five-tool player. He hit for average in the minors, but his power never fully materialized. A notorious hothead, he had some unpleasant clashes with umpires. In all, he would spend portions of six seasons on the farm before attaining full-time status in the big leagues.

His debut with the Expos in 2000 was inauspicious. He compiled a .221 batting average in 42 games. He was hitting just two points above that mark when he was traded to Cleveland in July of the following year. The Indians sent Bradley to Buffalo of the International League and then recalled him in September. The experience failed to improve his production at the plate as he collected just 4 safeties in 18 at-bats.

As was the case wherever he went, Bradley clashed with peers in the Forest City. Teammates used various unflattering terms to describe him, such as "lazy," "rude," and "hot-tempered." One day, he yelled at Hall of Fame coach Eddie Murray as Murray was trying to help him break out of a batting slump. He also had on-field disputes with Dodgers' catcher Paul Lo Duca and Yankees' first baseman Jason Giambi. On another occasion, he threw his bat and helmet in the direction of home plate umpire Bruce Froemming.

In February of '04, Bradley was sentenced to three days in jail after driving away from police during a traffic stop. A month later, he angered Cleveland manager Eric Wedge when he failed to hustle for a pop fly (which dropped for a hit) during an exhibition game. He was barred from training camp and placed on the trading block.

Bradley landed in Los Angeles, where his struggles continued. In June of 2004, he was suspended for four games after throwing a bag of balls onto the field following an ejection. He would later be forced to sit out the last five games of the season after slamming a plastic bottle (which had been tossed onto the field) at the feet of a fan sitting in the bleachers. He apologized for the incident and admitted that he might benefit from counseling to help him curb his temper. The Dodgers encouraged him to take an anger-management course in the off-season, but it failed to remove the sizable chip from his shoulder.

Bradley complained to reporters about second baseman Jeff Kent, claiming that he didn't know "how to deal with African American people." To Bradley's credit, the prickly Kent was disliked by several of his teammates. But Bradley went a step further, adding that white people in general have a tendency to ignore racial tensions even when they are evident. It was not the only time Bradley played the race card in Los Angeles. Tired of answering questions from *LA Times* reporter Jason Reid one day, he called Reid (who is African American) an "Uncle Tom."

After wearing out his welcome in Los Angeles and Oakland, Bradley was traded to the Padres in June of 2007. His season was preempted by a bizarre injury sustained while attempting to assault an official. During a loss to the Rockies, the fiery center fielder flipped his bat in disgust after being called out on strikes. This led to a confrontation several innings later with first-base umpire Mike Winters. Winters reportedly called Bradley a "piece of s—t." When Bradley lunged for Winters, he was restrained by Padres' skipper Bud Black. He tore his ACL and was out for the rest of the year. Winters was suspended for his role in the fiasco.

Granted free agency, Bradley signed with Texas for the 2008 campaign. Confident in his abilities, the Rangers shelled out more than $5 million to obtain his services. For the first time in a long time, he didn't disappoint, reaching career highs in homers (22) and RBIs (77). He also paced the circuit with a .436 on-base percentage. It was the only year in which he would lead his respective league in any category.

Sadly, Bradley's fine performance with Texas was not the turning point of his career. While playing for the Cubs in 2009, he was injured in spring training and sidelined until April. Upon returning to action, he was ejected from a game and suspended. During another bad day at the office, he lost track of how many outs there were and threw a live ball into the stands. Later still, he threw a tantrum in front of manager Lou Piniella and ended up being sent home.

There were issues of racism in Chicago as well. Bradley complained about prejudiced slurs being hurled at him by fans at Wrigley Field. He also claimed to have received bigoted hate mail. There may have been some truth to those reports. Former Cubs' standouts Jacque Jones and LaTroy Hawkins had both made similar charges while playing in the Windy City. But as usual, an embittered Bradley failed to handle the situation with tact. He openly stated that he didn't care about the outcome of games—he just wished they were over with quickly. He also commented that a "negative" environment in Chicago was to blame for the Cubs' failure to win a World Series since 1908. The latter remark led to his subsequent departure.

Bradley's last big-league stop was Seattle, where he caused more turmoil. In 2010, he flipped fans in Texas the bird and later screamed at manager Don Wakamatsu after being removed from a game in which he had struck out twice. In a scene reminiscent of his days with Los Angeles, he issued an apology and asked Wakamatsu and general manager Jack Zduriencik to help him work on his anger issues. For the second time in his career, Bradley completed an anger-management course. Improvement was evident, but a knee injury in July ended his season prematurely.

Bradley was cut loose by the Mariners in April 2011 following another ugly dispute with an umpire. Over the next two years, he would attack and threaten his wife repeatedly, resulting in multiple arrests. In January 2013, he was charged with more than a dozen misdemeanor counts of assault, which carried a maximum penalty of 13 years in prison along with $13,000 in fines.

Carl Mays became one of the most hated figures in baseball when he killed Indians' shortshop Ray Chapman with a pitch.
Library of Congress

Despite persistent rumors that Hal Chase (left) had been throwing games throughout his career, Giants' manager John McGraw (right) gave him one last chance in 1919. The experiment failed utterly as Chase was blacklisted from baseball before the 1920 slate.
Library of Congress

Chick Gandil, pictured here during his days with the Senators, was the self-proclaimed ringleader of the 1919 World Series fix.

Library of Congress

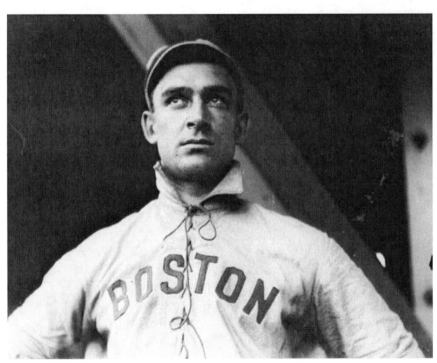

The cause of Chick Stahl's 1907 suicide has never been definitively determined. In the photo, he looks as if he's carrying the weight of the world on his shoulders.
Library of Congress

Among the first Cuban-born hurlers to meet with success in the major leagues, Dolf Luque's unstable temper was legendary. He was described by one contemporary as a "snarling, vulgar, cursing, aggressive pug."
Library of Congress

Ed Cicotte was on the mound for two of the White Sox's five losses during the ill-fated 1919 World Series. He won 209 games over a stellar 14-year career that was cut short by his lifetime ban from the sport.

Library of Congress

Fred Merkle was a more than capable first baseman who was unfairly stigmatized for a baserunning gaffe during his rookie season of 1908. The play would forever be referred to as "Merkle's Boner."
Library of Congress

The foul-mouthed George Stallings was one of the most superstitious managers in history. If something positive happened on the field, he was known to freeze like a statue and hold the pose, believing that the practice would prolong his team's good fortune.
Library of Congress

Juggling the Red Sox along with his theater interests, owner Harry Frazee sold most of his club's good players to the Yankees. Needless to say, he was an unpopular figure in Boston.
Library of Congress

Johnny Mostil was one of the premier center fielders in baseball before injuries and personal problems derailed his career. Mostil's grisly suicide attempt in 1927 was unsuccessful.
Library of Congress

HANLON, C. F. Detroits

Ned Hanlon as he appeared on his Old Judge Cigarette card.
Hanlon was manager of the 1890s Baltimore Orioles—one of the
nastiest teams ever to step onto a diamond.

Normally a sure-handed shortstop, Roger Peckinpaugh committed eight errors (an all-time record) in the 1925 World Series. His miscues directly affected the outcome of two games.
Library of Congress

Among the most crooked players ever to take the field, Heinie Zimmerman admitted to Giants' owner Charles Stoneham that he had thrown games while playing for the Giants. He was banished immediately thereafter.

Library of Congress

Baseball owner M. Stanley Robison (pictured here) and his brother Frank assembled the worst team of all time—the 1899 Cleveland Spiders. The hapless Spiders won just 20 games all year.

Library of Congress

It has been suggested by more than one researcher that Ty Cobb was a sociopath. His reputation as the meanest man in baseball was well deserved.
Library of Congress

While patrolling right field for the Orioles at Baltimore's Union Park, Willie Keeler almost always kept an extra ball hidden in the grass in case the one in play eluded him.

Library of Congress

Appointed commissioner of baseball after the World Series scandal of 1919, Judge Kenesaw Mountain Landis was faced with the daunting task of cleaning up the sport. He's all business in this photo.
Library of Congress

CHAPTER SIX

~

Scapegoats

Jack Chesbro

How degrading it must have felt to be remembered for one wild pitch. During a brief but productive major-league career, Jack Chesbro set an American League record for wins in a season and performed with enough consistency to be posthumously elected to the Hall of Fame. But during his lifetime, he was constantly reminded about the one that got away on the last day of the 1904 campaign.

Hailing from Houghtonville, a small village in North Adams, Massachusetts, Chesbro was the son of a shoemaker. He got his start in organized ball with various local sandlot teams. At age 20, he began working at a state mental hospital in Middletown, New York. He was consistently pleasant to patients and coworkers, a trait that reportedly earned him the nickname "Happy Jack." While playing for the hospital's baseball team (known as the "Asylums"), he was encouraged by catcher Pat McGreevy to pitch professionally.

Chesbro followed the advice, but his debut seemed star crossed as he played for two teams that folded before seasons' end in 1895. He ended up with Springfield of the Eastern League, where he logged a 2–1 record in seven games. Over the next two campaigns, he posted a .453 winning percentage in spite of miserly earned run averages. His fortunes improved significantly in 1899, when he was signed by the Pirates after going 17–4 in the Atlantic League.

Chesbro began his career as a fastball pitcher but eventually learned the deceptive art of the spitball. In order to throw it, the surface of the ball is moistened with saliva (as the name implies), causing pitches to behave in a manner similar to a knuckleball. Low pitches tend to drop dramatically while high ones often wobble and rise. Declared illegal in 1920, the "wet one" continues to be employed infrequently by some to the present day. Few hurlers can accurately predict where the pitch will go after it is released. In his time, Chesbro seemed to have complete command of the quirky offering, averaging just two walks per nine frames during his career.

Chesbro was one of many stars in Pittsburgh, a list that included eventual Cooperstown honorees Honus Wagner and Fred Clarke. During Chesbro's three full seasons in the Steel City, the Pirates won two pennants. His presence was felt most dramatically in 1902, when he compiled a 28–6 record and 2.17 ERA. A perennial holdout in spring training, Chesbro negotiated a contract to play for the New York Highlanders near the end of the '02 slate. When the Pirates learned that he was defecting to the rival American League, they excluded him from a series of postseason exhibition games in which players were allowed to split the gate receipts. There would not be an official World Series until the following year.

Chesbro was the Highlanders' first great pitcher. Later hailed by *Sporting Life* correspondent W. F. H. Koelsch as "king of the twirlers," he took his time reporting to spring training in '03. When he finally arrived in camp on April 1, having missed several practice games, he was a bit overweight. The New Yorkers were a middling squad managed by Hall of Famer Clark Griffith, who also shared pitching responsibilities. Chesbro won 21 games that year as the Highlanders finished in fourth place.

In the spring of '04, Chesbro was feeling rather ambitious. He reported to camp on time and in much better shape. He also started working on his spitball—a pitch that would forever change his career. Clark Griffith disliked the pitch, and backstop Jim McGuire was averse to catching it. But when the Highlanders got off to a lukewarm 5–5 start through April, both men conceded that something should be done to get the team going. Chesbro was encouraged to unleash the spitter in game situations.

The results were quite dramatic as the right-handed junk-baller won 14 straight games. Looking to ride his coattails into the postseason, Griffith handed Chesbro a cumbersome workload. Adding a changeup to his arsenal, the durable hurler made 28 starts on two days' rest and completed 48 of 51 assignments. The end result was one of the greatest pitching performances of all time: 41 wins, 12 losses, and a 1.82 ERA in 454.2 innings.

The Highlanders and Boston Americans would trade places at the top several times during the '04 slate. Offensively, New York was led by Hall of Famer Willie Keeler, who hit at a brisk .343 clip that year. Second baseman Jimmy Williams added 31 doubles while outfielder John Anderson gathered 82 ribbies—fourth best in the circuit. On the Boston side, the tireless Cy Young put up 26 wins at the age of 37. Outfielder Chick Stahl provided a lot of punch with 49 extra-base hits, including a league-leading 19 triples. A late-season surge put the Bostonians one and a half games ahead on the last day of the season. Scheduled to face them in a doubleheader at home, the New Yorkers had a chance to claim the pennant with a sweep.

The Highlanders were heavily favored in the first contest with Chesbro slated to take the hill. But opposing starter Bill Dinneen was no pushover, having logged his third consecutive 20-win campaign. The game remained scoreless until the fifth inning, when New York jumped out to a 2–0 lead. One of the runs was plated by Chesbro himself. Boston knotted the score in the seventh on a costly error by second baseman Jimmy Williams. In the top of the ninth, catcher Lou Criger beat out a roller to shortstop Kid Elberfeld—a remarkable development considering that Criger was so slow he stole just 58 bases in more than 1,000 career games. Bill Dinneen moved Criger to second with a sacrifice, and Kip Selbach followed with a ground ball out, advancing Criger to third. This brought Freddy Parent to the plate with two away. Parent was a capable hitter with some power, and Chesbro pitched carefully. Looking to polish off the dangerous Boston shortstop, Chesbro resorted to his most reliable pitch. Unfortunately, it sailed over the head of catcher Red Kleinow, bringing Criger home with the go-ahead run, which would hold up as the game winner.

Whenever the infamous game is recounted, a few details are typically left unmentioned: the crucial error by Jimmy Williams and the Highlanders' failure to rally in the bottom of the ninth. Chesbro would carry the brunt of the loss for the rest of his days and beyond. Some close friends tried to get the official scoring on the ill-fated play changed to a passed ball, but their efforts were in vain. Years later, Clark Griffith would contend that the pitch should have been caught by Kleinow. Kid Elberfeld insisted that it couldn't have been hauled in "with a crab net."

Hampered by weight issues and arm trouble, Chesbro's career went into a gradual decline following the 1904 slate. He reached the 20-win threshold in 1906 and then disappeared from the majors after compiling a 24–35 record over the next three seasons. A comeback attempt in 1912 was unsuccessful. In later years, he coached and pitched at the semi-pro level, remaining active until the age of 53. He operated a chicken farm until his death in 1931. Not surprisingly, the wild pitch was even mentioned in his obituary.

Ernie Lombardi

Many things have been written about Ernie Lombardi over the years, both flattering and otherwise. Even if he hadn't been unfairly blamed for the Reds' Game 4 loss in the 1939 World Series, he would still have been criticized for being a bit too slow and, at times, somewhat ham-fisted. But like so many talented players who have served as scapegoats over the years, he deserved much more.

Born Ernesto Natali Lombardi, he was raised in Oakland, California. His parents ran a grocery store in an Italian American neighborhood. At age 12, he played for Rivoli's Meat Market and established himself as one of the most talented youngsters around. He would carry a slew of nicknames in his lifetime, some of them disparaging, such as "Lumbago" and "Schnozz," which he received on account of his undeniably bulbous nose. Lombardi's nose was so large, in fact, that it protruded beyond the wires of his protective mask and occasionally took the brunt of foul tips.

Lombardi was a mountain of a man at 6-foot-3, 230 pounds. In his later career, he was even bigger, approaching the 300-pound mark. He was among the slowest runners ever to grace the diamond. Historian Bill James commented that his "center of gravity was four feet behind him." Another writer joked that he looked like he was carrying a piano on his shoulders while someone was still tuning it whenever he navigated the bases.

Lombardi earned his first professional roster spot with the Oakland Oaks. In 1929 and '30, Lombardi collectively hit .368 with 121 extra-base hits. He was signed by Brooklyn on the strength of his offense.

The hard-hitting backstop was not entirely a one-dimensional player. He had a rifle for an arm, foiling 47 percent of all attempted steals during his career. With the multitalented Al Lopez also on the '31 roster, the Robins (later known as the Dodgers) had a difficult decision to make. Lombardi split catching duties with Lopez that year, hitting at a solid .297 clip in 73 games. When Lopez proved to be slightly more adept behind the plate, manager Wilbert Robinson considered converting Lombardi to a pitcher but then opted to trade him instead.

For a decade, Lombardi was the Reds' first-string catcher. He led the National League in passed balls eight times while playing for Cincinnati but also made five straight All-Star appearances and captured an MVP Award. The lumbering backstop was among the greatest offensive forces of his era, hitting

.330 or better on five occasions while capturing a pair of batting titles. He was the last receiver to claim a batting crown before Joe Mauer did it in 2006.

Lombardi used a 42-ounce bat. He held it with interlocking fingers like a golf club. He resorted to a regular grip whenever he was in a slump and reported feeling "sort of funny" about it. He was known for his scorching line drives, undoubtedly a result of the bulky club he wielded. Because he was so slow afoot, infielders had the luxury of playing him very deep in an attempt to rob him of base hits. In a famous quote, Lombardi commented that he thought Dodger shortstop Pee Wee Reese was an outfielder for several seasons. He never hit more than 20 homers in a season and collected just 190 in 17 years of big-league service.

In the late '30s, the Reds climbed into contention with the addition of right-hander Bucky Walters, who was acquired from the Phillies. Walters formed a potent one-two punch at the top of the pitching rotation with perennial staff ace Paul Derringer. Together, the two hurlers averaged 42 wins per year from 1939 through 1941. With the clutch-hitting of Lombardi and first baseman Frank McCormick, Cincinnati captured two pennants in that span.

The '39 World Series would prove to be a miserable experience for Lombardi. The Yankees were a powerhouse that year, led by a gaggle of Cooperstown greats, among them Joe DiMaggio, Bill Dickey, and Red Ruffing. There was very little drama in the first three games as the Bombers outscored the Reds by a collective 13–4 margin. Looking to stay alive, Lombardi's crew fought valiantly in Game 4 at Crosley Field.

The Yanks jumped out to a 2–0 lead in the top of the seventh on solo homers by Bill Dickey and Charlie Keller. Refusing to roll over, the Reds came storming back with three runs in the bottom of the frame. Outfielder Ival Goodman doubled off reliever Johnny Murphy in the eighth, and Lombardi drove him home to put the Reds up, 4–2. With the dependable Bucky Walters on the mound, the game seemed well in hand. But the Yankees would not go quietly as Keller, DiMaggio, and Joe Gordon all singled in the ninth to even the score at four apiece.

In the 10th frame, Lombardi's reputation would be irrevocably stained as one of the most unusual plays in Series history unfolded. With Walters still on the mound, Frank Crosetti drew a leadoff walk. Red Rolfe sacrificed him to second. Charlie Keller followed with a grounder to shortstop Billy Myers, who muffed the play. With runners on the corners, Joe DiMaggio dropped a single in front of Ival Goodman in right field. Crosetti scored easily as Goodman mishandled the ball, bringing Keller around third. The throw home was late, and there was contact between Keller and Lombardi. In some accounts,

Lombardi took a knee to the head. In others, it was a shot to the groin. Keller himself reported that he ran right by Lombardi without touching him, but films of the play suggest there was impact. The big backstop explained afterward that it was a sweltering day in Cincinnati and he was "feeling dizzy." The force of the blow spun him around, and he lay motionless at the plate with the ball resting nearby. As DiMaggio circled the bases, Lombardi slowly recovered. (One has to wonder exactly where Bucky Walters was stationed during all this.) The play at the plate was close, but "Joltin' Joe" eluded Lombardi's tag with a nicely executed hook slide. The Reds failed to score in the bottom half of the 10th as the Yankees clinched the Series.

Historian Bill James described the press reaction as "the kind of negative media lightning that flashes across the landscape, scarring a random target." Ignoring the fact that DiMaggio's run was meaningless to the game's outcome, journalists painted Lombardi in an unfavorable light. To this day, the play is still identified as "Lombardi's Snooze," though variations such as "Swan Dive," "Swoon," and "Sit-Down Strike" also exist.

The 1940 season wasn't terribly uplifting for Lombardi either as he was in and out of the lineup all year with finger and ankle problems. Things took an ugly turn in August when backup catcher Willard Hershberger committed suicide at the Copley Plaza Hotel in Boston. Before slicing his own throat, he confided to manager Bill McKechnie that his father had committed suicide and he had been thinking about it himself. The regrettable incident took much of the luster away from the Reds' World Series victory over the Tigers that year.

In 1942, Lombardi was traded to the Braves following a salary dispute. He added another trophy to his case with a second batting title. Transferred to the Giants in '43, "Schnozz" closed out his major-league career with five relatively strong seasons in New York. He remained active in the minors through 1948, when his Oakland club won a league championship under Casey Stengel.

Life after baseball was tough for Lombardi. He ran a liquor store in San Leandro, California, before suffering a mental breakdown in 1953. While traveling to a psychiatric hospital at the insistence of his wife, he slit his own throat in the same fashion as former teammate Hershberger. He pleaded to be allowed to die and even wrestled with hospital attendants, but in the end, he made a full recovery.

Overlooked by the Baseball Writers Association of America for many years, Lombardi grew increasingly bitter, telling one reporter: "They can take the Hall of Fame and you know what they can do with it." He died the same year that Al Lopez—the catcher given preference over him in Brooklyn—

was enshrined as a manager. The forgotten backstop was finally elected to the Hall by the Veteran's Committee in 1986.

Bill Buckner

In the annals of New England sports history, few players have been as vilified as Bill Buckner. The mention of his name still evokes disapproval from a scattering of diehard Red Sox followers. Though the media would never let him forget the critical role he played in Boston's 1986 World Series loss, most reasonably informed fans realize that there were many other forces at work during that long ago October.

For the record, Buckner was a highly reliable if not exceptional player, who finished his career with 2,715 hits (among the top 100 totals of all time). Though he never won an MVP Award, he received serious consideration twice. He also made an All-Star appearance, won an NL batting title, and led the league in numerous defensive categories over the years. If not for recurring physical problems that repeatedly kept him out of action, there is no telling how many accolades he might have received.

Buckner grew up in Vallejo, California, and ended up being selected by the Dodgers in the second round of the 1968 amateur draft. In his first pro season, he hit .344, earning a promotion to the higher ranks. By the end of the '69 slate, he was wearing a Dodger uniform. After getting off to a .121 start in Los Angeles during the spring of 1970, he was sent down to Spokane for more conditioning. He was recalled in September and would remain at the major-league level for the next 20 years.

Buckner was one of several young players who would have a major impact in Los Angeles, a list that included Steve Garvey, Ron Cey, and Davey Lopes. By 1974, the Dodgers had assembled quite a crew, winning the NLCS over the Pirates before suffering a World Series loss to the A's. Buckner gathered five hits in the Fall Classic that year, one of them a solo homer in Game 3.

In 1975, the left-swinging outfielder was saddled with injuries, missing 70 games altogether. He was told by doctors that his left ankle was in bad shape. The joint was not moving properly, and there were numerous bone spurs present along with a ligament tear. Despite corrective surgery in the off-season, he was unable to play at full strength the following year. The ankle would give him periodic trouble for the rest of his career.

Feeling that he was damaged goods, the Dodgers shipped Buckner to the Cubs in January of '77. Admittedly bitter, the jilted fly chaser made negative comments about playing for a non-contender in a city he disliked. He regretted those words later as Chicago proved to be a good fit for him. Buckner would spend portions of eight seasons in the Windy City, hitting .280 or better on seven occasions. His crowning achievement came in 1980, when he edged out Keith Hernandez of the Cardinals for the NL batting title. He also paced the circuit twice in doubles.

The Cubs fared poorly during "Billy Buck's" tenure, and in 1984, newly appointed manager Jim Frey was looking to shake things up. Through the first 21 games of the season, Buckner was used mainly as a pinch hitter and a defensive replacement for Leon Durham at first base. Meanwhile, over in the American League, Boston was looking to get rid of right-hander Dennis Eckersley, who had been pitching inconsistently for the better part of two seasons. In a move that would prove beneficial to both clubs, Eckersley was dealt to Chicago for Buckner and minor-league prospect Mike Brumley.

Buckner was fairly optimistic about the trade, commenting: "You don't know how good you have it until you don't play." He made the most of the opportunity in his first full season with the BoSox, reaching career-high marks in doubles (46), hits (201), and RBIs (110). He remained highly productive in '86 with 59 extra-base hits and 102 ribbies. Boston had a well-balanced attack that year with Wade Boggs at the top of the order and Jim Rice regularly cleaning off the bags. Veterans Dwight Evans and Don Baylor pulled their weight as well, gathering 191 RBIs between them. In the pitching department, the Sox didn't even need the services of mound master Tom Seaver, who was fading at the age of 41. Roger Clemens turned in what was arguably the best season of his career with a 24–4 record and 238 strikeouts. The performance earned him Cy Young and MVP honors.

Boston climbed into first place in mid-May and then never let go the rest of the way. The ALCS was a hotly contested affair as the Sox climbed out of a 3–1 hole to dispose of the Angels in seven games. Making their first World Series appearance in a decade, the Hub Men had yet another chance to end a postseason drought dating back to 1918.

Their opponents—the Mets—were a colorful team driven offensively by prolific run producers Gary Carter, Darryl Strawberry, and Keith Hernandez. Right-handed strikeout specialist Dwight Gooden was a force to be reckoned with on the mound at the age of 21. Hurlers Bob Ojeda, Sid Fernandez, and Ron Darling made an excellent supporting cast as the Mets ran away with the pennant and disposed of the Astros in the League Championship Series.

Interestingly, the '86 Fall Classic did not favor the home teams. The Mets dropped the first two games in New York, and the Red Sox were defeated in both of their initial Fenway outings. In Game 5, the Mets squandered numerous scoring opportunities, stranding eight runners in a 4–2 loss. With the

Red Sox poised to clinch the Series, Boston fans prepared for a celebration that would never take place.

In front of 55,000 rabid fans at Shea Stadium, the Red Sox carried a tenuous 2–0 lead into the bottom of the fifth. The Mets scratched out a pair on a walk, a steal, and back-to-back singles, but the Sox pulled ahead, 3–2, thanks to a costly throwing error by third baseman Ray Knight in the seventh. An inning later, Lee Mazzilli led off with a single and then gradually circled the bases on a fielder's choice, a bunt, and a sac fly by Gary Carter. After nine innings of play, the score was knotted at 3.

The game should really have been clinched in the top of the 10th, when Dave Henderson homered and Wade Boggs doubled, later scoring on a timely single by Marty Barrett. But the Red Sox bull pen couldn't hold the lead. With two outs, reliever Calvin Schiraldi yielded three straight singles to Gary Carter, Kevin Mitchell, and Ray Knight. Right-hander Bob Stanley, who was called upon to put out the fire, uncorked a wild pitch, scoring Mitchell and tying the game. Mookie Wilson hit a routine bouncer to Bill Buckner, who had been left on the field with his notoriously bad wheels by manager John McNamara. The ball went straight through Buckner's legs, scoring Knight and forcing Game 7.

The rest, as they say, is history.

Why Buckner was chosen as the Series goat is mystifying. With Game 6 well in hand, most managers would have provided a defensive replacement for the 36-year-old first baseman. It was Calvin Schiraldi who surrendered the tying run in the eighth and failed to close the door later on. Bob Stanley was equally culpable with his stray toss that tied the game. Furthermore, Red Sox hitters collectively stranded 14 runners that night. The Hub Men had a chance to take the Series in Game 7 and even led 3–0 at one point before six different hurlers coughed up a slew of runs in a resounding 8–5 loss.

Buckner would be hounded relentlessly in the months that followed. A popular joke circulating shortly after Game 6 was as follows:

The Setup: Hey, did you hear what happened to Bill Buckner? He was so depressed over what happened, he stepped out in front of a bus.

The Punch Line: Luckily, it went straight through his legs.

The aging first-sacker soldiered on with Boston in '87, hitting at a respectable .273 clip before earning his release in July. Signed by the Angels, he would hit .306 for them the rest of the way. By '88, Buckner's career was coming to a close. Released by the Angels in early May, he signed as a free agent with the Royals. He spent portions of two seasons in Kansas City before returning for a curtain call in Boston.

The error continued to captivate fans after Buckner's retirement. In 1992, actor Charlie Sheen reportedly paid $93,500 for the infamous game ball. Buckner eventually moved to Idaho, where he could hunt, fish, and escape the enduring stigma of the '86 Fall Classic. He coached for the White Sox in '96 and '97 and then dropped out of baseball for a while. When the Red Sox finally won it all in 2004, Buckner described the experience as a "downer" since there were so many references made to him by the media. He groused that: "I feel like the guy who got put away for a crime he didn't commit." Four years later, he appeared at pregame ceremonies honoring Boston's 2007 World Championship squad. He received a warm ovation as he addressed the crowd and threw out the first ball that day. "I've got nothing bad to say about Red Sox fans," he later told reporters. "They were always good to me."

Mickey Owen

Life on the October stage can be cruel. One clutch hit can make you a household name. One costly error can destroy your credibility. Mickey Owen recovered from a miserable experience in the 1941 postseason, but he would forever be associated with the most infamous passed ball in World Series history.

Born in Nixa, Missouri, Owen carried the nickname "Preacher" in his minor-league days. He would later be known as "Mickey" on account of his resemblance to Hall of Famer Mickey Cochrane. Owen's professional career began in 1934 with the Rogers Rustlers of the Arizona State League. He moved to the Western Association the following year and fashioned two consecutive .300 seasons at the plate before joining the Cardinals in '37.

A lifetime .255-hitter, Owen was known primarily for his defense. He had a strong, reliable arm, foiling 50 percent of all attempted steals during his 13 years in the majors. He led the National League twice in that category while regularly placing among the top five in putouts, assists, and fielding percentage. The turning point of his career came in December of 1940, when he was traded to Brooklyn for veteran backstop Gus Mancuso. Mancuso would hit below .200 in three of the next five seasons as he slowly faded from the majors. Owen would make four straight All-Star appearances and guide his new club to the '41 pennant.

The 1941 Dodgers were managed by the fiery Leo Durocher, who once commented that he would trip his own mother if she were playing against him. Owen handled catching responsibilities brilliantly, setting an NL record for consecutive chances without an error (476). He worked with the top pitchers in the circuit—Kirby Higbe and Whit Wyatt, who won 22 games apiece. Right-hander Hugh Casey was Brooklyn's most often used reliever, collecting 14 victories in 45 appearances.

The offensive assault was led by center fielder Pete Reiser. Playing in his second major-league season, the 22-year-old phenom claimed the batting title with a .343 mark while also leading the league in runs scored (117), doubles (39), and triples (17). He finished second in MVP voting to teammate Dolph Camilli, who paced the loop with 34 homers and 120 RBIs. Corner outfielders Joe Medwick and Dixie Walker provided plenty of punch as well, collectively batting .314 with 159 ribbies.

The '41 Fall Classic was the first of seven postseason showdowns between the Yankees and Dodgers while both teams were located in New York. With six eventual Hall of Famers on their roster, the Bombers had finished 17 games ahead of the second-place Red Sox and were favored by many sportswriters to claim their fifth world championship in six years. The Dodgers fought hard to defy the odds, splitting the first two games in the Bronx and then dropping a 2–1 nail-biter at Ebbets Field. Looking to even things up, Durocher sent Kirby Higbe to the mound in Game 4 against sporadically used right-hander Atley Donald. Neither hurler would finish the contest.

The Yankees carried a 3–0 lead into the bottom of the fourth, when Donald issued consecutive walks to Owen and Pete Coscarart. Both men scored on a double by Jimmy Wasdell. An inning later, Donald was chased from the game following a two-run homer by Pete Reiser. The Dodgers would nurse a precarious 4–3 lead into the ninth inning.

Called upon to bail Johnny Allen out of a bases-loaded jam in the top of the fifth, Hugh Casey pitched four scoreless frames yet still managed to lose the match. In the ninth, he induced groundouts from Johnny Sturm and Red Rolfe. He then struck out the dangerous Tommy Henrich, swinging to end the game. Unfortunately, the ball eluded Owen's glove and rolled to the backstop, allowing Henrich to advance to first.

History has dictated time and again that it is a dangerous practice to give the Yankees a second chance. Casey couldn't buy an out, coughing up four runs on three hits before finally retiring the side—*again!* The stunned Dodgers went quietly in the bottom of the ninth to close out a heartbreaking 7–4 loss. The momentum completely shifted in favor of the Yankees as they clinched the Series in Brooklyn the following day.

After the demoralizing Game 4 defeat, Owen refreshingly made no excuses. He explained that Casey had two types of curveballs—an overhand slant with a big break and a smaller one with sharp movement like a slider. Before the ill-fated pitch, Owen had signaled for the curve and was apparently expecting the smaller one. When the big hook arrived instead, he got crossed up. "I was late getting my glove down there and it went right by me. My fault," he admitted. Years later, Owen described the shameful walk from the dugout to the clubhouse as follows: "It was like getting thrown to the lions. [Fans] were grabbing, cussing and throwing things."

In addition to being labeled a Series goat, Owen would later be known as an outlaw and a defector. Upon returning from navy service in 1946, he jumped to Jorge Pasquel's Mexican League. The son of a shipping magnate, Pasquel had been seducing established players with lucrative contract offers in the interest of creating a rival to the major leagues. Aside from Owen, the most prominent players to sign were pitchers Max Lanier and Sal Maglie. Yankee shortstop Phil Rizzuto reportedly balked at a $10,000 offer that included a brand new Cadillac as a bonus.

Owen soon found the conditions in Mexico disagreeable and returned home. Fearing that Pasquel's associates might apprehend him, he flew secretly into Brownsville, Texas. Back in the States, he received a rude awakening as he was blacklisted from the majors. Reinstated by Commissioner Happy Chandler in 1949, Owen served as a platoon catcher in Chicago. He was released after the '51 slate and spent two years in the minors before making his last major-league appearance with the Red Sox in 1954.

Life after the Big Show was fruitful for Owen as he founded his own baseball school and later moved on to a career in law enforcement. He served as sheriff of Green County, Missouri, for nearly two decades. On the 25th anniversary of the infamous passed ball, Owen received thousands of wires and letters from fans. Some included job offers and marriage proposals. He went to his grave in 2005 with the knowledge that he had been forgiven for his regrettable World Series faux pas.

Roger Peckinpaugh

There are legions of players who have been forced to contemplate the impact of a costly postseason error. Roger Peckinpaugh had several to think about. In the 1925 Fall Classic, he set an all-time record with a total of eight miscues. Though he captured MVP honors that year, he would never atone for the role he played in the Senators' disappointing World Series loss.

Peckinpaugh was born in Wooster, Ohio. He learned the basics of the game from his father, who had played at the semi-pro level. While still a boy, Peckinpaugh moved into the same neighborhood as Napoléon Lajoie—Cleveland's preeminent diamond hero. It was Lajoie who discovered Peckinpaugh after he blossomed into a multisport star at East Tech High School in Cleveland. The aspiring infielder spent just two years in the minors before becoming a mainstay in the Cleveland lineup.

Traded from the Naps (later known as the Indians) to the Yankees in 1913, Peckinpaugh established himself as one of the top defensive players of the era. He also earned lavish praise for his leadership abilities after serving as interim manager at the end of the 1914 slate. The youngest skipper in baseball history at 23 years of age, he guided the New Yorkers to a respectable 10–10 finish down the stretch. He would later be described by one writer as having a "steadying influence" wherever he played.

Offensively, Peckinpaugh was little more than competent, hitting .280 or better just four times during his career. According to one contemporary, opposing fielders were able to regularly rob Peckinpaugh of base hits by shifting to the left since he was a dead-pull right-handed hitter. When he did reach base safely, he demonstrated above average speed, swiping more than 200 bases in 17 seasons.

With the addition of several high-impact players in the early '20s, the Yankees immediately climbed into contention. The 1921 World Series was an offensive disaster for Peckinpaugh as he hit just .179 in eight games against the Giants. He was traded to Boston in December and then shipped to Washington before the start of the '22 slate.

The Senators had gone without a postseason appearance in their first two decades of play. Peckinpaugh was one of several players who helped turn things around—a list that included homegrown stars Sam Rice, Joe Judge, and Bucky Harris. With the illustrious Walter Johnson slinging bullets from the mound, the Capital City crew won a tight pennant race in 1924 and squeaked out a narrow Series victory over the Giants. It would be the only world championship for the Senators of old.

Retaining the same cast of characters with a few useful upgrades, Peckinpaugh's troops finished more than eight games ahead of the second-place Athletics in 1925, earning the right to appear in their second consecutive Fall Classic. Occupying the opposing dugout, the Pirates were hoping to end a lengthy postseason dry spell that stretched all the way back to 1909. Their offense was powered by a trio of Cooperstown greats: Pie Traynor, Max Carey, and Kiki Cuyler, all of whom had hit .320 or better during the regular season. In the pitching department, there was scarcely a weakness to be found as five different hurlers posted a minimum of 15 victories. To be certain, the Senators had their work cut out for them.

Before the Series started, Peckingpaugh was named AL MVP on the strength of his defense and intangible leadership qualities. Despite that ringing endorsement, he delivered one of the most abominable performances in postseason history. A sign of bad things to come, his wild throw in the fifth inning of Game 1 allowed George Grantham to reach base safely. Though this particular error was inconsequential to the game's outcome (a 4–1 Washington victory), several of Peckinpaugh's impending blunders would prove far more costly.

With the second game tied at 1 in the bottom of the eighth, Peckinpaugh muffed a grounder by leadoff hitter Eddie Moore. Moore eventually scored on a homer by Cuyler, and the run ended up being highly significant as the Pirates held on for a 3–2 victory. Peckinpaugh committed forgivable errors in three of the next four contests before almost single-handedly blowing the Series for the Senators in Game 7.

The final match looked like a runaway affair when the Senators tagged hurlers Vic Aldridge and Johnny Morrison for four runs in the first inning. Things got interesting in the third frame as the Pirates rallied for three runs of their own. With the Senators leading 6–4 in the seventh, Peckinpaugh dropped an easy pop fly by second baseman Eddie Moore. Max Carey drove Moore home with a double as the Bucs ended up tying the game at 6.

Peckinpaugh nearly redeemed himself in the top of the eighth with a towering homer off Ray Kremer. But the Pirates were not nearly finished, battering Walter Johnson for a pair of doubles in the bottom of the frame. With two on, two outs, and the game tied at 7, Peckinpaugh cemented his status as the Series goat when he botched a relay to second, loading the bases for Pittsburgh. Firpo Marberry, the American League's top closer, was well rested in the Senators' bull pen, but manager Bucky Harris opted to stick with his exhausted veteran. It was a move that would draw later criticism as Johnson surrendered a two-run double to Cuyler before retiring the side. The Senators failed to score in the top of the ninth, dropping the game and the Series.

In all, Peckinpaugh's miscues led to four unearned runs and directly influenced the outcome of two Washington losses. To his credit, the conditions in Game 7 were so damp that gasoline was burned on the infield to dry it off. The even-tempered shortstop later commented that some of the errors were the result of "stinko calls" by the official scorer. There were many who begged to differ with that statement.

In the wake of Peckinpaugh's horrific Series performance, one reporter joked that he should have been named NL MVP as well. No one was more deserving of the AL honor than Al Simmons, whose 253 hits for the A's were second most by any junior circuit batsman during the 20th century. In the years that followed, writers would wait until after the World Series was over to give out the award.

By 1926, Peckinpaugh was nearing the end of his playing days. He compiled a substandard .238 batting average for Washington that year. Traded to the White Sox in '27, he raised his average to .295 before calling it quits. He moved on to a moderately successful managerial career in Cleveland, guiding the Tribe to a .500 record in five of his seven seasons there. He also piloted two minor-league squads. In later years, he was a manufacturing representative for the Cleveland Oak Belting Company—producers of friction products and conveyor components. He reportedly worked until the advanced age of 85.

Fred Merkle

Forget all you may have heard about Fred Merkle. Contrary to the opinions of numerous contemporaries, he was far too intelligent to be labeled a "bonehead" or a "leather skull." In fact, the play that inspired those enduring epithets was actually quite pardonable in hindsight. Even so, poor Merkle was among the most maligned players of his era.

Merkle grew up in Toledo, Ohio, earning wide acclaim for his football and baseball skills. He began his career as a pitcher, toeing the rubber for various semi-pro teams in his hometown. In 1906, he shifted to third base for Tecumseh of the South Michigan League. He was converted to a first baseman shortly afterward.

After leading the league in homers during the '07 minor-league slate, Merkle accepted a $2,500 offer to player for John McGraw's Giants. He joined the team in September and hit just .255 while committing seven errors. The performance failed to earn him the starting first-base job as he played behind veteran Fred Tenney the following year.

The most memorable contest of Merkle's career took place on September 23, 1908, at the Polo Grounds. Tied for first in the National League, the Giants and Cubs engaged in an epic battle that afternoon. Merkle was installed as a substitute for Tenney, who had awoken that morning with severe lower-back pain. With the game deadlocked at 1 in the bottom of the ninth, Merkle sent teammate Moose McCormick to third with a single. Al Bridwell followed with another base hit up the middle that reportedly knocked umpire Bob Emslie to the ground. McCormick scored what should have been the winning run as hometown fans rushed onto the field.

In the resulting confusion, Merkle stopped short of second base and headed toward the center field clubhouse. Outfielder Artie Hofman relayed to Cubs' second baseman Johnny Evers, but the throw never reached its destination as Giants' hurler Joe McGinnity intercepted the ball and threw it into the stands. Evers, who loved to argue, was not so easily deterred, producing a different ball and appealing to home plate umpire Hank O'Day that Merkle had not touched the bag. O'Day ruled Merkle out on a force and declared the game a tie since clearing the field at that point would be a daunting task. The call was upheld despite a later appeal, and the contest would directly affect the outcome of the pennant race as the Giants and Cubs remained tied for first at the close of play on October 7.

A one-game playoff on October 8 produced pandemonium in New York. Tickets were available on a first-come, first-served basis, and when the gates opened, thousands were lined up. The stadium was completely sold out in a short span. Trying desperately to gain entry into the Polo Grounds, a horde of fans burned down a fence and had to be repelled by police with fire hoses. Others snuck into the park via a sewer entrance. Thousands of others watched from whatever vantage points they could find. At least one fan was killed in a fall from an elevated subway platform.

According to multiple sources, the umpires were bribed at some point before the contest by an undisclosed party. The offer was refused and the incident reported to the league office. (Umpire Bill Klem would later accuse Joseph Creamer, Giant's team physician, of the indiscretion.) John McGraw sent Joe McGinnity, who was not scheduled to pitch that day, over to provoke a fight with Frank Chance, hoping that the Cubs' player/manager would get thrown out of the game. Resisting the urge to spar with McGinnity, Chance encouraged his players to heckle opponents all afternoon.

The Cubs won 4–2 behind the strong pitching of Mordecai "Three Finger" Brown. On the way to the clubhouse, Chance was attacked by angry fans, sustaining a minor neck injury. Pitcher Jack Pfiester allegedly had his shoulder slashed while several other Chicago players were struck by projectiles. New Yorkers continued to vent their frustration the following day as the Cubs received multiple death threats at their hotel. One misguided fan even threatened to blow up the team's train.

Merkle, who was just 19 years old at the time of the incident, had difficulty dealing with the media onslaught and the scathing reaction from fans. McGraw adamantly defended the young infielder, retaining his services for the following year. Relentlessly harassed in New York, Merkle slumped to .191 in 257 plate appearances during the '09 slate. At one point, he suggested that McGraw trade him.

Merkle's career did eventually take off. He remained with the Giants for eight full seasons, hitting .283 or better four times while regularly appearing among the league leaders in homers, RBIs, and stolen bases. He saw postseason action on five occasions with three different clubs, coming out on the losing end each time. His enjoyed his most productive Series against the Red Sox in 1912, gathering nine hits, scoring five runs, and driving in three more. He was a lifetime .239 hitter in the Fall Classic.

Merkle ended his 16-year big-league run with the Yankees in 1926. He played and managed for Reading of the International League the following season. After his retirement, he operated a fruit farm in Daytona Beach, Florida. He later invested in a company that produced fishing lures. Through the years, Merkle went out of his way to avoid reporters, who invariably inquired about his infamous blunder. In his *Historical Baseball Abstract* (first published in 2001), Bill James placed Merkle at number 84 among the top 100 first basemen of all time.

CHAPTER SEVEN

~

Meddlesome Managers

George Stallings

When it comes to running a baseball club, there is more than one way to attain a goal. Some have achieved favorable results by employing a nurturing approach, while others have resorted to outright tyranny. In the pages of diamond history, few managers have been as overbearing as George Stallings. During a turbulent career that spanned 13 big-league seasons, Stallings clashed with players and executives repeatedly. Interpersonal problems aside, he guided his 1914 squad to one of the most astonishing World Series sweeps in history.

During his playing days, Stallings served primarily as an outfielder and catcher, languishing in the minors for three full seasons before earning a brief trial with Brooklyn during the 1890 slate. He failed to hit in 13 plate appearances and was subsequently released. He would play in three more games while managing the Phillies in 1897–98, gathering just 2 safeties in 20 lifetime at-bats.

Perceived by many as cultured and genteel off the field, he was unrefined in the dugout. Some have compared his temperament to that of John Mc-Graw—one of the most volatile personalities ever to adorn a major-league bench. Like McGraw, Stallings ran his clubs in dictatorial fashion and regularly treated his players to prolific streams of verbal abuse. One writer asserted that Stallings could "fly into a schizophrenic rage at the drop of a fly ball." Another reported that he seldom allowed his pledges to go through a game "without cussing them to the full limit of his wonderful vocabulary."

111

In one G-rated (and possibly apocryphal) episode, the Braves were behind in the late innings of a losing cause. With a 3–0 count on catcher Hank Gowdy, Stallings loudly announced: "If he gets on base, I guess I'll let 'Ol' Bonehead' take a crack at the ball." Seconds later, the petulant skipper noticed several of his players heading out of the dugout with bats in their hands.

Stallings accepted his first managerial position in 1893, piloting his hometown crew—the Augusta Electricians of the Southern League. His first big-league opportunity surfaced in 1897 with the Phillies. He guided the club to a pitiful 10th-place finish in his first season and then quickly wore out his welcome the following year. Players openly revolted against his heavy-handed style as one of his charges griped to the press: "We are fed up with the way Stallings has been riding us. . . . For weeks he's been handling us like a lot of cattle." With the club mired in a 19–27 funk, Stallings was replaced by Bill Shettsline, who led the team to a 59–44 record the rest of the way.

The following year, Stallings took over the Tigers, then of the Western League. He would remain with Detroit after the circuit was renamed and elevated to major-league status. In their 1901 big-league debut, the Motor City crew finished third with a highly respectable 74–61 record. Unfortunately, Stallings clashed with AL president Ban Johnson, who accused him of deliberately trying to sabotage the fledgling circuit by negotiating the sale of the Tigers to National League rivals. Stallings asserted he could not have completed the transaction in the first place since Johnson owned a majority share of the club's stock. Either way, the dispute marked the end of Stallings's tenure in Detroit.

For the next several seasons, "Gentleman George" managed the Buffalo Bisons and Newark Indians of the Eastern League. In 1909, he agreed to take charge of the floundering New York Highlanders, who had finished dead last in '08 with a woeful 51–103 record. The club placed fifth in Stallings's first season at the helm and got off to a hot start the following year before major controversy arose. Midway through the 1910 slate, Stallings became convinced that first baseman Hal Chase was deliberately lying down in games. This led to a confrontation between the two that nearly ended in a fistfight. Interviewed for Lawrence Ritter's classic work, *The Glory of Their Times*, Highlanders' infielder Jimmy Austin revealed that Chase lodged numerous complaints against Stallings to owner Frank Farrell. When Farrell failed to act on Stallings's suspicions, the disgruntled skipper resigned from his post. He was subsequently replaced by Hal Chase, who would later be blacklisted from the majors for doing exactly what Stallings had accused him of.

In addition to frequent interpersonal conflicts, Stallings exhibited various odd behaviors during games. His superstitions became legendary as he was compelled to keep the dugout free of peanut shells and scraps of torn paper, which made him extremely uncomfortable. Opponents would sometimes throw litter in front of the dugout just to upset him. When something positive happened on the field, he was known to freeze in place and hold the position, believing that the practice would prolong his team's good fortune. By some accounts, he nervously slid up and down the bench during games, wearing out numerous pairs of pants in the process.

Stallings's crowning achievement as manager came in 1914, when he led the Braves from last place to first in the span of a few months and then pulled off an amazing upset of the heavily favored Athletics in the World Series. He described the 1914 squad as: "One .300 hitter, the worst outfield tandem that ever flirted with sudden death, three pitchers and a good working combination around second base." The lone .300 hitter was outfielder Joe Connolly, who lasted just four seasons in the majors before serving as a state senator. The three pitchers were Bill James, Dick Rudolph, and Lefty Tyler—an efficient rotation that produced 68 victories. The working combination around second base consisted of Rabbit Maranville and Johnny Evers, two of the most gifted glove men in history. The outfield tandem was a worrisome aggregation of nearly a dozen players who combined for more than 40 errors.

The Braves remained out of contention until late summer, slowly clawing their way to the top with a 45–11 record through August and September. They finished with a ten-and-a-half-game lead over the second-place Giants. Having won three of the previous four World Series, the A's were picked by most experts to make quick work of Stallings's crew. But when the dust had settled, the Braves had defied the odds with an astounding sweep that would inspire Philly manager Connie Mack to completely overhaul his roster.

Though Stallings would be hailed as a "Miracle Man," he soon ran out of magic in Boston as the club settled back into the second division within three years. After a dismal 62–90 showing in 1920, Braves executives decided it was time for a change, handing the reins to Fred Mitchell. Stallings managed in the International League until his retirement in 1928. Diagnosed with heart disease that same year, he was allegedly asked by his doctor if he knew what had caused the ailment. As legend has it, he responded in typical gruff fashion: "Bases on balls, you son of a bitch!"

Ossie Vitt

In order to run an efficient ball club, a manager must earn the respect of his players. In a different scenario, things can fall apart in a hurry. During the

1940 slate, Cleveland skipper Ossie Vitt chose to berate and embarrass his subordinates. The result was an outright player rebellion and a late-season collapse that cost his team the pennant.

Born in San Francisco, Vitt got his professional start with the Seals of the Pacific Coast League. He performed respectably enough to be selected by the Tigers in the Rule 5 draft during the fall of 1911. He would remain a backup player in Detroit for three seasons before assuming full-time responsibilities at third base. When Vitt joined the Tigers in 1912, he was bullied relentlessly by Ty Cobb. One day, catcher Oscar Stanage stepped up on Vitt's behalf and threatened to punch Cobb so hard it would "send [him] all the way back to Georgia." Cobb was not afraid of anyone, but he did respect Stanage, and the harassment reportedly stopped after that. In early photos, Vitt is often seen smiling and clowning around, a habit that contradicted his sour attitude later on.

Vitt had a fairly long playing career, remaining in the majors from 1912 through 1921. There were a number of things he was adept at—for instance, the art of the sacrifice. He averaged 26 per year, finishing among the top 50 of all time in that category. Another aspect of Vitt's game worthy of praise was his defense, as he paced the circuit in fielding percentage and assists three times apiece. Offensively, Vitt rarely broke the .250 mark, but he drew a fair amount of walks and was a difficult man to strike out. He assembled his finest season at the plate in 1915, scoring 116 runs while gathering 32 extra-base hits and 48 RBIs. The Tigers came within one game of the AL lead in mid-September that season before eventually conceding the pennant to Boston.

After the 1918 slate, Vitt was traded to the Red Sox for three players of little note. His arrival preceded owner Harry Frazee's purging of the Boston roster. The sale of Babe Ruth to the Yankees in January of 1920 marked the beginning of a mass exodus that would leave the city with a non-contender for many years. Vitt was cut loose after the '21 slate when he managed a sickly .191 average in 78 games. He continued in the PCL with the Salt Lake City Bees and Hollywood Stars, logging his last minor-league at-bat in 1929.

A long and successful managerial career would follow as Vitt led the Stars to three straight league finals before jumping to the International League in 1936. His '37 Newark squad is still considered among the best minor-league clubs in history, housing a slew of future Yankee greats, among them, Joe Gordon and Charlie Keller. The Bears won the pennant by a large margin and then captured the Junior World Series. It would prove to be the turning point of Vitt's career as he took over the Cleveland Indians the following season.

There are many words that have been used to describe Vitt's style of managing, not all of them terribly flattering. Among the phrases that leap off the page are "hard-assed" and "degrading." One writer opined that "by 1940, the boys who would be The Greatest Generation were too soft and spoiled for the likes of Ossie Vitt." But Vitt would have been difficult to play for in any era as he was quick to point fingers, slow to offer support, and fond of criticizing his pledges in front of peers.

Vitt had an All-Star cast in Cleveland with Lou Boudreau, Hal Trosky, and Ken Keltner manning the infield—all of whom were considered among the best of the era. The pitching staff was anchored by illustrious fireballer Bob Feller, with right-hander Mel Harder playing a strong supporting role. From 1932 through 1939, Harder would collect no fewer than 15 victories and finish his career with a total of 223—among the top totals in franchise history.

Though the club remained in contention throughout the 1940 slate, Vitt rode his players mercilessly until mid-June, when several of his pledges decided they had had enough. Events came to a head during an abysmal East Coast road trip in which the Indians posted a 5–8 record. After a 9–2 loss to the Red Sox on June 11, Vitt denigrated starter Bob Feller within earshot of the entire bench. The following afternoon, he pulled Mel Harder from a game and rudely stated that the hurler wasn't worth the money he was being paid. He had previously griped to reporters that his players weren't hustling enough. Frustrated with the situation, team captain Hal Trosky vented to Frank Gibbons of the *Cleveland Press* (off the record) that the Indians could not win the pennant with Vitt in charge. Gibbons advised Trosky not to do anything rash.

After considerable debate, players decided to consult owner Alva Bradley about the problem. Mel Harder was appointed spokesman. On June 13, Trosky was called away unexpectedly to attend the funeral of his mother. In his absence, Harder—accompanied by nearly a dozen teammates—met with Bradley to discuss Vitt's dismissal. Bradley promised to investigate the matter thoroughly and advised players to keep the meeting secret.

Naturally, the press got a hold of it almost immediately as the *Cleveland Plain Dealer* plastered the headline across the front page. Incredibly, the article was given more prominence than Hitler's invasion of Paris. Bradley was forced to state for the record that he would take no immediate action before talking things over with Trosky. In the end, Vitt remained at his post, and the press bestowed various disparaging labels upon players, including "Vitt's Crybabies," "The Bawl Team," and "Half Vitts."

The playoff race continued undaunted as the Indians and Tigers exchanged places at the top several times in the second half. During a September series at Detroit, Cleveland players were reportedly pelted with eggs and rotten tomatoes after stepping off their train. At Briggs Stadium, the Indians' dugout was mockingly adorned with a baby carriage and diapers. Vitt found time to pose for a photograph with Detroit manager Del Baker.

The cracks began to show as the Indians stumbled in the season's final month, producing a 15–15 record while generating significantly less offense. They had a chance to claim the pennant with a three-game sweep over Detroit on the final three days of the season, but hopes were dashed in the series opener at Cleveland when they failed to get anything going against no-name right-hander Floyd Giebell. Feller pitched a three-hit gem for the Tribe in a 2–0 loss. After winning the pennant by a slender margin, Detroit ended up dropping the World Series to Cincinnati in seven games.

Vitt finished his career in the PCL, managing Portland in 1941 and then Hollywood in 1942. He was inducted into the league's Hall of Fame the following year. In an unexpected turn of events, Alva Bradley drafted a memo in 1951, revisiting the topic of the "Crybaby" squad. Published in the *Cleveland News*, Bradley's note stated unequivocally that the Indians should have won the 1940 pennant and that the complaints lodged by players against Vitt that season were "one hundred percent correct."

Eddie Stanky

Known for his highly quotable witticisms, Leo Durocher once described Eddie Stanky as follows: "He can't hit, can't run, can't field. . . . All the little SOB can do is win." Though Stanky was a bit more adept than Durocher gave him credit for, most contemporaries would agree that he got by more on hustle and grit than natural ability. In later years, he managed exactly how he had played, hammering opponents and working every angle. Though he had many admirers, he made plenty of enemies as well.

Stanky grew up in the blue-collar neighborhood of Kensington, Pennsylvania. The family's name was Stankiewicz, but his parents changed it when Stanky was quite young. Though he hit just .243 during his senior year at Northeast High School, he ended up being signed by the A's. He began his pro career in the East Dixie League, becoming homesick after just a few months and wiring his mother for train fare. She told him that quitters were not welcome in her house.

In the minors, Stanky was coached by his father-in-law, Milt Stock, who placed him in a leadoff role and encouraged him to be more patient at the plate. Stanky lost hearing in one of his ears as a result of a serious beaning. The injury would keep him out of military action. While many players were joining the armed forces in 1942, Stanky was busy compiling a .342 batting average for Milwaukee of the American Association. He was promoted to the majors the following year.

In his Chicago Cubs' debut, Stanky scored 92 runs and drew the same number of walks on the way to compiling a handsome .363 on-base percentage. Traded to Brooklyn in 1944, he endeared himself to fans with his hard-edged style of play. Stanky employed any means necessary to get on base. He tried everything from an illegal crouch to repeatedly calling for time during a pitcher's windup. He even took to wearing a jersey that was several sizes too large and heavily starched in the hope of getting nailed by a pitch. One sportswriter joked that "Eddie was the only guy who could get a double on a hit by pitcher." The scrappy second baseman was appropriately nicknamed "the Brat" because he was such a nuisance to hurlers. One moundsman complained: "First you lose Stanky, then you lose your temper, then you lose the game."

Consistently appearing among the league leaders in putouts, assists, and fielding percentage, Stanky was known to get creative on defense as well. Until the 1950s, players habitually left their gloves on the field between innings. It was a dangerous practice when Stanky was around. Giants' infielder Bill Rigney recalled Stanky filling his glove with dirt and tobacco. "Whatever he could find, he'd put it in the finger of your glove," Rigney once told a writer.

Stanky's underhanded tactics directly led to a rule change in 1950. During a contest against Boston that year, he attempted to distract Braves' slugger Bob Elliott by standing in front of second base and waving his arms. After Elliott struck out, Stanky decided he had discovered a magic bullet. He employed the same strategy a few days later against Andy Seminick of the Phillies. Seminick complained to Al Barlick, but the arbiter insisted that Stanky wasn't violating any rules. Home-plate umpire Lon Warneke finally put an end to the practice the following day when Stanky added jumping jacks to his routine. Stanky was ejected and sternly reprimanded by President Ford Frick. A new clause was added to the rule book prohibiting such actions in the future.

The resourceful Stanky helped three different clubs to pennants, making World Series appearances with the Dodgers, Braves, and Giants. In 1952, he doubled as a manager for the Cardinals, slowly phasing himself out of the lineup. Though he was named Manager of the Year by the *Sporting News* in his managerial debut, he was not terribly popular with players in St. Louis. Hall of Famer Enos Slaughter commented: "The Cards were all fine people except one. That was Eddie Stanky."

Stanky carried the same win-at-all-costs attitude into his managerial career, occasionally resorting to outrageous schemes. In 1954, he was fined and suspended for delaying a rain-soaked game at Sportsman's Park that had not yet become official by repetitively changing pitchers. In Chicago, he was accused of conspiring with the grounds crew to deaden baseballs (a practice that had begun with Stanky's predecessor Al Lopez). With a slew of sinker-ball pitchers on the Sox staff in the late '60s, head groundskeeper Gene Bossard was encouraged to keep the infield grass high and the area near home plate soggy. Catcher J. C. Martin commented: "You couldn't have driven a ball past our infield with a cannon."

While piloting the White Sox for portions of three seasons, Stanky employed a "run-and-gun" philosophy. He utilized 144 pinch runners in 1966 and 127 the following year—more than twice the major-league average. His methods sometimes left players shaking their heads in bewilderment. "He was unique in his own way," said shortstop Ron Hansen. "Eddie always had a reason at least for wanting to do something." But Stanky's plans didn't always work to an advantage. During a tight pennant race in '67, he tried to rattle Carl Yastrzemski of the Red Sox with a series of disparaging remarks made to the press. "Yaz" ended up raking White Sox pitching for 21 hits in 18 games, including 4 homers.

Few would argue that Stanky was an easy man to work for. He imposed fines for the simplest transgressions. He was gruff and insensitive. He once left Vice President Hubert Humphrey standing outside the clubhouse for an interminably long time while he addressed players after a 3–2 loss. Told that Humphrey was waiting to meet the team, he barked: "Humphrey can't hit. What do I need with him?"

Fired in St. Louis and Chicago, Stanky moved on to a 14-year coaching career at the University of South Alabama, guiding the club to a slew of NCAA Tournament appearances. Steve Kittrell, who played for Stanky and later became a coach, commented: "He brought the University of South Alabama from just about point-zero to a national power in three or four years." Stanky's efforts were not forgotten as he was inducted into the Alabama Sports Hall of Fame in 1977. The university's playing field is named after him.

Billy Martin

Jim Murray of the *LA Times* once said of Billy Martin: "Some people have a chip on their shoulder. Billy has a whole lumberyard." The pugnacious Martin rarely backed down from a fight during his 27 years in the majors, pummeling opponents into submission both literally and figuratively while finding his way to the postseason on 10 occasions. In addition to holding an unconfirmed record for most cubic feet of dirt kicked on umpires, he also had the distinction of being fired more times than any manager in Yankee history.

Martin grew up on the rough side of Berkeley, California, and turned pro in 1946. After stints in the Pioneer and Arizona–Texas Leagues, he was promoted to the Triple-A level. Enamored with his aggressive style of play, Oakland Oaks manager Casey Stengel took a shine to him. When Stengel took over the Yankees in 1949, he encouraged the club to sign Martin.

Martin played alongside some of the greatest Bronx idols of all time, such as Mickey Mantle, Yogi Berra, and Whitey Ford. Serving primarily as a second baseman, he played in five Fall Classics for the Yankees, compiling an impressive .333 postseason batting average. His defining moment was a game-saving catch in Game 7 of the 1952 World Series. With two outs in the seventh inning and the bases loaded with Dodgers, Jackie Robinson launched a weak pop fly that nearly eluded the entire Yankee infield staff. Martin alertly scrambled in from second base to make a knee-high grab that helped preserve a 4–2 Series-clinching victory.

Despite being a bit on the lean side at 5-foot-11, 165 pounds, Martin was not afraid to tangle with anyone. In 1957, he was involved in a scuffle at a New York bar that left a Bronx delicatessen owner with a concussion and broken jaw. General manager George Weiss believed that Martin was a bad influence on teammates, particularly Mickey Mantle, and arranged for him to be traded to the A's. The fighting and the dismissals would continue for more than two decades.

While playing for the Reds in 1960, the tempestuous infielder threw his bat at Jim Brewer of the Cubs following a brushback pitch and then headed out toward the mound. While Brewer was reportedly trying to hand the bat back, Martin punched him in the eye, breaking his cheekbone and necessitating a lengthy hospital stay. The Cubs sued for loss of the hurler's services but eventually dropped the case. Brewer pursued the matter in civil court, receiving $10,000 in compensation several years after the fact.

After playing for seven teams in a five-year span, Martin retired as a player and became a scout for the Twins. He was installed at the helm of the PCL Denver Bears in 1968, earning a promotion to Minnesota. He led the Twins to an AL West title but fell out of favor with upper management when he beat up one of his own pitchers outside a Detroit bar. He returned to a manager's role with the Tigers in 1971.

Martin led Detroit to a playoff berth in '72, the same year he posed for an infamous Topps baseball card photo with his middle finger extended. After a somewhat disappointing follow-up, he was replaced by Joe Schultz in August of '73. He finished the season with the lowly Rangers. Though he led the club to a second-place finish the next year, he became embroiled in controversy yet again when he punched traveling secretary Burt Hawkins following a petty dispute. Martin left Texas behind in 1975, beginning the first of many stints with the Yankees.

Though Martin could turn a team upside down with his inappropriate conduct, he was an ingenious strategist. On the second day of the 1976 campaign, Don Money of the Brewers hit what appeared to be a game-winning grand slam. Having seen his team rally from a 6–0 deficit, the Yankee skipper was not about to give up so easily. He charged out of the dugout and confronted umpire Jim McKean, claiming that time had been called for by Yankee first baseman Chris Chambliss prior to pitcher Dave Pagan's windup. McKean admitted that he had approved the time-out and, in a rare reverse ruling, discounted the homer. The Yankees went on to win, 9–7.

The shrewd Yankee pilot nearly stole another victory away from the Royals in 1983. With the Bombers leading 4–3 in the ninth inning of a July contest at Yankee Stadium, reliever Goose Gossage coughed up a two-run homer to George Brett. After Brett crossed home plate, Martin asked umpire Tim McClelland to inspect the bat. Yankee personnel had noticed in earlier games that Brett's bat was slathered with pine tar, and Martin had filed the information away as potentially useful since the rule book clearly states that a bat cannot be covered by a substance more than 18 inches from tip to handle. In one of the most controversial decisions of all time, Brett's bat was found to be in violation of those guidelines, thereby nullifying the homer. Video footage of Brett flying out of the Kansas City dugout in a blind rage has become legendary. Responding to an official protest from the Royals, AL president Lee MacPhail later restored the round-tripper and ordered the game replayed at the point it had been disrupted. When the contest resumed on August 18, Martin put pitcher Ron Guidry in center field and first baseman Don Mattingly at second. The Yankees lost, 5–4.

Martin is perhaps best remembered for his stormy relationship with Yankee owner George Steinbrenner. To Martin's credit, Steinbrenner was nearly impossible to work for, going through 19 managers, 5 team presidents, 15 pitching coaches, and 13 general managers between 1973 and 1990. Martin was hired and fired by Steinbrenner five times during a turbulent but fruitful Yankee career that included two pennants and one world championship. He once admitted that he sometimes did just the opposite of what "the Boss" wanted him to do because he loathed having anyone tell him how to manage. He joked that "the only real way to know you've been fired is when you arrive at the ballpark and find your name has been scratched from the parking list."

Unsavory incidents in the Bronx were numerous during Martin's reign, but the most infamous one occurred during a nationally televised game at Fenway Park during the '77 slate. Martin pulled superstar Reggie Jackson off the field for not hustling, and when Jackson told him he didn't appreciate being shown up, Martin went ballistic and had to be physically restrained. The feud continued the following year when the troublesome slugger was suspended for bunting against Martin's orders. Shortly afterward, Martin was told by White Sox owner Bill Veeck that Steinbrenner had approached him with the idea of a managerial swap. Fed up with the entire state of affairs, Martin ripped the outfielder and owner, saying: "The two of them deserve each other. One's a born liar and the other's convicted." He was forced to resign from his post.

Rehired in 1979, Martin's pugilistic lifestyle got him in trouble again after he fought a marshmallow salesman named Joseph Cooper at a Minneapolis hotel. He was dismissed for the second year in a row only to return for three more shifts at the Yankee helm. Some believe that Steinbrenner deliberately manipulated Martin over the years. Bob Hertzel of *Baseball Prospectus* writes: "It was nothing but a game to [Steinbrenner]—toying with the unstable manager's emotions and laughing at the reaction it would draw each time he brought him back." The two lampooned their tempestuous relationship in a pair of 1970s television commercials—one for Miller Beer and another for Pepto-Bismol.

Martin's last stint with the Yankees was in 1988, when he was replaced by Lou Piniella before the All-Star break. His chronic alcohol problems persisted after his managerial career ended. He was intoxicated at the time of his death in a 1989 car crash, though he reportedly wasn't driving. It was rumored that Steinbrenner was planning on bringing him back for a sixth appearance in the Bronx.

John McGraw

Few managers have been as successful as Giants' skipper John McGraw. From 1902 to 1932, he guided the club to ten pennants and three world championships. A bona fide celebrity in his day, he attracted actors, politicians, and business tycoons. But he was extremely unpopular with players, many of whom resented his dictatorial approach and notoriously foul temper.

McGraw was an imposing figure on the diamond. Hall of Famer Christy Mathewson once commented that he was "as welcome as a man with the black smallpox" in some cities. Sportswriter Grantland Rice observed that "his very walk across the field in a hostile town was a challenge to the multitude." He maintained absolute control of his team, telling players exactly how to play the game while treating them to verbal abuse when they failed to live up to his standards. His own conduct was often in question as he drew frequent suspensions and was ejected from more than a hundred contests during his career.

McGraw's explosive temper may have stemmed from his early childhood, which was about as difficult as they come. The oldest of eight children, he lost his mother and three siblings to a diphtheria epidemic in the winter of 1885. He was beaten severely by his alcoholic father and taken in by a widow named Mary Goddard, who ran a neighborhood hotel. She raised him along with her two sons.

The young McGraw took an active interest in baseball and became a star pitcher for a local team in Truxton, New York. When the club's manager bought into a New York–Pennsylvania League franchise, McGraw pleaded successfully to be included on the roster. He made a slew of errors in his first game and was released shortly thereafter but soon found a home in the Western New York League, where he fashioned a .364 batting average in 24 games for Wellsville. He earned a call-up from the Baltimore Orioles the following year.

The Orioles of the 1890s were a rough lot, and McGraw was bullied by teammates upon his arrival. One day, after literally being pushed off the bench, he proceeded to beat up his oppressors in front of fans. He was rarely taunted after that. McGraw became one of the nastiest players on the club, resorting to underhanded tactics, such as physically restraining runners at his third-base post. He helped the Orioles to three straight pennants.

Offensively, McGraw was a patient batsman, accruing on-base percentages in excess of .400 for 12 straight seasons. From 1899 through 1901, he reached base safely in more than 50 percent of his plate appearances. A lifetime .334 hitter, he demonstrated superior speed on the base paths, swiping 436 bags in 1,099 career games.

During the '01 and '02 slates, he clashed with American League president Ban Johnson over a variety of issues. Johnson frequently sided with umpires in their disputes against McGraw, which were numerous. After receiving an indefinite suspension in '02, McGraw defected to New York, where he would remain for the rest of his career. As a retaliatory gesture, he brought several Orioles' players with him, including luminaries Joe McGinnity and Roger Bresnahan. When the Giants won the NL pennant in '04, McGraw thumbed his nose at Johnson yet again, boycotting the World Series that year.

McGraw worked hard to keep his club in contention. He was known for his frequent transactions and the farming of prospects long before he allowed them to play regularly. He used pinch runners, pinch hitters, and relief pitchers far more often than contemporaries. He developed signs for every type of play and permitted "no deviations from instructions." According to multiple sources, he once fined utility man Sammy Strang $25 for hitting a homer with orders to bunt.

Narrow minded and insensitive, McGraw alienated players with his harsh criticisms. He once berated star second baseman Larry Doyle in front of teammates, calling him "a miserable yellow thing." He did the same to Frankie Frisch, inspiring the future Hall of Famer to leave the team. Edd Roush, another Cooperstown inductee, commented: "I didn't enjoy playing for [McGraw]. . . . When he traded me, I couldn't have been happier."

McGraw's behavior frequently invoked controversy. In May of 1905, he brawled with Pirates manager Fred Clarke and then wandered the Polo Grounds before game time the next day shouting insults at Pittsburgh owner Barney Dreyfuss. McGraw accused Dreyfuss of controlling NL umpires through league president Harry Pulliam. Outraged, Dreyfuss lodged a formal protest and alleged that McGraw had invited him to accept a $10,000 wager on the outcome of a game. Giants' owner John T. Brush successfully overturned McGraw's subsequent suspension by obtaining a superior court injunction.

McGraw fought with fans, security guards, and even inspired a police officer to take a swing at him one day in Cincinnati after he referred to the city as "home of the Huns." The darkest moment of his career came in June of 1917, when he made a snotty remark to umpire Bill "Lord" Byron, who subsequently needled him about being run out of Baltimore. McGraw punched Byron in the face, and the two grappled until players broke it up. McGraw received a $500 fine—the largest ever imposed upon a manager to that point. While serving a lengthy suspension, he bad-mouthed NL president John K. Tener, charging that he was out to sabotage the Giants. Forced to explain himself to league magnates, he retracted the statement and apologized. He was strapped with an additional $1,000 fine.

In 1919, McGraw became vice president and minority owner of the Giants. His personal life came into question the following year, when actor John Slavin was found badly beaten in McGraw's New York apartment. Questioned by authorities, both parties denied that a fight had taken place, though McGraw was charged by prohibition agents for possessing a bottle of whiskey. The charge didn't stick, and the two combatants later settled their differences out of court.

After a World Series loss at the hands of the Senators in 1924, the Giants failed to capture a pennant for the remainder of McGraw's career. He grew increasingly irritable and dispassionate. In 1929, he was accused of damaging team morale by verbally abusing players and handing out impulsive fines. McGraw admitted to fining certain players and to having been absent from the clubhouse for a lengthy period. As time wore on, he sometimes failed to show up at the ballpark altogether.

In 1933, the iconic field general was replaced by first baseman Bill Terry, who promptly led the club to a World Series victory over the Senators. McGraw died the following year of prostate cancer and renal failure. He was posthumously inducted into the Hall of Fame. His widow inherited his shares of Giants' stock and frequently attended games into the 1950s. She was reportedly quite distraught when the club left the Big Apple in '57.

Leo Durocher

Some men are larger than the game itself. Leo Durocher was one of those characters. A free-spender who loved to dress to the nines, he fit in nicely with the Hollywood crowd, maintaining friendly relationships with the likes of Frank Sinatra and Dean Martin. Loquacious and self-confident, he freely dispensed his baseball philosophies to the masses, leaving behind a legacy of quotable one-liners. Even casual fans are familiar with some of his quips— especially the one about him tripping his own mother if she were rounding third base with the winning run. "I'd pick her up and brush her off and say 'Sorry, Mom,'" he added, "but nobody beats me."

Durocher was a lifetime .247-hitter with little power. When he caught on with the Yankees in 1928, Babe Ruth took to calling him the "All-American Out." What he lacked offensively, he made up for with his glove as he led AL shortstops in fielding percentage three times. Notoriously fond of the high life, he allegedly asked Yankee general manager Ed Barrow for a $1,000 raise before the 1930 campaign to pay off a large hotel bill. When Barrow refused, Durocher cursed him out, prompting a trade to Cincinnati. Rumors would later surface that Durocher had been stealing money and valuables from Babe Ruth.

Traded to the Cardinals in 1933, Durocher ended up in debt to the club for his cash advances nearly every year. Executive Branch Rickey referred to them as "bonuses," never formally giving the frivolous infielder a raise. Durocher was a member of the "Gas House Gang," one of the most colorful ball clubs of all time. When the team was on a winning streak, players refused to change their uniforms. "We looked horrible, we knew it and we gloried in it," Durocher later reminisced. With the muscle of Joe Medwick, the speed of Pepper Martin, and the showmanship of Dizzy Dean, the Cardinals defeated the Tigers in the '34 World Series.

Durocher helped out any way he could. He and Dean allegedly had a ruse going in which the hurler would toss the ball too short when he needed an out pitch. Durocher, who kept a sharp point on his belt buckle, would rough up the baseball and throw it back. Dean would then use a slider with extra movement to polish off hitters.

As St. Louis gradually fell out of contention, skipper Frankie Frisch became convinced that Durocher was after his job and complained to the front office about it. Durocher was shipped to the Dodgers before the 1938 campaign. He replaced Burleigh Grimes as manager a year later. Appropriately nicknamed "the Lip," Leo experienced his fair share of problems in Brooklyn as he and general manager Larry MacPhail were like an early version of Billy Martin and George Steinbrenner. Though Durocher once claimed that he was fired 40 times during his 9 years with the Dodgers, sportswriter / traveling secretary Harold Parrott joked that he could only verify 27.

"There is a thin line between genius and insanity," Durocher later said of the erratic general manager, "and in Larry's case it was sometimes so thin you could see him drifting back and forth." Less than two months into his new job as player/manager, Durocher attended a country-club dinner and stuck around for bingo afterward. He took the grand prize that evening and treated the entire house to champagne with his winnings. The next morning, MacPhail reprimanded him for being a "gambler" and fired him. He was rehired in time to lead the Dodgers to a third-place finish and capture Manager of the Year honors.

The most infamous row between Durocher and MacPhail took place after Brooklyn had clinched the 1941 pennant. Durocher was told that the team's train would stop at 125th Street to avoid the large crowd waiting at Grand Central Station. Durocher, who rarely followed orders, felt that his players deserved a warm welcome after securing their first pennant in 21 years. He told the conductor to continue past the 125th Street platform. What he didn't know was that MacPhail was waiting there to join the celebration. Incensed at being stranded at the station, he fired and later reinstated Durocher for the umpteenth time.

Describing Durocher's penchant for creating chaos, team president Branch Rickey once remarked that the spirited manager had a knack for taking "a bad situation and making it immediately worse." In 1940, he incited a riot at Ebbets Field on the heels of a disparaging extra-inning loss to the Reds. A famous photograph from the incident depicts a grossly overweight fan punching umpire George Magerkurth. Durocher was fined and suspended for his part in the fracas.

On July 10, 1943, players staged an open revolt against Durocher after he suspended the club's top hurler, Bobo Newsom, for insubordination. Just before game time, shortstop Arky Vaughan turned in his uniform and refused to play. Durocher appealed for volunteers to take the field and managed to recruit only two—pitcher Curt Davis and backup catcher Bobby Bragan. Branch Rickey interceded as the Dodgers won 23–6 that day with a full squad. Vaughan never patched up his differences with Durocher, sitting out the next three seasons.

Controversy of a darker nature surfaced in 1945, when "the Lip" was accused of using brass knuckles to hit a fan named John Christian, who was heckling the Dodgers during an 8–7 win over the Phillies. Durocher allegedly landed the punch while Christian was being restrained by a police officer beneath the Ebbets Field grandstands. Criminal charges were dismissed in April of '46, but Christian received nearly $7,000 in damages.

The year 1947 was Durocher's finest hour, though he ended up sitting out the entire season. While playing an exhibition series in Panama, the fiery manager learned that several of his pledges were refusing to play if Jackie Robinson ended up being promoted to the club. Durocher had been in favor of desegregation for years, openly commenting about the wealth of untapped potential in the Negro Leagues. Rousting Dodger players out of bed for a team meeting, he explained to them what a great player Robinson was and how everyone would profit in the long run. "I'm interested in one thing: winning," he said. "I'll play an elephant if he can do the job and to make room for him, I'll send my own brother home."

In spite of those words, Durocher would not have a chance to manage Robinson in his big-league debut. Instead, he received an unexpected one-year suspension from Commissioner Happy Chandler. The charges were vague, based on Durocher's involvement with gamblers and his marriage to actress Laraine Day, who was 15 years his junior and married at the time the two cemented their relationship. Most sources agree that Durocher fell prey to the complex interpersonal politics of Branch Rickey and Larry MacPhail, who had defected to the Yankee organization and allegedly made a play at getting Durocher to do the same.

The jilted Dodger skipper returned to the helm in '48 but ended up being traded to the Giants when Brooklyn got off to a slow start that year. Durocher would remain a thorn in the Dodgers' side for seven full seasons, capturing two pennants and one world championship with the other New York club. His tour of duty did not pass without a fair share of scandal. Not only was he accused of setting up a spy operation in '51 designed to steal signs from opposing teams, but also he played a major role in keeping the Dodgers' hottest hitter out of action during the '53 pennant stretch. In the second inning of a 5–3 loss to Brooklyn, Durocher ordered pitcher Ruben Gomez to throw a beanball at Carl Furillo, who was leading the National League with a .344 batting average. Furillo was restrained from rushing the mound but not from entering the Giants' dugout and taking a wild swing at Durocher. In the ensuing brawl, Furillo had his hand stepped on by a Giants' player and would not return to action until the World Series. His average was frozen at .344—good enough to claim the 1953 NL batting crown.

After "retiring" in '55, Durocher worked as an NBC broadcaster and made scattered appearances on television shows such as *The Munsters*. He later served as a Dodger coach until 1966, when he returned to a manager's role with the Cubs. In '69, Chicago maintained a healthy lead over "the Miracle Mets" until an epic late-season collapse landed them in second place. The Cubs would fail to capture a pennant during Durocher's tenure, which ended in 1972.

Not finished with the game yet, Leo piloted the Astros for portions of two seasons. In 1975, he wrote his autobiography, *Nice Guys Finish Last*, which became an enduring baseball classic. In it, he recounted all the feuds, controversies, and unconventional tactics that had made him a household name. He died in 1991, just three years before his election to the Hall of Fame.

CHAPTER EIGHT

~

Onerous Owners

Gerry Nugent and William Cox

Whenever stories of perpetual baseball failure are recounted, the Philadelphia Phillies figure prominently into the mix. Among the least successful franchises in major-league history, the club captured just one world championship during the 20th century and went without a Fall Classic appearance every year from 1916 through 1949. The most fruitless period by far was presided over by owner Gerry Nugent, who spent the entire decade of the 1930s trading away the club's brightest stars and most hopeful prospects.

Nugent served in World War I and was decorated twice for bravery. By some accounts, he was a leather merchant and, by others, a furniture salesman. The fact that he was an avid Phillies fan has never been in question. He attended games regularly, daydreaming about what he might do to improve the club's fortunes. He eventually became acquainted with Philly owner William F. Baker and married his secretary, Mae Mallon. Impressed with Nugent's many ideas, Baker hired him as an assistant in 1925.

When Baker died four years later, Nugent's wife inherited nearly half of the club's stock. (The rest would fall into her hands with the eventual passing of Baker's widow.) Lewis C. Ruch succeeded Baker as team president, and upon his retirement in 1931, Nugent aspired to the position. He would serve in that capacity until 1943. By then, he had run the team into the ground.

Many phrases have been tossed around in conjunction with Nugent over the years. His colossal failure in Philadelphia has endured the test of time as David Schoenfield of ESPN.com ranked him among the top-ten worst MLB owners in 2011. *Business Insider* referred to him as "despicable" in a similar survey that same year. In his day, Nugent earned scathing criticism for his inability or unwillingness to hang on to key players. He made no apologies for his inclination to barter with other clubs, complaining that the Phillies were forced to get by on the worst attendance in the league.

The scarce fan base could be at least partially attributed to the fact that the Phillies played in one of the most unattractive venues in the majors. Built on an oddly shaped parcel of land, the Baker Bowl was an eyesore, featuring irregular facets, such as a hump in the outfield created by a railroad tunnel underneath. The most prominent abnormality was a towering tin-plated wall in right field situated a mere 280 feet from home plate. Outfielders spent many long afternoons chasing the unpredictable caroms as opponents circled the bases. Aside from its ungainly dimensions, the park was architecturally unsound. Sections of the seats collapsed on two separate occasions, killing 12 and injuring close to 300. Nugent had little money to spend on repairs during his tenure, and one writer quipped that the Phillies' home "bore a striking resemblance to a run-down men's room." The club eventually began playing games at Shibe Park, home of the Athletics, midway through the 1938 campaign. By 1939, they had abandoned their crumbling edifice for good.

During the 1930s, the Phillies never exceeded 300,000 in attendance. The low point came in '33, when the club attracted just 156,421 patrons—an average of less than 2,100 per game. Nugent did very little to promote the team and, in fact, weakened its fan base with an endless series of ill-advised transactions.

In 1932, the club posted a 78–76 record and finished in the first division under manager Burt Shotton. Within three years, Nugent had sold off most of the positional players that had helped make that promising finish possible. Among the first to go was Pinky Whitney, a slick-fielding third baseman and reliable RBI-man. Chuck Klein, an eventual Hall of Famer who captured MVP honors during the '32 slate, would soon follow. Catcher Spud Davis, who topped the .300 mark in five consecutive campaigns with Philadelphia, received his walking papers in '34 along with first baseman Don Hurst, whose 143 ribbies were tops in the NL during the '32 slate. Acquired in the Hurst deal, slugger Dolph Camilli pulled his weight for several seasons before being shipped to Brooklyn in March of '38. Nugent missed the boat on that one, too, as Camilli topped the 100-RBI mark four times for the Dodgers and won an MVP Award in 1941.

Nugent cited pitching as the root of his club's troubles more than once but was equally fickle in his dealings with hurlers. Between 1932 and 1942, the Phillies accrued the worst ERA in the National League on 10 occasions, peaking at a dreadful 5.17 in '39. Whenever promising starters appeared on the roster, they were up on the auction block soon afterward. Nugent's list of dismissals included Kirby Higbe, Bucky Walters, Claude Passeau, and Curt Davis, who collectively earned 14 All-Star selections during their careers.

In 1941, Nugent received a $500,000 offer to buy the club from a syndicate headed by John B. Kelly, a former Olympic champion who served as director of civilian physical training for the U.S. Defense Department. The group reportedly badgered league officials to make the sale compulsory, but President Ford Frick refused to get involved. In the end, Nugent rejected the offer. Though Frick expressed optimism about the Phillies' future at seasons' end, he would eat those words the following year.

Before the '42 campaign was under way, Nugent secured an advance from league officials to cover his spring training costs. The club lost more than 100 games for the fifth year in a row as home attendance sagged to 230,183. When Nugent announced his intentions of selling several of his best players in the off-season, NL officials grew increasingly concerned. At Nugent's request, a meeting was held in November to discuss the situation. No action was taken, but Frick openly stated that he would not lend money to Nugent.

At the annual league meetings in February, Nugent was told to find a buyer for the Phillies. When the floundering executive failed to deliver, National League officials purchased the club's stock and assumed responsibility for outstanding debts. Nugent told the press that he was "fully satisfied" with this outcome. In mid-February, a syndicate headed by lumber baron William D. Cox purchased the team, setting up another ugly chapter in Philly history.

Born in NYC, Cox had attended New York University and Yale. A sports enthusiast, he assumed ownership of the New York Yankees—an AFL football team—in 1941. He promptly changed the club's moniker to the "Americans" and signed a Heisman Trophy winner to play for him. He later ascended to the title of league president before the advent of WWII forced the circuit to shut down. Cox's interests shifted to the lumber trade as his Oregon-based company supplied all the pilings used for the Panama Canal.

In the spring of '43, Cox breathed life into the ailing Phillies franchise with the hiring of Bucky Harris as manager. Harris had led the Senators to consecutive pennants in 1924–25. His low-key style and superior knowledge of the game had earned him universal respect throughout the baseball community. With a competent man now at the helm, Cox proceeded to raise the team's payroll and funnel much-needed resources into player development. For the first time in years, fans were buzzing about the Phillies.

The 33-year-old Cox had played baseball at Yale and still considered himself an outstanding athlete. Adopting a hands-on approach, he hired his high-school track coach as team trainer and personally participated in workouts. He even took to regularly showing up at the clubhouse before games. The impact was initially positive as the club climbed into fourth place on the final day of June—a position unfamiliar to them so late in the season.

In July, the Phillies hit a rough patch, compiling an 11–24 record. Cox took no comfort in the fact that the club had nearly matched its win total from the previous season with two full months still left to play. Instead, he announced to reporters that he was firing his veteran skipper.

Harris had no prior notice, and when the news reached him, he was utterly flabbergasted. "This is the most shocking thing that has happened to me in my entire life," he told reporters. Players were outraged at Cox's lack of etiquette as well and threatened to go on strike, but Harris talked them out of it. Instead, he launched a counterattack, calling Cox an "all-American jerk" and accusing him of betting on Phillies games.

The allegation found its way to the office of Commissioner Landis, who began a full investigation. In early November, Cox was forced to formally explain himself. He admitted to making "sentimental bets," but insisted he didn't know that it was illegal. He even went so far as to claim that the bets were a "trap" to ensnare a disloyal employee who had been betting on games. Landis didn't buy the story, issuing a lifetime ban.

Cox appealed the decision and (according to the *United Press*) testified at a December open hearing that he had made a few friendly bets of hats, cigars, and dinners but never on the outcome of games. In a particularly damaging assault on Cox's character, Nathan Alexander—a Philly front-office assistant—charged that the executive was drawing a $25,000 salary despite having assured stockholders that he would take $5,000. Alexander also cited "gross mismanagement" on Cox's part since he had made player purchases against the advice of his manager and scouts. At least one of those players had turned out to be ill equipped for major-league service.

Later in the proceedings, which lasted for six hours, Cox was incriminated even further when Bucky Harris testified to having overheard a secretary, Dorothy Massey, inquiring about betting odds over the phone on the owner's behalf. When Harris asked her if Cox was wagering on games, she allegedly responded: "I thought you already knew." At the hearing's conclusion, Landis stuck to his original decision, stating for the record: "There is nothing I can do for Mr. Cox."

Harris was replaced with Freddie Fitzsimmons, an excellent pitcher in his prime but a managerial novice. The Phillies finished in seventh place with a 64–90 record. Cox returned to the lumber trade and also pursued other sports interests, founding the International Soccer League. He was never reinstated to baseball. The team was sold to the Carpenter family, who fielded at least one first-division squad in every decade of ownership. They were largely responsible for the team's only world championship of the 20th century, which would finally be attained in 1980.

Marge Schott

At the height of her power, Marge Schott had lunch with a president and was granted an audience with a pope. Had either known that Schott would be run out of baseball for an ongoing series of racist comments, they almost certainly would have avoided any association with her.

The daughter of a wealthy lumber baron, Marge Unnewehr was teased in school about her unusual last name. She once described her father as an "achtung German" who was so entitled he would ring a bell to summon her mother. The second of five children (all of them girls), Marge received a Christian education and learned the fundamentals of business from Edward Unnewehr himself.

In the early '50s, Marge married Charles Schott, owner of several successful enterprises—among them a General Motors car dealership. When Charles died of a heart attack at the age of 42, Marge took control of her husband's affairs. General Motors did not believe she was qualified to run her newly acquired Buick franchise, and it took more than a year of wrangling to win a contract designating her as the company's first female dealer in a major market.

In 1981, Schott assumed minority ownership of her hometown Reds. By then, most of the prominent players from the '70s dynasty were gone, but the club was still quite respectable—placing second in both halves of the strike-shortened '81 slate. They soon tumbled out of contention, inspiring Schott to claim the position of managing general partner. Few women had owned ball clubs to that point, and even fewer had actually made executive decisions. With Schott operating behind the scenes, the Reds finished second in four consecutive campaigns. Manager Pete Rose's banishment from baseball derailed the '89 pennant run, but the team would rise from the ashes the following year.

Schott shared her expansive home with a St. Bernard named "Schottzie," which she appointed as team mascot. The dog was allowed to roam Riverfront Stadium freely, and sometimes did its business on the field, much to the chagrin of players and coaches. Schott earned a reputation as a tightwad, shutting off the lights in the team's offices and threatening to dismiss all the team's scouts, who (according to her) did virtually nothing for the club. The frugal executive remained popular with the public by keeping the prices of tickets and concessions reasonably low. She also made herself accessible to fans, especially children, in her executive seat at the ballpark.

In 1990, the Reds swept the A's in the World Series, but Schott sullied the affair by slighting her star outfielder, Eric Davis. Davis was injured in Game 4 while diving for a ball. He suffered a lacerated kidney that required surgery. Upon his release from an Oakland hospital, he was forced to pay his own way home. He was less than enthusiastic about it, commenting acerbically that Schott's dog received better treatment than he. The caustic owner would soon prove that there was some truth to that statement.

In 1991, Schott was sued by former Reds' marketing director Tom Sabo, who claimed that he was dismissed after challenging her refusal to hire black people. Testimony included damning statements from several front-office employees, all of whom claimed to have heard her use racially offensive terms. In particular, she was accused of referring to Eric Davis and slugger Dave Parker as "million dollar n—rs." She admitted that the word was in her vocabulary but denied using it in conjunction with the players.

Schott did little to help her own cause after she came under fire. She admitted to displaying a Nazi armband with a swastika on it in her home. She also went on record saying that "Hitler was good in the beginning, but went too far." Bud Selig, acting as chairman of baseball's executive council, released a 10-page report detailing Schott's offensive rhetoric. She was subsequently strapped with a $25,000 fine and one-year suspension.

Seemingly unable to curb her acidic tongue, Schott would land herself in hot water several more times before her career was finished. Addressing the Ohio County Treasurer's Association in '94, she denigrated players with pierced ears, proclaiming that "only fruits wear earrings." She also meddled in the personal affairs of manager Davey Johnson that year, threatening to fire him if he didn't marry his live-in girlfriend. When umpire John Mc-Sherry tragically died of a heart attack during the Reds' home opener in '96, Schott told reporters she "felt cheated" by the game's postponement. She allegedly approached umpire Harry Wendelstedt two weeks later only to have him literally turn his back on her. Later in the season, she issued more derogatory remarks aimed at Asian Americans, Japanese, and homosexuals. She also made positive statements about Hitler (again) on ESPN, commenting that he "built tremendous highways and got the factories going." This drew a scathing reaction from members of the Anti-Defamation League, who classified her remarks as "profoundly ignorant and offensive."

Served with an ultimatum from MLB, she abandoned day-to-day control of the Reds through the '98 campaign. Before the '99 slate had begun, she was again pressured by the commissioner's office to get out of baseball. Over 70 years old and in failing health, she finally sold her controlling interest in the Reds. The club had not heard the last of her as she sued CEO Carl Lindner in 2003 over the placement of her seats at Great American Ballpark. In later years, she was quite generous with her wealth, giving charitable donations to various organizations she deemed worthy, such as the Boy Scouts and the Cincinnati Zoo. When she died in 2004, her estate was valued at over $120 million.

Harry Frazee

Boston fans are a superstitious lot. Mention owner Harry Frazee's name to any diehard Red Sox follower and you're liable to hear about the "Babe Ruth curse"—a popular myth based upon Frazee's sale of Ruth to the Yankees in 1920, which allegedly doomed the franchise to a long championship drought. But there is far more to the story than Ruth. In fact, Frazee stocked the Yankee roster with a multitude of players that would make them a powerhouse for years to come. Painted as a hapless victim by some and a shameless villain by others, a careful examination of the facts colors Frazee as an ambitious executive at odds with a league magnate and desperately trying to keep his business interests solvent.

During the first two decades of American League play, the Red Sox were the most successful franchise in the loop, capturing five world championships before the "roaring 20s" arrived. They played in one of the most unique stadiums in the majors, and only a handful of teams had a larger following. That fan base would dwindle dramatically as the club finished last in 9 of 11 seasons between 1922 and 1932. Though Frazee cannot be single-handedly blamed for this complete reversal of fortune, he undeniably set the winds of change in motion.

A New York–based theater producer and director, Frazee purchased the Red Sox from Joseph Lannin in 1916 for a reported sum of $1 million. He assumed responsibility of a club heavily laden with the game's brightest talent. This included the corner outfield tandem of Harry Hooper and Duffy Lewis along with a formidable pitching staff anchored by 21-year-old Babe Ruth, who had not yet revealed his prodigious power at the plate.

The transaction was the first to take place without the intercession of American League president Ban Johnson. Johnson, who had traditionally run the league in dictatorial fashion, resented Frazee's independent spirit and began campaigning behind the scenes for the Boston proprietor's removal from baseball. In those days, the sport was presided over by a three-man executive committee, which consisted of a chairperson and two league presidents. In response to Johnson's maneuverings, Frazee went so far as to approach former U.S. president William Howard Taft with the idea of creating a "one-man National Baseball Commission" that would curtail Johnson's power. Frazee was also quite vocal in his disapproval of Johnson's handling of wartime affairs during the 1918 slate.

Things came to a head the following year when Boston's star hurler Carl Mays walked off the mound in the middle of a game against the White Sox. Johnson clamored for his suspension, but Frazee had other ideas, selling the insubordinate hurler to the Yankees. From that point on, Johnson worked diligently to limit Frazee's ability to engineer deals with most junior-circuit clubs. The Yankees, now officially on Johnson's bad side, would remain willing trade partners along with the White Sox and A's, who also had axes to grind with the domineering AL chief.

By the end of the 1919 slate, Frazee was on shaky financial ground. He still owed Joseph Lannin a substantial sum of money from the original purchase of the Red Sox. In the wake of WWI, attendance was on the decline. Frazee's theater business had suffered as well and was not earning nearly enough to cover his baseball shortfalls. In need of some quick cash, he began to consider the unthinkable.

In 1919, Babe Ruth had enjoyed a coming-out party, playing more than 100 games in the outfield for the first time. Proving he belonged in the lineup every day, he led the league in runs scored, RBIs, slugging percentage, and total bases while setting a new single-season record for homers with 29. He liked hitting so much, in fact, he began to gripe about having to pitch. In January of 1920, Frazee made his move, selling his most valuable player to the Yankees for a then record $100,000. Additionally, he borrowed money from Yankee owner Jacob Ruppert to set his other affairs straight.

Things turned sour when Lannin sued for ownership of Fenway Park and Frazee ended up on the losing end of the settlement. The entire sum of Ruth's sale went to Lannin along with most of the Yankee loan. Frazee told reporters after the fact that the team's finances were secure and the club would soon be purchasing players, but the statement did not hold water. In fact, the opposite took place as Frazee helped build a Yankee dynasty piece by piece.

After the 1920 slate, the misguided Red Sox owner got rid of Hall of Fame right-hander Waite Hoyt and veteran catcher Wally Schang. The following December, he added two more talented hurlers to the Yankee staff: Bullet Joe Bush and Sad Sam Jones. Further enabling the Bombers' rise to supremacy, he traded away slick-fielding shortstop, Everett Scott, who would set the record for consecutive games played while in pinstripes (later broken by Lou

Gehrig). In '22 and '23, Frazee completed a string of ill-advised transactions by donating infielder Joe Dugan and southpaw Herb Pennock (another Hall of Famer) to the Yankee cause. The results were highly predictable as New York won six pennants during the 1920s while the Red Sox went in a completely different direction.

With few players of any worth left to sell, Frazee dished the Red Sox to a syndicate headed by Bob Quinn (former vice president of the Browns) in 1923. The following year, Frazee left his financial misery far behind as his play *No, No Nanette* became a smash hit. It would be his last successful theatrical venture as the sequel, *Yes, Yes Yvette*, was a flop. In 1929, Frazee died of a kidney ailment.

Though he invited scathing criticism from such notable sportswriters as Shirley Povich and Fred Lieb, Frazee was neither the first nor the last owner to auction off a baseball team. Connie Mack had done it after the A's suffered a humiliating World Series sweep at the hands of the Braves in 1914. Charles Finley would break up another A's dynasty six decades later with the sale of all his top players. Following in those footsteps, Florida Marlins owner Wayne Huizenga held a fire sale on the heels of a world championship in 1998.

Frank and M. Stanley Robison

Though the Robison brothers put some fine teams on the field during the 19th century, they will forever be remembered for building the worst squad in baseball history—the 1899 Cleveland Spiders. The name itself has become a punch line.

How bad were they?

So bad that they lost 24 straight games at one point and managed to string together a pair of consecutive wins just once all year.
So bad that they were forced to play most of their games on the road because virtually no one would pay to see them at home.
So bad that when Orioles pitcher Jerry Nops lost to them one afternoon, he was fined and suspended by his manager, John McGraw.

One has to wonder: how could the Robisons assemble such a dud? The answer is stranger than fiction.

Frank and Stanley were born in Pittsburgh. They spent their childhood years in Dubuque, Iowa. Seven years older than his brother, Frank got a head start in the business world, attending Delaware University and teaming with his father-in-law to establish street railway systems all over the U.S. and Canada. In 1889, he founded the Cleveland City Railway Company, merging with Marcus A. Hanna a few years later. He reportedly lost his shirt when broker John Shipherd fraudulently sold the stock to Hanna and kept the proceeds. A court settlement gave Robison a substantial interest in the company.

In 1887, Frank and Stanley purchased the Cleveland Blues, an American Association squad. After two mediocre campaigns, the team moved to the National League as the Cleveland Infants (a.k.a. the "Babes"). At some point during the spring of '89, a reporter observed that the players were gaunt and "looked like a lot of underfed spiders." The nickname caught on. Determined to build a reliable following, the Robisons financed the construction of a new stadium (known as League Park) on East 66th and Lexington Avenue. It opened in 1891.

The Spiders soon climbed into contention under hard-nosed manager Patsy Tebeau, who was categorized by one writer as a "cutthroat" and given credit for founding "the new rowdy game." Taking over in 1892, Tebeau's aggressive style sparked Cleveland to a league championship over Baltimore in 1895. It would prove to be the pinnacle of the Robison dynasty.

In 1898, the United States became entangled in a war with Spain. Late in the season, all of the Spiders' games were transferred to rival cities. Criticized for the move, the elder Robison remarked that baseball was a business and not a public service. At the time, the National League was a loosely governed collection of 12 teams. There were no rules in place to stop owners from buying multiple franchises. After the Spiders had dropped to fifth place in 1898, the Robisons made a bold maneuver, purchasing the St. Louis Browns from bankrupt proprietor Chris von der Ahe. Then came the shocking announcement: the two teams would be switching cities.

The Browns had been a dominant club in the 1880s but had fallen to ruin in later years, finishing last in '97 and '98. The '98 squad was particularly inept, winning just 39 games all year. Sensing disaster for baseball in the Forest City, the *Cleveland Plain Dealer* denounced the outrageous plan in a series of derisive articles. Addressing concerns that the Spiders would become equivalent to a minor-league franchise, Frank commented: "Cleveland will not, contrary to the impression that some persons have been trying to get abroad, be a farm for the St. Louis team. Not a single man who is now with Cleveland will be transferred to St. Louis this season." This would stand as a bold-faced lie when multitalented player/manager Lave Cross was shipped out after the Spiders got off to an 8–30 start. He joined a trio of future Cooperstown honorees in St. Louis—pitcher Cy Young, outfielder Jesse Burkett, and shortstop Bobby Wallace.

As the newly christened Perfectos battled to a respectable 84–67 record, the Spiders struggled to stay afloat. At one point during spring training, Cross had asked the Robisons for a couple of players to help the team and received the following reply from Frank: "I am not interested in winning games here. Play out the schedule. That's your job."

The Spiders had a long road ahead of them—literally. Rarely attracting more than a few hundred fans at home, many of their games were relocated to rival cities. Beginning on July 3, they completed the longest stretch of "away" games in major-league history. During this 50-game tour of the entire circuit, the team went 6–44, falling 55 games out of first place and 20 games behind the 11th-place Washington Senators. At one point during the season, Cleveland sportswriter Elmer Bates wrote a humorous column listing the advantages of playing for the Spiders. Among the perks listed were:

"Defeats do not disturb one's sleep."

"You are not asked 50 times a day, 'what's the score?'"

Near the end of the '99 campaign, trouble arose between players and owners. On October 1, the *Cleveland Plain Dealer* reported that players had not been paid in six weeks and were growing increasingly discontent. Frank Robison insisted that it was against club policy to pay his men on the road. He invited players who were strapped for cash to draw from the club treasury as needed. All would eventually receive their back pay but not until November.

After compiling the worst record in major-league history at 20–134, the Robisons retained 15 players for the following year. None would wear a Spiders' uniform as a series of contractions occurred in the off-season, reducing the National League to a far more manageable eight-team circuit. Baltimore, Louisville, Cleveland, and Washington were all dropped, and syndicates were outlawed. The Spiders would reappear in the American League as the Naps, Blues, and Indians under different ownership.

The Perfectos were renamed the Cardinals in 1900. They were an annual source of disappointment to the Robisons as they finished below .500 ten times between 1900 and 1911. The club got off to such a poor showing in 1905 that Stanley took over as manager for the last 50 games of the season. He led the squad to a lackluster 19–31 record. Frank Robison passed away in 1908, and Stanley retained sole ownership of the St. Louis franchise until his own death in 1911. The Cardinals would remain without a world championship until 1926.

George Steinbrenner

George Steinbrenner was a walking contradiction. He could be stubborn, demanding, and impossible to please as evidenced by the 19 managers he employed from 1973 to 1990. At the same time, he was "generous, caring," and "compassionate." Those words were used by Yogi Berra to describe the man he knew as "the Boss"—the same man who had fired him impulsively just 16 games into the 1985 slate. Steinbrenner's commitment to the Yankees was never in doubt as he used his bulging wallet to lure the game's brightest talent to the Bronx for nearly 40 years. When he passed away in 2010, he had 7 world championships and 11 pennants in his pocket.

The Yankee icon was born in Rocky River, Ohio. His father was owner of Kinsman Marine, a highly successful shipping company. George had a privileged childhood, growing up in Bay Village—a wealthy community near Cleveland. He took an active interest in sports, participating in football and track at Culver Military Academy before graduating from Williams College in Massachusetts.

The listless Steinbrenner spent two years in the Air Force and then coached basketball and football at St. Thomas Aquinas High School in Columbus, Ohio. He would move on to greener pastures as a coach at Northwestern and Purdue Universities. Finding no satisfaction in those positions, he returned to his father's shipping business, which he helped rejuvenate in 1957.

Steinbrenner's first professional sports venture was a disappointment. He bought the Cleveland Pipers of the National Industrial League with a group of investors and then moved them into the American Basketball League. After winning a championship, he laid plans for merging his club with the NBA. It would never happen as the team couldn't generate enough revenue despite the presence of former Ohio State All-American Jerry Lucas. The Pipers went bankrupt, and the American Basketball League folded before the completion of the 1962–63 season.

In 1967, Steinbrenner became CEO of the American Ship Building Company. He tried to invest a portion of his substantial earnings in the Cleveland Indians, but owner Vernon Stouffer wouldn't sell to him. He was not the kind of man to take "no" lightly, and in 1973, his aspirations of owning a baseball team became a reality when he assembled a group of financiers to purchase the New York Yankees from CBS. He promised to be hands off and insisted that he would "stick to building ships," but those words could not have been further from the truth.

A year later, Steinbrenner got indirectly caught up in the Watergate presidential scandal. Prior to the start of the '74 season, he was indicted on

14 criminal counts and later pleaded guilty to making illegal contributions to Richard Nixon's reelection campaign. He was fined $15,000 by a U.S. district court and suspended by Commissioner Bowie Kuhn for two years. That penalty would later be reduced by nine months.

When "the Boss" returned in '76, he became increasingly domineering, enforcing a strict grooming code. This didn't sit well with some players, especially outfielder Lou Piniella, who challenged Steinbrenner: "You mean to tell me that if Jesus Christ came back down with his long hair, you wouldn't let him play on this team?" In response, Steinbrenner led Piniella to a pool located behind a nearby motel. "If you can walk across the water in that pool, you don't have to get a haircut," he allegedly said.

Much has been made of the love/hate relationship between Steinbrenner and Billy Martin, who was fired several times in New York. But Martin was not the only high-profile manager to feel the sting of George's rash decisions. In September of 1981, Gene Michael was summarily dismissed and replaced with Bob Lemon, who had stepped in for Martin during the '78 pennant run. Michael was reinstated in place of Lemon 14 games into the '82 slate only to be fired again after guiding the club to a mediocre 50–50 record through early August. Recognizing his own impulsiveness, Steinbrenner once commented: "I am tough. Sometimes I am unreasonable. I have to catch myself once in a while."

Steinbrenner had no qualms about insulting the highest paid Yankee players. He once called Japanese pitching prospect Hideki Irabu, who had been signed to a 12.8-million-dollar contract, "a fat pussy toad." His treatment of outfielder Dave Winfield was even worse. In 1980, Winfield inked a lucrative 10-year deal with the Yankees. Though he compiled impressive statistics in the Bronx, Steinbrenner was resentful of him. After a three-game losing streak in the second half of the '85 slate, the disgruntled Yankee owner approached reporters and asked where Reggie Jackson was. "We need a Mr. October or Mr. September," he said. "Dave Winfield is Mr. May."

In the late '80s, Steinbrenner hired gambler Howard Spira to uncover scandalous information about Winfield. Nothing was ever found, and when Commissioner Fay Vincent got wind of the scheme, he suspended "the Boss" from day-to-day operations of the Yankees for life. Steinbrenner was reinstated by acting commissioner Bud Selig in 1993. Winfield would have his comeuppance when he sued the Yankee owner for $300,000 promised but never delivered to the Winfield Foundation, which provides services to underprivileged youth and families in need. The icing on the cake, when Winfield was inducted into the Hall of Fame in 2001, he was enshrined as a member of the San Diego Padres despite the fact that his longest tenure had been with the Yankees. This reportedly irked Steinbrenner although the two made nice in public.

In Steinbrenner's final years, he more or less stepped aside, allowing Joe Torre to quietly manage the club from '96 through 2007. There were (of course) a few instances of George being George, but his presence was not nearly as oppressive as it had been in the early days. As his health slowly declined, he let his sons Hal and Hank take over his affairs and granted fewer interviews. He showed up at the new Yankee Stadium just a handful of times, the most memorable appearance being the 2010 home opener, when he was presented with his seventh World Series ring by Derek Jeter and Joe Girardi.

Perhaps the most enduring image of "the Boss" was a caricature created by Larry David for the *Seinfeld* show. The Emmy Award–winning writer/producer provided the voice-over for Steinbrenner's recurring character, who referred to himself as "the Big Stein" and never revealed his face to the camera. The Yankee owner was portrayed as chatty and meddlesome, accusing one of the show's major characters, George Costanza, of various indiscretions, such as stealing equipment and secretly being a communist. He also made poor decisions and bad trades. One episode included a running joke about the transfer of Jay Buhner to the Mariners. A top Yankee slugging prospect at one time, Buhner would smash close to 300 homers with Seattle. The real Steinbrenner maintained a sense of humor about the *Seinfeld* parody. "I'm really 95 percent Mr. Rogers and only 5 percent Oscar the Grouch," he once remarked. Some would say that his math was a bit fuzzy.

~

CHAPTER NINE

Fanatical Fans

Ivonne Hernandez

The Yankees / Red Sox rivalry has been described as one of the fiercest in all of sports. Over the years, the epic clashes between the two clubs have brought out the best and worst in both players and fans. In May of 2008, a passionate Yankee supporter named Ivonne Hernandez went to the ultimate extreme when she struck and killed a Red Sox enthusiast with her car in a New Hampshire parking lot.

Entering the 2012 slate, Boston and New York were dead even in their ongoing regular season series. But it wasn't always that way. In the first two decades of the 20th century, the Yankees could hardly compete. Playing as the "Highlanders" from 1903 through 1912, they finished in the second division six times. The name change didn't help them much as they remained out of the running until 1919. In contrast, the Red Sox enjoyed one of their most fruitful periods, capturing six pennants and five world championships before 1920.

The rivalry began after financially pressed owner Harry Frazee sold off all his best players to the Yankees, leaving Boston's roster in virtual ruin. The Sox eventually recovered but would fail to win a championship for the remainder of the century. The Yankees, on the other hand, became the most successful franchise in baseball history. The Bean Town faithful were at a loss to explain their club's ongoing misfortune, and in the 1990s, the "Curse of the Bambino" became a widely distributed urban legend. The idea of a hex originating with the 1920 sale of Babe Ruth to New York was officially debunked in 2004, when the Sox finally won their sixth World Series. But the postseason triumph failed to inhibit the ongoing resentment between the two clubs and their fans.

Even today, players seem to take the game to a higher level each time the Yankees and Red Sox lock horns. Most encounters are marathon affairs involving an exhaustive series of strategic maneuvers. Traditionally, the meetings have been marred by brawls, among the most memorable being a '76 donnybrook instigated by notorious hotheads Lou Piniella and Carlton Fisk. Another infamous bout occurred during the 2003 ALCS, when Don Zimmer was thrown roughly to the turf by Yankee nemesis Pedro Martínez. The following year, Jason Varitek and Alex Rodriguez went at it, providing fodder for an infamous photograph.

The story of Ivonne Hernandez is a sad example of how alcohol and sports rivalries don't mix. After consuming several beers at the 603 Club, a watering hole located less than an hour from Boston in the heart of Red Sox territory, Hernandez ran into a small group of Boston fans who were leaving Slade's Food and Spirits—another popular bar situated on the same street. Hernandez's car was parked in the Nashua City Hall lot, and when the group of Red Sox followers noticed a large Yankee decal stuck to the window of her vehicle, a verbal exchange took place.

According to Hernandez's testimony, the Sox fans began taunting her, and one of them punched her in the back of the head. Prosecutors begged to differ, stating that Hernandez had been the one to throw a punch, striking a woman named Brooke Garger in the face. The full truth will likely never be known, but Hernandez hopped into her car and drove into a dirt lot across the street. She turned around, gunned the engine, and piloted her vehicle straight into the jeering throng.

An investigation later revealed that the car's brakes were never engaged—compelling evidence that Hernandez's act was intentional. Twenty-nine-year-old Matthew Beaudoin slammed into the windshield and was catapulted violently to the pavement when Hernandez hit a parking meter. He died of massive head trauma. One of Beaudoin's companions, Maria Hughes, was also clipped by the car, but her injuries were minor. Arrested at the scene, Hernandez admitted to consuming alcohol and then refused a breath test. She told police that she felt threatened by the group of hecklers and had only meant to frighten them.

At the police station, she was charged with second-degree murder, reckless conduct, and drunken driving. Responding to a provocatively phrased question from an investigator, she admitted that she intended to do more than scare her antagonists. She later claimed that the testimony was coerced and should therefore be discounted.

There was enough evidence to convict her anyway as she was sentenced to prison for 20–40 years. During the trial, she read a tearful apology to Beaudoin's family and pleaded for forgiveness. The *Nashua Telegraph* reported that Beaudoin's mother was largely unmoved.

Hernandez, who stood to be separated from her daughter until she was a senior citizen, appealed the decision, claiming that detectives had tricked her into a confession by promising that her remarks would be kept off the record. The appeal was overturned in November of 2011. The incident remains among the most senseless tragedies in recent baseball history.

Bill Veeck's Disco Demolition Night

Bill Veeck was more mad scientist than baseball owner. He preferred to be called a "hustler" and wrote an entire volume on the topic, appropriately entitled *The Hustler's Handbook*. A true maverick who was resentful of the baseball establishment, he believed that any club relying solely on the sport itself to draw fans would soon be out of business. And so, he spent his entire career trying to give the masses something more.

His intrinsic desire to be different inspired him to generate a string of popular innovations and zany promotions. In Cleveland, he opened a daycare center at the ballpark and integrated the American League with the signing of Larry Doby. In Chicago, he planted ivy on the outfield walls. On the South Side of the Windy City (where the White Sox still reside), he installed a shower in the bleachers, allowed fans to manage his team, and unveiled an exploding scoreboard. He also executed the strangest gag in baseball history when he sent 3-foot-7 Eddie Gaedel to the plate in a game against the Tigers. He pulled that one off as owner of the St. Louis Browns.

Veeck got his first job in baseball at age 11, working as a vendor and office boy at Wrigley Field. He bragged that he was the "only human being ever raised at the ballpark." He attended two prestigious prep schools and later studied at Kenyon College, cutting his studies short when he went to work for the Cubs. After parting ways with the club in 1941, he teamed with former Cubs' infielder Charlie Grimm to purchase the Milwaukee Brewers of the American Association. It was there that his wild promotions began to take off as Brewers' games featured live bands and unusual prize giveaways, such as lobsters and guinea pigs. Defying baseball standards, he also introduced morning games, during which fans were served coffee and cornflakes.

Veeck enrolled in the Marines and lost his left leg in action. He would undergo many surgeries during his lifetime. After the war, his travels brought him to numerous cities, where he succeeded in piquing the interest of fans. He fell ill in the early '60s and dropped out of baseball for a spell. After recovering his health, he wrote the classic autobiography, *Veeck as in Wreck*. Eager to get back to his roots, he purchased the White Sox again in 1975.

Two of Veeck's least successful promotions occurred at Comiskey Park. Determined to spiff up the club's dreary uniforms, he decked players out in dark shorts with black and white striped knee-high socks for the first game of a 1976 doubleheader. The matching uniform shirts (which the ChiSox wore all season) had high sleeves with a fanned out collar. Surprisingly, Veeck's unconventionally clad crew stole four bases in a 5–2 triumph over Kansas City. One can only hope that the pilferers went in standing up. In a now famous quote, Royals' first baseman John Mayberry taunted his opponents: "You guys are the sweetest team we've seen yet." Perhaps inspired by the derogatory remark, the Southside crew changed back into full-length pants before the nightcap.

Veeck's most disastrous promotion was actually the brainchild of his son Mike. It took place before the second game of a doubleheader in July of 1979. Billed as "Disco Demolition Night," the event coincided with a campaign led by Chicago deejay Steve Dahl to eradicate disco music from the airwaves. Dahl had lost his job at a local radio station when the musical format was converted to all disco. Hired by a rock station known as WLUP the "Loop," he created the "Anti-Disco Army," which at one time boasted 7,000 associates. Mike Veeck happened to be the sports commentator at WLUP, and together, he and Dahl sold the rebellious White Sox owner on the idea of destroying disco records during a game. The three had no idea what trouble it would bring.

Inspired by the 98-cent admission price offered to anyone who brought a vinyl record to be demolished, nearly 60,000 fans mobbed the stadium, creating standing-room conditions. Outside the park, 20,000 more were left as police blocked exit ramps from the interstate to discourage new arrivals. One writer described the scene as "an invasion of drunken, stoned, long-haired teens sporting Sabbath and Zeppelin t-shirts."

Before the game even started, a beefed up security force had their hands full as fans rushed the turnstiles and began climbing Comiskey's two-story chain-link fence. A bin designated to collect the LPs and 45s filled up quickly, and fans took their records inside, tossing them recklessly onto the field. Rusty Staub of the Tigers later commented: "I've never seen anything so dangerous in my life." Tiger players unabashedly put their helmets on to protect themselves against projectiles, which also included fireworks, beer cups, and hot dogs.

After the Tigers had won the first game by a 4–1 margin, Dahl—clad in a green army helmet—played master of ceremonies for the "demolition." The bin of records was placed in the outfield, where it was obliterated with an explosive charge. The crowd roared its approval as pandemonium ensued.

Fans swarmed the field, tearing up grass, setting fires, and overturning the batting cage. Numerous fistfights broke out, and when Bill Veeck personally appealed to the marauding crowd to settle down, his pleas were ignored. Even Harry Caray's rendition of "Take Me Out to the Ballgame" failed to bring the mob under control. Eventually, a horde of riot-clad cops were dispatched, quickly restoring order.

Veeck wanted the second game to commence, but the field was in such disarray that umpires were forced to postpone it. The following day, AL president Lee MacPhail declared the contest a forfeit in favor of the Tigers. The besieged White Sox owner criticized the decision but ultimately accepted responsibility for the unfortunate turn of events. He would later refer to the promotion as a "mistake." Veeck died in 1986, gaining entry into the Hall of Fame in 1991, the same year Comiskey Park was demolished—literally this time.

Jeffrey Maier

Jeffrey Maier was an early bloomer. Before he was even out of middle school, he had made multiple television appearances and received the ceremonial keys to New York City from Mayor Rudy Giuliani. It was a tough act to follow for an adolescent.

A die-hard Yankee fan, Maier was attending his first playoff game at Yankee Stadium when he carved a place for himself (albeit a small one) in baseball history. Some perceived his actions as meddlesome and felonious, while others (mostly New Yorkers) painted him as heroic. Maier, himself, said he was just a "12-year-old kid trying to catch a ball." Either way, his name would not be soon forgotten.

The Yankees of 1996 were a team loaded with homegrown talent such as Derek Jeter, Bernie Williams, Andy Pettitte. Climbing into first place in late April, they built a 10-game lead in August only to see it nearly evaporate a month later. They were chased all year by the Orioles, who occupied second from May 31 to season's end. Baltimore was a club heavily stocked with talented veterans, including Hall of Famers Roberto Alomar, Cal Ripken, and Eddie Murray. Their pitching staff was filled out by aces Mike Mussina and David Wells, both of whom would later see World Series action with the Yankees.

Maier reportedly received his ticket to Game 1 of the '96 ALCS as a present. Though many youngsters can only daydream idly about playing a role in a championship game, the boy from Old Tappan, New Jersey, would put his dream into action. With the Yankees trailing the Orioles 4–3 in the bottom of the eighth inning, Derek Jeter launched a deep fly to right field off reliever Armando Benitez. Tony Tarasco settled under it and was poised to make the catch when Maier interfered with the play, reaching over the wall and deflecting the ball into the bleachers.

Fans are allowed to keep souvenirs hit into the stands but are not permitted to tamper with live balls on the field. Spectator interference is called on such occasions with the play being ruled dead and the batter being called out or awarded a discretionary number of bases by the umpire. In the case of Jeffrey Maier, arbiter Rich Garcia evidently didn't have a clear view of Jeter's hit as he declared it a game-tying homer. Tarasco argued vehemently with Garcia until manager Davey Johnson took over for him. The appeal was not enforced. After the Yankees won in the 11th inning on a memorable walk-off homer by Bernie Williams, the Orioles lodged a protest to AL president Gene Budig. It was refuted since judgment calls cannot be protested.

After thoroughly reviewing the play, Garcia later admitted that Maier had interfered with the ball—though he held firm that it was not catchable. Before Game 2, the official was seen on national television laughing with New York fans and signing autographs. The Yanks went on to win the World Series against the Braves—their first championship in nearly two decades as Maier was elevated to folk-hero status in the Big Apple. After the game, Derek Jeter commented: "Maybe I should send him something. That's our boy." Maier received the biggest gift of all when the *New York Daily News* allowed him to sit behind the Yankee dugout later in the postseason.

Life went on for Maier after the publicity faded. He played ball for Northern Valley Regional High School in Old Tappan. He matured into a solidly built third baseman / outfielder for Wesleyan University—a private liberal arts college in Middletown, Connecticut. As a senior in 2006, he broke a school record for career base hits. Though he expressed interest in becoming a major-league player, his chances were slim since Division III teams don't attract too many scouts. A National League headhunter told the *New York Times* in '06 that Maier was not "on anybody's radar."

He enjoyed a fruitful college-baseball career nevertheless—and his name was not forgotten. During a 2004 game against Williams College in Massachusetts, he was pelted with snow and ice by some Red Sox fans who still resented him for his actions on that long-ago October night. The game was stopped as Maier deserted his center-field post to avoid being hit. Ten years after the fact, Jeter still remembered the incident as well. "It's good that he is doing something now on his own and has his own memories," the Yankee shortstop commented.

Maier eventually earned a tryout with the Yankees but was not selected. He scouted for the Cape Cod League and later became a consultant for the New Haven County Cutters, of the independent Can-Am League. He also appeared as an extra and helped teach baseball skills to actors for ESPN's *The Bronx Is Burning*, a miniseries recounting the story of the 1970s Yankees. In 2008, he was the subject of a novelty song performed by the New York Sports Band.

Kitty Burke

Throughout the course of baseball history, women have been largely excluded from play. Though MLB and the Hall of Fame do not officially recognize it, a nightclub entertainer named Kitty Burke became the first woman to bat in a major-league game during the 1935 campaign. Her name may be absent from the historical register, but Burke had 30,000 witnesses who could have vouched for her.

Burke was not the first woman to appear on a professional diamond. In 1898, Lizzie Arlington pitched one inning for the Reading Coal Heavers of the Atlantic League (never logging a plate appearance). In 1931, Jackie Mitchell joined the professional baseball ranks when she signed a contract with the Double-A Chattanooga Lookouts. Hit hard by the Depression, Chattanooga owner Joe Engel was in search of a novelty to draw fans to the ballpark. Mitchell, a spirited southpaw with an effective sidearm drop curve, made a name for herself in an April exhibition game against the Yankees. Called upon in relief to face the heart of the New York order, she struck out the game's most fearsome hitters, Babe Ruth and Lou Gehrig, in succession. Ruth got caught looking on a 1–2 pitch while Gehrig swung through three of her offerings. She was removed from the game after walking Tony Lazzeri and then declared ineligible to play before she had a chance to bat. Commissioner Kenesaw Mountain Landis voided her contract on the preposterous pretense that baseball was "too strenuous for a woman to play." Ruth and Gehrig, who posed for a picture with her, may have been of a different mind-set.

In 1935, a banner year for baseball, the Reds hosted the first night game in major-league history at Crosley Field in Cincinnati. Franklin Delano Roosevelt played a role in the momentous event, using a telegraph key that sent a signal to officials standing by at the ballpark. On the president's cue, more than 600 incandescent lights were turned on at once, slicing through the dark and aweing the crowd of 20,000-plus. Two months later, Crosley Field was the sight of another unprecedented event.

Making her living as a burlesque dancer, Kitty Burke was one of 30,000 spectators who turned out on July 31 to see the Reds face the St. Louis Cardinals—defending world champions. The park was ill equipped to handle such a large crowd, so fans were allowed to stand on the field in foul territory. Reds' left fielder Babe Herman commented that conditions were so cramped, "you couldn't see the game from the dugout."

Burke, described by one reporter as "a pretty young blonde in red," had been heckling players all evening, and when Cardinals' outfielder Joe Medwick shouted back at her, the sultry entertainer was determined to show him up. In the bottom of the eighth, while Babe Herman was waiting to hit in the on-deck circle, Burke wove her way through the crowd and approached the slugger.

"Give me your bat," she demanded.

"What do you want with it?" Herman inquired.

"I want to bat," she told him.

"Go ahead," he conceded, handing her the implement.

The home plate umpire was a man named Bill Stewart, who doubled as an NHL referee in the off-season. For whatever reason (perhaps he was impressed with Burke's shapely curves), he decided to play along. He shouted, "Play ball!" as Burke took her place in the batter's box. St. Louis's hurler, Paul "Daffy" Dean—brother of Dizzy Dean and winner of 19 games the previous season—was hesitant about pitching to Burke until she taunted him in front of the standing room only crowd, calling him a "hick" and suggesting he go back to the farm and milk some cows. Dean found the insult amusing and lobbed an underhand toss to the plate, which she grounded solidly back to the box. The congenial moundsman fielded the ball and waited for her at first base, but she ducked back into the crowd, later commenting suggestively: "If he wanted me, he'd have to chase me." Herman added a comical quote of his own, telling reporters: "That's the first time a broad ever pinchhit for me."

Since there were two outs at the time and Stewart had allowed Burke to hit, Cardinals' manager Frankie Frisch argued that her groundout should end the inning. Stewart disagreed since she was not officially on the Cincinnati roster. Babe Herman stepped up to the dish and blasted a double, sparking a two-run rally. The Reds won in extra innings, 4–3.

After the game, Burke was allegedly given a Reds' uniform, which she incorporated into her act. She toured the burlesque circuit touting herself as the first woman to bat in a major-league game. Technically, the claim was accurate. In honor of her unofficial achievement, a company called Cincy Shirts offered Kitty Burke T-shirts in 2012. The shirts featured a 1930s-era publicity photo of Burke holding a bat with a narrative of the event in the background.

Vasili Sianis

Anyone who follows baseball must periodically ask oneself: will the Cubs ever win another World Series? It's the most mystifying conundrum in all of sports—how any team can play for over a hundred years without garnering a championship. In probability theory, the "law of large numbers" infers that the likelihood of an expected outcome increases with the number of trials. Yet the Cubs have defied the odds year after frustrating year while continuing to draw fans to their ballpark.

Only three venues have lured more spectators through the turnstiles: Yankee Stadium, Dodger Stadium, and Fenway Park. Opened in 1914, Wrigley Field is one of few remaining structures from yesteryear. Like the Red Sox in Boston, the Cubs have been resistant to change, waiting until the 1980s to install lights. They've also been resistant to winning. When the Cubs last prevailed in a Fall Classic, President Theodore Roosevelt was wrapping up his second term in office and the first Model T Ford had just been produced. Since then, the club has lost 13 postseason showdowns, including seven World Series, three League Championship Series, and three Division Series. When the *Chicago Tribune* purchased the long suffering franchise in the early '80s, sportswriter Bob Verdi quipped: "I don't know why we bought the Cubs. We already had a perfectly good company softball team." Commenting on the possibility of managing the club in 1999, former Chicago outfielder Billy Williams inquired jokingly: "They can't kick you out of the Hall of Fame, can they?"

At the root of the Cubs' failure lies a legend and a curse. Vasili Sianis, nicknamed "Billy Goat" for the goatee he sported, was a Greek immigrant and an innovative promoter. During the 1930s, he purchased the Lincoln Tavern near Chicago Stadium on a bounced check he reportedly made good on after his first weekend in business. Thinking outside the box, he petitioned the State Department to issue him the first restaurant license for the moon and later lured members of the 1944 Republican Convention to his establishment by hanging a sign in the window stating that party members were not welcome.

Sianis hatched his most infamous scheme October 6, 1945, when he showed up at Wrigley Field for Game 4 of the World Series accompanied by a goat named Murphy. The animal was adorned with a sign reading: "We Got Detroit's Goat." Though employees at the turnstile were hesitant to honor the two box seats Sianis produced, they granted him access. The events that followed would inspire the eccentric businessman to unleash his dreaded curse.

Shortly before game time, Murphy wandered onto the field and began grazing. The animal was subsequently taken into custody by stadium security. Reporters wanted pictures, and Sianis was allowed to stand on the field and be photographed. After that, he was asked to leave. By some accounts, a heated discussion ensued, during which Sianis argued that rules prohibiting animals from attending games were not prominently displayed on Wrigley Field tickets. Security guards were swayed by this appeal.

Sianis could do nothing about Murphy's odor, however, which was intensified by a light rain that had been falling that day. Fans sitting in proximity found it objectionable and issued multiple complaints to security. Sianis was ejected from the park—this time for good. Standing outside the stadium, he put an Old World hex on the club. After the Cubs lost the game, he allegedly sent a telegram to owner P. K. Wrigley that said: "Who smells now?" (The legitimacy of this remains in question, but it makes for an amusing twist.) In another interpretation, the telegram stated ominously that the Cubs would never win a World Series again.

According to multiple sources, Wrigley was a superstitious man who was receptive to the prospect of a curse. In 1950, he composed a letter to Sianis. In it, he apologized for the insult to the goat and petitioned Sianis to remove the hex. The request was denied.

Beginning in 1947, the Cubs fell on hard times, failing to register a winning record for 16 straight seasons (they would finish at an even .500 once in that stretch). During the 1960s, they began to improve with the presence of Cooperstown greats Ernie Banks, Billy Williams, and Ron Santo. In '69, Sianis had an abrupt change of heart, informing the *Chicago Tribune* that he intended to lift the curse. He wrote a letter to Wrigley requesting four seats to Chicago's World Series games that year. Most fans know the story: the Cubs faded down the stretch and were overtaken by the "Miracle Mets"—the other loveable losers. When it was over, Sianis reinforced the fact that the jinx had been removed and attributed the Cubs' second-place showing to the fact that the Mets had "played like hell."

When Sianis died, the tavern passed into the hands of his nephew Sam, who was also an enthusiastic Cubs' supporter. In '73, Sam showed up at Wrigley Field in a limousine encumbered by a goat with a sign that read: "All is forgiven. Let me lead you to the pennant. Your friend, Billy Goat." Members of the Wrigley staff that day, who had perhaps been recently born or living under a rock for several decades, denied the goat access. The curse persisted despite numerous other ceremonial attempts to dispel it. Sianis's tavern, on the other hand, prospered greatly, growing into a chain that expanded to Washington DC in 2005.

In studying the sizable body of literature pertaining to the plight of the Cubs, one can't help but wonder if there is some validity to the hex. In a 2011 ESPN interview, Cubs' manager Mike Quade called the whole idea "comical" and insisted that none of his players thinks about the goat when they take the field. In the absence of a psychological explanation, the supernatural can be at least halfheartedly entertained.

William Ligue Jr. and Eric Dybas

In one of his best known compositions, singer-songwriter Jim Croce asserted that the South Side of Chicago was "the baddest part of town." The neighborhood lived up to that billing during the summer of 2002 and spring of '03 when a pair of shocking on-field incidents unfolded during White Sox games. In the aftermath, serious questions were raised about the character of the ChiSox fan base and competency of their security staff.

The first ugly disturbance occurred on September 19, 2002, during a game against the Kansas City Royals. The Sox were having a mediocre season, entering the contest with an even .500 record. They stood a distant second to the Minnesota Twins in the AL Central and had only a slim chance of capturing a wild-card berth. With one out in the top of the ninth, a drunken spectator named William Ligue Jr. rushed onto the field accompanied by his teenage son, Bill. Entering from the first-base side, the two viciously attacked 54-year-old Royals' coach Tom Gamboa, leaving him with permanent hearing damage.

Ligue had a history of behavioral problems. In 1986, he was convicted of burglary. In '96, he was sued for unpaid child support. A year before the Comiskey Park incident, he was charged with beating up his girlfriend and throwing a brick through the window of her house. The ballpark attack was premeditated, as Ligue called his sister at some point before the episode and told her to watch the game because he was going to be on TV. When she couldn't find it on any channels, he instructed her to watch the news.

Referred to as "shirtless buffoons" by one writer, both assailants were charged with battery. In addition to hitting Gamboa, the younger Ligue also struck a White Sox security guard, who happened to be an off-duty cop. While in police custody, the elder Ligue accused Gamboa of flipping his son the bird. He later admitted to being an alcoholic and to suffering from drug addiction. He was sentenced to 30 months of probation and forced to enter a substance-abuse program in addition to attending parenting classes. His son was sentenced to probation and community service as well.

The penalties were perceived as flagrantly lenient to some. Outraged, Tom Gamboa groused: "To me, probation is nothing." Likewise, Major League Baseball's security chief Kevin Hallinan commented that: "For [Ligue] not to be held accountable is disappointing." The disgruntled Gamboa opted to file a suit against several parties, including Comiskey Park security. In an unfortunate turn of events, he was released by the Royals near the end of the '03 campaign.

The punishments had no lasting effect as Ligue committed another offense while still on probation, breaking into a car in March of '06. This time, he ended up with a five-year prison sentence. His son was also less than penitent, posting pictures of the attack and boasting about it on his Myspace Web page years after the fact. Before the case against Ligue had even been settled, the White Sox were forced to deal with the fallout of another senseless act of fan violence.

In April of 2003, another spectator, Eric Dybas, stormed the field (again from the first-base side) and grabbed umpire Laz Diaz. This time, it was the arbiter who got the upper hand as Diaz used his U.S. Marine training to subdue the inebriated trespasser. Players got in a few shots as well, leaving Dybas scraped and battered when he left the stadium in police custody. Shortly after the attack, Diaz was seen laughing with other members of the umpiring crew.

Dybas had reportedly consumed ample amounts of alcohol while attending a Cubs game earlier in the afternoon. His attorney made a play for leniency, but William Ligue Jr. had set a dangerous precedent several months earlier, and officials wanted justice to be served this time around.

Chicago Alderman James Balcer proposed an increase in the fines imposed upon spectators who disrupt sporting events by running onto the field. Illinois State senator Mattie Hunter successfully sent a bill to Congress making attacks on coaches or officials at any level of play punishable by stiff prison sentences. The commissioner's office endeavored to complete a full review of security protocol at major-league ballparks. The White Sox took their own precautions, beefing up their security force while prohibiting fans with upper deck seats to enter other levels of the ballpark, which was renamed US Cellular Field in 2003.

As for Dybas, he pleaded guilty to an aggravated battery charge and was sentenced to 6 months in jail along with 30 months of probation. He later dropped out of the public eye.

Ten-Cent Beer Night

The Cleveland Indians have traditionally had difficulty maintaining a fan base. From 1960 through 1974, the club placed fifth or lower on 12 occasions. And though some talented players passed through that region of Ohio, such as Frank Robinson, Gaylord Perry, and Graig Nettles, the Indians averaged less than 10,000 patrons per game in that span. The lack of support was made glaringly obvious night after night by Cleveland Municipal Stadium's spacious capacity of more than 70,000. The run-down edifice came to be mockingly referred to as the "mistake by the lake."

In 1974, Executive Vice President Ted Bonda called a board meeting to discuss the club's sagging attendance and how to improve it. Someone suggested they follow the example of the Texas Rangers, who had hosted a successful "10-Cent Beer Night." The board agreed, and the date for the promotion was set for June 4. It would turn out to be an evening that would live in baseball infamy.

To begin with, the Indians failed to request the presence of Cleveland Municipal Police—a big mistake. There were few, if any, on-duty cops at the stadium to help control the sizeable crowd of 25,000, many of whom showed up drunk or stoned at the onset. There were also no regulations in place to control the distribution of beer. Fans were allowed to buy up to six cups at a time. There were no safeguards to prevent people from buying the prescribed six, handing them off to anyone in the stadium and promptly returning for more. Even the choice of opponents that night ended up being awkward. Less than a week before, a full-scale brawl had broken out during a game between the Indians and Rangers at Arlington Stadium. There was still some bad blood between the two when Texas arrived on June 4 to open a three-game set.

The Rangers jumped out to a second-inning lead on a homer by designated hitter Tom Grieve. With the beer flowing freely and half the attendees exhibiting "the glow," a woman ran into the Indians' on-deck circle and bared her breasts. It was only the beginning. After Grieve had homered in the fourth to put the Rangers up 3–0, a naked man ill-advisedly slid into second base. In the bottom of the frame, the crowd joined together in a hostile chant when Texas pitcher Fergie Jenkins was struck in the stomach by a line drive. The stadium reverberated with a chorus of: "Hit him again! Hit him again! Harder! Harder!"

The frat party continued in the fifth, when two more men hopped over the wall and mooned Rangers' outfielders. Numerous other fans in various states of undress were dragged off the field by security as the evening wore on, prompting a rain of beer cups, batteries, and golf balls. At one point, firecrackers were tossed into the Rangers' bull pen.

The demand for beer became so great that fans were allowed to line up in front of the Stroh's distributor trucks and fill their cups directly. The alcohol continued to negatively affect the behavior of the crowd as fans on the third-base side conspired to tear the padding off the left-field wall. They were thwarted by the grounds crew. By the seventh-inning stretch, patrons with families could be seen filing out of the stadium in droves. Team executives, among them Ted Bonda, followed suit shortly afterward.

Unbeknownst to many in attendance, there was a heck of a game going on. Trailing 5–1 in the sixth, the Indians rallied to tie the score in the bottom of the ninth. They had the winning run on second base when a man jumped out of the stands and tried to steal right fielder Jeff Burroughs's cap. Burroughs turned to defend himself and clumsily fell over. In the Texas dugout, manager Billy Martin had seen enough. He armed himself with a bat and headed toward the outfield. His players trailed behind him as chaos ensued.

Rangers' personnel soon found themselves surrounded by drunken hooligans, some holding knives, chains, and blunt instruments torn from stadium seats. Realizing the peril their baseball brethren were in, Cleveland players sprang into action under orders from manager Ken Aspromonte. Indians' reliever Tom Hilgendorf was hit on the head with a chair. Rangers' first baseman Mike Hargrove threw a fan to the ground and beat the man senseless. Texas backstop Duke Sims sparred with several thugs. Banding together, the players escaped to their clubhouses with their wounded in tow. Billy Martin later commented: "Maybe it was silly of us to go out there, but we weren't about to have a man on the field unprotected."

With insufficient security to control the crowd, the mob rioted for nearly a half hour, stealing bases and anything they could get their collective hands on. Umpire Nestor Chylak was nearly hit by a thrown hunting knife. He was bleeding from the back of his head when he declared the game a forfeit and exited the field with the rest of the crew. Speaking to members of the press, he referred to the crowd as "f—ing animals."

Cleveland police finally arrived and officially put an end to the most disastrous promotion in club history. There were nine arrests. Though the Indians had three more 10-Cent Beer Nights planned, AL president Lee MacPhail pulled the plug on all of them after a full investigation of the riot. The team finished fourth that year with a 77–85 record and would place no higher than that in the standings until 1994.

Steve Bartman

In the 1920s to early 1930s, alluring actress Greta Garbo developed a reputation for evading the spotlight. A major box-office draw and four-time Academy Award nominee, Garbo avoided Hollywood functions, answered no fan mail, and refused numerous interviews, commenting that she wished "to be let alone." The behavior gave rise to the expression "pulling a Garbo." In 2003, a Cubs' fan named Steve Bartman was forced to employ the same strategy when he was single-handedly blamed for Chicago's failure to win the pennant.

Bartman received that condemnation after Game 6 of the '03 NLCS at Wrigley Field. The Cubs held a 3–2 Series edge over the Marlins and stood within five outs of advancing to the World Series for the first time since 1945. Staff ace Mark Prior was in the midst of a three-hit shutout when Florida's Luis Castillo lofted a pop fly near the left-field corner. Chicago's Moisés Alou drifted over and appeared to have a play on the ball, which had sailed into the seats. Sitting in the front row, Bartman instinctively reached for the ball and deflected it from Alou. The infuriated outfielder slammed his glove down in frustration and screamed at several fans. The Cubs (mainly Alou and Prior) argued in favor of interference, but the appeal was denied by umpire Mike Everitt since the ball had clearly left the field of play. The events that followed were nothing short of a nightmare for Bartman and the rest of the Chicago faithful.

Castillo drew a walk. The fourth ball was a wild pitch that advanced Florida's Juan Pierre to third base. Ivan Rodriguez followed with a single, putting the Marlins on the board, 3–1. The most critical event of the inning had nothing to do with Bartman or the foul ball. Miguel Cabrera hit a grounder to Alex Gonzalez at short that could easily have been an inning-ending double play. The ball took a funny hop, and Gonzalez, who had led NL shortstops in fielding percentage that year, mishandled it. The bases were loaded with the dangerous Derrek Lee coming to the plate. The result was too painful for many to watch as Lee pounded a two-run double, tying the score. By the time reliever Mike Remlinger put an end to the rally, the Marlins had sent 12 men to the plate and opened up an 8–3 lead. Meanwhile, various media sources were already engaged in a disjointed effort to ruin Steve Bartman's life.

Television announcers singled Bartman out as the play was rerun over and over again during the broadcast. Immediately after the ball had settled in the seats, *Chicago Tribune* columnist John Kass, who was sitting nearby, asked Bartman ominously: "Do you realize what you've done?" The crowd soon turned ugly, and sensing danger for the 24-year-old software specialist, Wrigley Field security ushered Bartman out of the stadium for his own good. As he made his shameful exit, he was peppered with insults and debris flung at him by ignorant fans. Erika Amundsen, a security guard assigned to the detail, remembered a disconsolate Bartman asking: "Did I really ruin the game?" She assured him that he had done nothing wrong.

Had Alou caught the ball, the Cubs would still have been four outs away from advancing to the World Series. Bartman was in no way responsible for the eight runs, five hits, and three walks surrendered by Chicago pitchers in that disastrous inning. He wasn't even the only fan reaching for the ball. He just happened to be the one to get his hands on it. Nevertheless, his life became a living hell in the months that followed.

The young computer professional attempted to deflect negative publicity by issuing a public apology, which was read to the press by his brother-in-law. By that time, he had already been named by nearly every major media source in Chicago. Bartman's official statement, which remains the only one he has ever made to date, was brief and sincere. He apologized from "the bottom of his Cubs' fan's broken heart." He explained that he had been following the flight of the ball and had been unaware that Alou was tracking it. "Had I seen Alou approaching," he asserted, "I would have done whatever I could to get out of the way and give Alou a chance to make the catch."

Bartman's apology might have been accepted had the Cubs won Game 7 of the Series. But it was not to be as the Marlins went on to knock off the Yankees in the '03 Fall Classic. Bartman's attempt to maintain anonymity would prove quite challenging after the *Chicago Sun-Times* released his home address to the public. Major League Baseball's online message boards also offered various tidbits of personal information. Illinois governor Rod Blagojevich didn't help matters either when he jokingly stated that Bartman would "never get a pardon" from him. As a result, the mild-mannered Cubs' fan was bombarded with death threats. TV trucks surrounded his house for weeks. At one point, it got so bad that Florida governor Jeb Bush offered him asylum.

The Cubs attempted to put out the fire by issuing their own statement, which proclaimed that it was "inaccurate and unfair to suggest that an individual fan is responsible for the events that transpired in Game 6." Likewise, pitcher Mark Prior went on record saying that the Cubs had "numerous chances to get out of that situation." Alou commented long after the fact that he wouldn't have caught the ball anyway. In a different interview, he forgot all about the remark, telling a reporter from the *Palm Beach Post*: "If I said that, I was probably joking to make [Bartman] feel better."

In the end, Bartman "pulled a Garbo," dropping off the grid completely. He moved to an undisclosed location and avoided the talk-show circuit altogether. Though a Facebook profile still bears his name as of the time of this writing, Bartman himself has nothing to do with it. He doesn't use Twitter either. His family, friends, and employers have all conspired to help sequester him from public scrutiny. In short, he is little more than a ghost.

Bartman could have profited considerably from his infamy as he received numerous lucrative offers over the years. He declined them all and asked that donations given to him be forwarded to the Juvenile Diabetes Research Center. In 2011, a documentary about the ballpark incident was released by Academy Award–winning filmmaker Alex Gibney. Though Bartman's presence was requested during production, he politely refused.

The infamous ball was grabbed by a Chicago lawyer and sold at auction for more than $100,000. In February of 2004, it was detonated in a publicity stunt. In a bizarre development that seems too strange to be true, the remains of the ball were reportedly used by a restaurant. The fragments were boiled and the steam was distilled and then added to a pasta sauce. Bartman's seat in section 4, row 8 remains a tourist attraction at Wrigley Field.

~

CHAPTER TEN

The Grand Finale:
Just Plain Nasty!

Joe Medwick

Simply stated, Joe Medwick was a great ballplayer but a difficult man to get along with. During his 17 years in the majors, he sparred both verbally and physically with teammates and opponents while treating members of the press with contempt. Believing himself to be among the greatest players in the National League, he once commented that baseball was all about "base hits and buckerinoes." His self-serving attitude led to a trade from the Cardinals during the prime of his career. It may also have been at the root of his 20-year wait to gain entry into the Hall of Fame.

Medwick was born to Austro-Hungarian immigrants in Carteret, New Jersey. Sturdily built at 5-foot-10, 187 pounds, he became a multisport star in high school, excelling at football and basketball in addition to his game of choice. He was signed by the Cardinals off the New Jersey sandlots while still a teenager, rapidly working his way up through their farm system. In 1930, he collected 53 extra-base hits and fashioned a .419 batting average in 75 games at the Class-C level. He was promoted to Class-A the next year. In two seasons with the Houston Buffaloes, he cumulatively hit .328 with 93 doubles and 45 homers. By 1933, he was a fixture in the Cardinals' outfield, where he would remain until June of 1940.

Medwick was a free-swinger who loathed walks. A notorious bad-ball hitter, his finest campaign occurred in 1937, when he led the National League in a dozen major offensive categories, including homers (31), RBIs (154), and batting average (.374). As of 2012, he remained the last NL player to have claimed a Triple Crown. The feisty New Jersey native would finish among the top five in batting average on six other occasions while leading the league in RBIs for three straight seasons (1936–38). Opposing pitcher Dutch Leonard once commented that: "I think he shouldn't be allowed to carry a bat to the plate. Make him use his fists to swing. Then he'd only hit singles."

Medwick was no stranger to using his fists. Unpopular with teammates in St. Louis, he fought with Ripper Collins and Tex Carleton, reportedly knocking both men down. When relief pitcher Ed Heusser accused him of not hustling in a 1936 contest, a round of fisticuffs followed. Reports of that scrape vary, though most agree that Heusser landed a blow to Medwick's chin. Medwick exchanged angry words with both of the Dean brothers as well—Dizzy and Daffy.

Leo Durocher, who managed him in Brooklyn for several years, commented that Medwick was "the meanest, roughest guy you could imagine." Medwick had proved that definitively during Game 7 of the 1934 World Series. The Cardinals were leading the Tigers by a score of 7–0 in the sixth inning when Pepper Martin led off with a single. He ended up at second base when Detroit's Goose Goslin mishandled the ball. After two fly ball outs, Medwick hit a deep drive to the right field wall. Martin scored easily, and Medwick, digging all the way despite his team's enormous lead, decided to go for a triple. At third, Marv Owen stepped on Medwick's leg (his motive remains unclear—it could have been unintentional). This provoked the ire of Medwick, who retaliated by kicking Owen in the stomach with both of his spikes. The two tangled briefly and were separated by umpires. Medwick later scored on a Ripper Collins single, and the Cardinals carried an airtight 9–0 lead into the bottom of the frame.

When Medwick took his place in left field, Detroit fans booed him lustily and tossed garbage, mostly fruit, onto the field. Antagonizing the crowd, Medwick began playing catch with some of the fruit. This invited a fresh rain of debris. Umpires halted play three times and called for order, but the fans would not stop. Paul Gallico of the *New York Daily News* wrote: "Every face in the crowd, women and men, was distorted with rage." Finally, after a conference with Commissioner Mountain Landis, Medwick was removed from the game for his own safety. He required a police escort off the field. With Medwick out of action, the Cardinals tacked on two more runs to claim the world championship. After the last pitch had been thrown, Landis stood by his decision, commenting: "I saw what Medwick did and I couldn't blame the crowd for what it did."

Medwick could be quite selfish at times. St. Louis's third baseman / outfielder Pepper Martin was highly superstitious and believed that finding hairpins brought good luck. In Cincinnati one day, a pair of beat writers purchased a package of them and scattered them about the lobby of the Cardinals' hotel to give Martin a mental boost. Unfortunately, Medwick arrived first and began picking them up. When reporter Roy Stockton told Medwick they were for his teammate, Medwick allegedly said: "To hell with Martin. Let him find his own hairpins."

When it came to negotiating contracts, the self-confident Medwick could be equally standoffish. During one particular salary dispute, Cardinals owner Sam Breadon supposedly told Medwick he would rather throw $2,000 out the window than include it in Medwick's pay. "Mr. Breadon," Medwick replied sarcastically, "if you threw $2,000 out the window, you'd still be holding on to it when it hit the sidewalk." St. Louis management eventually tired of Medwick's attitude and traded him to the Dodgers in June of 1940.

Medwick stirred up trouble for himself in Brooklyn as well. One week after his transfer, he got into a verbal altercation with Cardinal pitcher Bob Bowman in a hotel elevator. Bowman, who was scheduled to pitch against the Dodgers that day, became quite agitated, warning Medwick and his companion, Leo Durocher: "I'll take care of both of you!" When Medwick came to the plate in the first inning of Bowman's start, he was hit in the head with a brushback pitch and carried off the field on a stretcher. At the hospital, the ailing slugger reportedly tried to get out of his bed to confront the hurler. Dodgers' owner Larry MacPhail successfully lobbied for an investigation of the incident, but Bowman was cleared of any criminal negligence. In 1941, Medwick agreed to use a special batting helmet designed by a pair of Johns Hopkins doctors.

Before Medwick was finished, other incidents would follow. In June of '42, he was ejected and fined for inciting a brawl after spiking Cardinals' shortstop Marty Marion. While playing for the Giants two years later, he was disciplined by management for confronting an umpire over a disputed catch. The ball he had trapped was still in play when he ran in from left field to confront the official. Two Cincinnati runners scored during his temper tantrum.

Though he still posted highly respectable batting averages, Medwick's power numbers tapered off after being hit with the pitch from Bowman. Signing with the Cardinals again in 1947, he closed out his career with the team that had made him famous. Upon falling from the major-league ranks, he managed in the Florida International League and Carolina League. He would take a job as a Cardinal minor-league batting instructor in '66. At some point after his retirement, Medwick traveled to Italy and met the pope. Asked to state his occupation, he said: "Your holiness, I'm Joe Medwick. I, too, used to be a Cardinal."

Over the years, Medwick was abrasive to members of the press, often telling them to "get lost." It came back to haunt him as members of the Baseball Writers Association of America waited until 1968 to elect him to the Hall of Fame. Medwick's 1975 obituary described him as a "controversial player."

Burleigh Grimes

Burleigh Grimes forged his own path in life. As a boy, he worked in a lumber camp from 4:30 a.m. to 9:00 p.m. for just a dollar a day. He began experimenting with a spitball in his early teens and had just about mastered the craft by the time his father told him to "go out and make something" of himself at the age of 16. Pursuing what he liked best, he turned to baseball.

His professional career began in 1912 with the Eau Claire Commissioners of the Minnesota–Wisconsin League. He would spend five years in the minors, fashioning a 76–52 record with a miserly ERA before joining the Pirates in September of 1916. Explaining his game philosophy to a reporter, Grimes once said: "There was only one man standing between me and more money and that was the guy with the bat. I knew I'd always have to fight the man with the bat as if he were trying to rob me in a dark alley."

That mind-set made Grimes one of the most formidable pitchers of his era. His preferred method of loading up the baseball was to chew slippery elm bark, which he reportedly cut right off of trees. On the days he pitched, he refused to shave since the elm resin irritated his skin. His unkempt appearance earned him the nickname "Ol' Stubblebeard." According to numerous sources, he moved with an overconfident gait that irritated opponents, and when he stared them down, his face would contort into a snarl. Intimidation was one of his key strategies, and he further accomplished this by throwing at batter's heads. He did it so often that players came to expect it.

One day, as a Pullman train porter was set to dust off the clothes of Cubs' catcher Gabby Hartnett, the Hall of Famer quipped: "Never mind—Grimes will dust me off this afternoon." Pittsburgh teammate Pie Traynor once claimed that he had seen Grimes knock down five batters in a row. During a September match against the Cubs in 1924, it was reported that he issued brushbacks to six Cubs' hitters in the first two innings. One particular volume of *The Baseball Hall of Shame* alleges that the fiery hurler once threw at a man in the on-deck circle. Grimes beaned 101 batters during his playing days, a number that landed him among the top-100 headhunters of all time.

Grimes's major-league career got off to a slow start in Pittsburgh. The Pirates were a second-division club in those days, and the victories weren't piling up for him in the early going. At one point during the 1917 slate, he had dropped 13 games in a row, prompting manager Hugo Bezdek to skip his spot in the rotation. Grimes protested, and Bezdek questioned the right-hander's competitive spirit. What followed was a bloody battle between the two men that involving biting and choking. Traded to Brooklyn in 1918, Pirates' owner Barney Dreyfuss commented: "I know we dealt away a fine young pitcher, but that Grimes just fights with everyone, friend or foe."

Known for having an engaging personality off the field, Grimes was a tyrant on the diamond. In 1919, a long-standing feud began with Cardinals' infielder Frankie Frisch after the "Fordham Flash" allegedly spiked Grimes on a close play at first base. The two shouted at one another and then started punching. After that, Grimes threw at Frisch every time he faced him for the next 10 years. Frisch commented that he expected exactly three dusters during each confrontation. When the hurler unleashed a fourth one day, Frisch hit the dirt so fast that he "literally fell from under his cap" according to one source. As player and cap landed (in that order), Grimes just stood there on the mound laughing. "It was one of the few times in baseball that I was really scared," Frisch said.

Grimes was not afraid to taunt some of the best hitters in the game. During a start against the Philadelphia Athletics in the 1930 World Series, he stuck his thumbs in his ears and wiggled his fingers at Mickey Cochrane, poking fun at the backstop's protruding ears. He also mimicked Al Simmons's habit of flicking dust from his uniform. When Jimmie Foxx strode to the plate, Grimes grabbed his throat in a gesture of mock terror. He lost both of his postseason starts that year but surrendered just 10 hits in 17 innings of work.

Losing was something that Grimes did not take lightly. When he dropped two decisions during the 1920 World Series, he shifted the blame to others, insisting that several of Brooklyn's top players had broken curfew the night before Game 7 and showed up at the ballpark in poor playing condition. He also faulted the scout who had told him to serve high fastballs to Elmer Smith. Smith had victimized Grimes for a grand slam in the first inning of Game 5. On another occasion, the petulant moundsman became irritated with what he perceived as substandard defensive play from his Brooklyn teammates during a 1922 contest. In frustration, he grooved a pitch to Cincinnati's Jake Daubert, who crushed it for a homer. Back in the dugout, Grimes treated manager Wilbert Robinson to a stream of unbridled profanity. He was fined $200 for the incident.

The Dodgers were willing to tolerate Grimes's sour attitude since he posted stellar numbers year after year. During his nine seasons in the Flatbush, he won 20 games four times and led the league in numerous statistical categories. He also helped his own cause with a bat, hitting .250 or better on three occasions during that span. He peaked at .306 in 1920. Tired of arguing with him over his salary on an annual basis, the Dodgers traded Grimes to the Giants in 1927. He failed to gel with dictatorial manager John McGraw and was transferred back to Pittsburgh in '28. On the heels of yet another fiscal dispute, he was dished to the Braves in April of 1930. He was injured shortly afterward and dealt to the Cardinals two months later. He would be involved in several more transactions before his big-league career came to a close in 1934.

In his prime, Grimes had five pitches in his arsenal: a fastball, changeup, curve, and slider. Of course, there was the ever-present spitter, which he was allowed to throw (due to a grandfather clause) even after the pitch was banned in 1920. He appeared to have lost his effectiveness at one point when the Phillies suddenly began knocking him all over the yard every time he faced them. Initially, Dodger personnel believed that their signs were being stolen and theorized that there was a spy with binoculars stationed inside the scoreboard at the Baker Bowl. When Grimes suffered the same fate at Ebbets Field, that theory fell through. Finally, a Brooklyn batboy noticed that Grimes's cap was so tight that it wiggled while he was preparing a spitball. The hurler's dominance continued when he took to wearing a larger hat.

Upon retiring as a player in 1934, he managed in the Three-I League and the American Association before the Dodgers handed the reins to him for the '37 slate. He spent two years at the Brooklyn helm, getting himself into trouble on more than one occasion. While counseling a young pitcher who was off to a rough start in the majors, Grimes took offense to the hurler's insubordinate attitude and smacked him in the mouth. The ill-tempered Hall of Famer has also been accused of punching a 12-year-old autograph seeker on the heels of a disparaging loss one afternoon. Later, while managing in the Michigan State League, he allegedly spat in the face of umpire Robert Williams while arguing a call.

Grimes waited a long time to get into the Hall of Fame but finally gained entry in 1964. He lived to the ripe age of 92 and died in the same region of Wisconsin in which he had been born. His *New York Times* obituary labeled him as a headhunter.

Albert Belle

According to sabermetric measurements, Albert Belle should have been a lock for the Hall of Fame. When he logged his eighth consecutive 30-homer, 100-RBI season in 1999, only Jimmie Foxx, Babe Ruth, and Lou Gehrig had duplicated the feat. A few years earlier, he had become the first man in major-league history to collect 50 doubles and 50 homers in a season. Between 1991 and 2000, he averaged 37 long balls and 120 RBIs per year. He accomplished this (presumably) without the use of steroids in an era when they were rampant. About the only thing keeping Belle off Cooperstown ballots was his poor attitude.

Rick Woolf, a sports psychologist who counseled Belle for several years, referred to the troubled slugger as "brilliant" and "complex." According to Woolf, Belle was a "perfectionist" who "couldn't deal with the frustration of baseball." Born and raised in Shreveport, Louisiana, Belle's quest for perfection was evident early on as he attained the rank of Eagle Scout and later became a member of the National Honor Society. A baseball standout at Huntington High School, he made the all-state team twice and was selected to play in the 1984 Junior Olympics, helping the United States capture a silver medal.

Offered sports scholarships to several colleges, Belle opted to stick close to home, attending Louisiana State University. He assembled a stellar collegiate baseball career, hitting .332 with a .670 slugging percentage in 184 games. Behavioral problems began to surface in the spring of 1987, when he went up into the stands after a heckler who had been directing racial slurs at him. During the College World Series that year, he was suspended for not hustling on a ball he had hit off the outfield wall.

Drafted by the Indians, Belle was initially known as "Joey" (his childhood nickname) to fans and peers. Though he was considered a top prospect, he was labeled a high-risk player due to his hot temper and heavy drinking. In his 1989 major-league debut, he hit just .225 in 62 games. He would spend 10 weeks in an alcohol rehabilitation clinic the following year after tearing apart a bathroom while playing for the Colorado Springs Sky Sox. Looking for a fresh start, he reverted back to his birth name of Albert.

By the time Belle was forced into retirement at the age of 34 due to degenerative osteoarthritis in his right hip, he had left behind a legacy of unpleasant anecdotes. Though he was one of the most productive hitters in the game, he never won an MVP Award largely on account of his troubled relationship with the press. He outright refused to speak to writers most of the time, and when he did, he was often churlish or dismissive. During the 1995 World Series, he directed a profanity-laden outburst at Hannah Storm of NBC. The Indians wanted Belle to issue a statement of regret, but he did no such thing, commenting: "I apologize for nothing." The media would have their revenge as Belle never finished higher than second in MVP voting between 1993 and 1998. On the basis of numbers alone, he should have won it at least once. At the end of his career, he was referred to by one New York writer as a "surly jerk" while another Gotham scribe bluntly labeled him an "a-hole" in print. Throughout his playing days, Belle was indifferent to the perceptions of the press, wondering: "Why does everyone want to talk to me, anyway?"

It was whispered in baseball circles that Belle might be certifiably crazy. Many observed that his moods were highly unstable, due in part to the fact that he drank coffee excessively and was constantly on edge as a result. He was known to throw watercoolers, break phones, and toss food around the clubhouse. Once, he even destroyed a boom box belonging to Kenny Lofton. He preferred the clubhouse thermostat to remain around 60, earning the nickname "Mr. Freeze." When an unidentified teammate made an adjustment one day, Belle turned the heat back down and then smashed the device with a bat.

In one of the most memorable misadventures of his career, Belle was accused by White Sox manager Gene Lamont of using a corked bat during the '94 slate. A superficial examination of the bat by officials revealed nothing out of the ordinary, but the implement was confiscated and placed in the umpires' dressing room. Belle later conspired with teammates to retrieve the impounded bat and replace it with one from the collection of Paul Sorrento. Shortstop Omar Vizquel later explained that Sorrento's bat was used because Belle's entire cache was corked. Pitcher Jason Grimsley crawled through the cramped ceiling space at Comiskey Park and successfully pulled off the switch but left behind remnants of broken ceiling tiles in the process, alerting arbiters that something was amiss. The original bat was returned, and after a detailed examination, cork was indeed discovered inside the barrel. Belle was suspended for seven games.

October of 1995 was a rough month for Belle. After yelling at Hannah Storm before Game 3 of the Fall Classic (a move that would cost him $50,000), he went after a group of unruly trick-or-treaters who were throwing eggs at his house. He was charged with willful disregard of safety and fined for his actions.

In April of the following season, Belle was at it again, throwing a ball at *Sports Illustrated* photographer Tony Tomsic after Tomsic took pictures of him while he was stretching. By that point, AL president Gene Budig had seen enough of Belle's reckless behavior. He ordered the troublesome outfielder to undergo counseling and perform community service. It would take more than that to effectively alter Belle's conduct. Two weeks later, after being hit with a pitch in the eighth inning of a game against the Brewers, the ornery slugger flattened Milwaukee infielder Fernando Viña, who was blocking Belle's route to second base. It wasn't a conventional slide—Belle used his forearm to upend Viña. The act appeared particularly heinous since

Viña was 4 inches shorter and 20 pounds lighter. Belle was suspended for five games (reduced to two on appeal) and fined $25,000. For many, it would prove to be the defining moment of his career.

Belle's numbers never really tapered off. He surpassed the century mark in ribbies during his final season of 2000 and went deep in his final major-league at-bat. His bad behaviors continued to the very end as well. In '97, he was fined $5,000 after making an obscene gesture at Cleveland fans. The following year, he was charged with domestic violence for allegedly hitting his girlfriend (those charges were later dropped). In '99, he was benched by Orioles' manager Ray Miller when he failed to run out a ground ball. This broke his streak of 392 consecutive games played—the longest active skein in the majors at the time. That same year, he shunned reporters completely. A sign above his locker directed them to his website for quotes.

There were few who wept for Albert Belle following his premature retirement. But there was a side of the man rarely mentioned by the media. Over the years, he donated scholarships of up to $4,000 apiece to 38 residents of Shreveport. Since he seldom talked about it, one can only assume he did it out of the kindness of his troubled heart.

Believed to be a shoo-in for Cooperstown enshrinement at one time, he was removed from Hall of Fame ballots in 2007 after he failed to garner the minimum number of votes. Told that Jose Canseco had singled him out as one of few superstars of his era to avoid the use of steroids, Belle commented in typical fashion: "Great. I have a criminal on my side." Belle became a felon himself the previous year when he was sentenced to 90 days in jail and 5 years of supervised probation after admitting to stalking his former girlfriend.

Tim Hurst

Hall of Famer Clark Griffith, who served as a pitcher, manager, and owner at different points in time, once commented: "There is a great deal of sympathy wasted on umpires. As a rule, they are very well able to take care of themselves." That statement was poignantly accurate when applied to one of Griffith's contemporaries, arbiter Tim Hurst. Though Hurst stood only 5-foot-5 and was sometimes referred to as "Tiny Tim," he instilled fear and respect in the hearts of players with his quick wit and no-nonsense demeanor.

Hurst was born in Ashland, Pennsylvania, and was somewhat of an athlete himself before serving as an official. He took part in a number of running competitions as a young man and was described as having "considerable ability." According to the *Sporting News*, his first certified experience calling balls and strikes was in the State Pennsylvania League during the 1888 season. The *New York Times* traced his umpiring debut to a Southern League contest that was to decide the pennant. Under fire from players, one of the umpires suddenly quit, prompting Hurst (who was a spectator at the game) to come out of the stands and volunteer his services. As the story goes, his offer was accepted. In the final inning, he called one of the home team's players out on a close play at the plate. The run would have tied the game, and realizing he might have to defend the decision, Hurst reportedly pulled a gun from his pocket. His ruling went without protest.

Hired by the National League in 1891, Hurst would establish himself as one of the most colorful men in the game. He often exchanged barbs with dissenting players, solving disputes with wry sarcasm. Umpiring crews were much smaller in those days, and officials had to cover a lot of ground. One day, a player was disputing a call Hurst had made on a foul ball, inviting him to come inspect the chalk line where the ball had landed. Hurst countered acerbically: "Why don't you move the line over here? My feet are tired." On another afternoon, he called a rookie out, claiming he had not touched the plate. "Guess you think it's the size of a feed plate, eh?" the freshman griped. "Oh, no," retorted Hurst, "if it were, you'd slide hands first."

Despite Hurst's diminutive stature, fellow umpire Bill Klem described him as "the toughest umpire of them all." In a game between Baltimore and Brooklyn in 1895, a foul tip shattered Hurst's mask, driving a wire into his forehead and hitting an artery. Remarkably, he stayed in the game. Longtime Giants' manager John McGraw once reminisced that he "never saw an umpire display more nerve in a critical situation" than Hurst. In particular, he referred to a game between Baltimore and Cleveland during the 1890s, when McGraw was playing for the Orioles. Accommodations in Cleveland were somewhat primitive as players dressed in a small shack beneath the grandstand. Inside Cleveland's cramped dressing room was an even smaller chamber set aside for umpires. It proved to be an awkward arrangement for Hurst when he made a controversial call on Patsy Tebeau in the bottom of the ninth, nullifying a bases-clearing triple that would have won the game for the Spiders. While players threatened Hurst with all kinds of bodily harm, the arbiter walked calmly through the hostile Cleveland dressing room to his own quarters undeterred. "It took real courage to do that, but Tim never flinched," McGraw commented.

Hurst was not always given to diplomacy. He had a nasty temper and a tendency to retaliate when provoked. Following an 1896 match between Pittsburgh and Washington, Hurst slapped or punched (reports vary) Pirates' players Jake Stenzel and Emerson Hawley in the face for being verbally abusive to him throughout the game. According to one reporter: "Neither player resented the attack." When Hurst made a call that went against the hometown Reds in August of the following season, a disgruntled Cincinnati fan hurled a beer stein onto the field. Hurst threw it back into the stands, hitting a fireman named John Cartuyvelles over the right eye and cutting him badly. The irascible arbiter was carted away by police and suspended. He returned to manage the Browns in 1898.

Hurst's jaunt into managing was an unmitigated disaster as the Browns finished dead last with a 39–111 record. According to various sources, Hurst was among the most notorious umpire baiters in the league. Not too many calls went his way that season as the pitching-poor Browns compiled the highest ERA in the NL while failing to shut out opponents on a single occasion. The offense failed to step up as well, as the Browns ranked last in hits, runs, and cumulative team batting average. The entire squad would be moved to Cleveland the following year and renamed the Spiders when Frank and M. Stanley Robison purchased the ailing franchise from bankrupt owner Chris von der Ahe. They compiled the worst record in major-league history at 20–134.

In January of 1899, Hurst served as a fight referee, presiding over a high-profile bout at the Lenox Athletic Club in New York City. Since boxing had a seedy reputation in those days, baseball owners John T. Brush (of the Reds) and Andrew Freedman (of the Giants) successfully rallied to have Hurst banned from National League games. In an official statement, the spiteful owners objected "to having a man of that type associated with their grounds, where ladies and gentlemen watch games."

Shunned by the NL, Hurst turned to boxing as a primary occupation, serving as a referee and promoter. In one of his more ambitious ventures, he imported six British fighters (all holding titles in their respective weight classes) to the States and arranged to have them compete in a tournament. According to reports, the endeavor proved to be unsuccessful for him. He would eventually return to baseball in the American League, where he continued to stir up periodic controversy.

During a 1906 game between the Highlanders and Senators, Hurst engaged in a lengthy argument with New York's player/manager Clark Griffith. The latter followed Hurst all over the field, spouting verbal abuse and gesturing wildly. Griffith crossed the line when he stepped on Hurst's foot. Hurst responded with a blow to Griffith's face. By some accounts, Griffith was knocked out cold.

Over the course of his career, Hurst issued 57 ejections, including 5 to his favorite target—Hall of Famer Joe Kelley. The year 1909 was his darkest hour as he was fired by the American League for an ugly on-field incident. Trailing the White Sox 4–1 at Philadelphia on August 3, the A's scored six runs to take the lead. With runners on base in the eighth, Philly infielder Eddie Collins singled and moved to second, where he appeared to be safe due to a dropped throw. Hurst may not have had a good angle on the play, ruling Collins out. Incensed by the blown call, Collins (a future Hall of Famer and lifetime .333-hitter) hounded Hurst, using various derogatory terms such as "yellow," "blind bat," and "crook." Hurst's mercurial temperament only allowed him to stand so much. He turned and spit in Collins' face. It would prove to be his undoing as a professional umpire. After the game, police fought to restrain fans for nearly a half hour as they flung cushions and bottles in Hurst's direction. He was suspended the following day pending a full investigation by league executives. On August 12, he was officially dismissed from his duties.

Despite all the unpleasantness, Hurst was well liked by contemporaries. Catcher Roger Bresnahan, the first backstop to be enshrined at Cooperstown, felt that the loss of Hurst damaged the game's entertainment value. "The game suffered when the fire-eaters were driven into the woods," he commented. After branching off into wrestling and motorcycle racing, Hurst eventually left the sporting life behind, pursuing a living in real estate. He had trouble making the transition, waiting until his old headquarters on 23rd and Broadway in New York City was set to be demolished before moving out. Supposedly, the wrecking crew was several days into the project when Hurst finally vacated the premises.

The colorful Pennsylvania native died somewhat suddenly in 1915 at the age of 49. The cause of his demise was listed as ptomaine poisoning—an erroneous term applied to the ingestion of spoiled food. He had apparently been ill for some time, but his condition was not deemed serious. He remains among the most vibrant personalities the game has ever produced.

The 1890s Baltimore Orioles

The Orioles were established in 1882 as members of the fledgling American Association, which started out as a six-team circuit. They fared poorly that year under manager Henry Myers, compiling a 19–54 record and finishing dead last. As the league expanded, Baltimore would continue to flounder in the standings, placing no higher than sixth until 1887. They never won a pennant while they were associated with the AA, and in 1890, they dropped out briefly only to reappear as a replacement for the bottom-feeding Brooklyn Gladiators club, which folded in late August due to lack of fan support.

When the American Association dissolved in 1891, the O's joined the National League. The '92 squad included a trio of future Cooperstown inductees, among them 20-year-old left fielder Joe Kelley, catcher Wilbert Robinson, and center fielder Ned Hanlon, who was on the cusp of a brilliant managerial career. Despite the presence of such competent men, Baltimore failed to compete, losing 69 percent of their games that season.

Hanlon's official online Hall of Fame bio describes him as "a shrewd trader, innovative tactician and master of inside baseball." Over the next several years, he transformed the lowly Orioles into a baseball juggernaut, signing a slew of superstars while fashioning a game strategy the likes of which had never been seen. Among the players who joined the squad were Willie Keeler, John McGraw, Hughie Jennings, and Dan Brouthers—all of whom would eventually join their pioneering manager in Cooperstown.

The Orioles mastered the art of "small ball," an approach that featured tight pitching and crisp defense. Hanlon's squad was among the first to utilize relays and cutoffs. On offense, they manufactured runs the hard way: by bunting, stealing, and sacrificing. They stretched singles into doubles and doubles into triples while sailing daringly around the base paths. They were also among the first to employ the "hit and run," a tactic that gives runners a head start with a contact hitter at the plate.

From 1894 through 1897, the National League held a best-of-seven postseason series pitting the circuit's top two teams against each other. It came to be known as the Temple Cup in reference to the trophy that was awarded to the winner, a silver chalice donated by business tycoon William Chase Temple. The Orioles appeared in all four matchups, winning two before the series was discontinued due to player apathy and lack of fan interest.

In addition to their novel strategic approach, the Orioles found other ways to beat opponents, mainly through intimidation. John McGraw commented of his days in Baltimore: "We'd go tearing into a bag with flying spikes as though with murderous intent. We were a cocky, swashbuckling crew and wanted everybody to know it." There is little doubt that everyone knew it. In fact, there was no way to ignore it. According to McGraw, the Orioles kept a row of files hanging on the wall outside the visiting players' clubhouse and would sit there sharpening their spikes in full view of opponents. This was probably more for show than anything, as evidenced by the scarcity of documented spiking incidents. But examples of rule bending among members of the Orioles abounded.

Union Park in Baltimore had been carefully designed to put visiting teams at a disadvantage. The grounds crew groomed the baselines so that bunts would stay fair. The path to first base had a downward slope that benefited

Orioles' speedsters. Soap flakes were mixed with the soil around the pitchers' mound to make the hands of perspiring pitchers slippery when they reached into the dirt. Orioles' hurlers knew well enough to keep a handful of untainted soil in their pockets. The infield was mixed with clay and rarely watered, creating a surface similar to concrete. Players slashed down on the ball (the origin of the term "Baltimore chop") and were well on their way to first before opposing infielders could get their hands on it. The right-field area of Union Park was ruddy and riddled with weeds. A downward slope kept Willie Keeler partially obscured from the umpire's view. Keeler almost always had an extra ball hidden out there in case the one in play couldn't be retrieved in a timely fashion.

There were other less civilized ways to gain an edge over opponents and the Orioles tried them all. Umpire baiting and bench jockeying were an intrinsic part of the Baltimore strategy. According to multiple sources, the Orioles were much freer in their use of profanity than most clubs. So free, in fact, that the National League adopted a resolution in 1898 (championed by Cincinnati owner John T. Brush) that imposed mandatory expulsions upon players who used "villainously foul" language. An official document drafted by league officials and labeled "unmailable" was laughably profane, listing nearly a dozen examples of players using language that would be deemed vulgar even by today's standards.

When none of these other strategies worked, the Orioles resorted to brute force. In an 1896 contest, Hughie Jennings plowed over Reds' third baseman Charlie Irwin as he was waiting for a relay from Bid McPhee. As was so often the case during the 19th century, no infraction was called on the play. After Jennings had scored what turned out to be the game-winning run, umpire Bob Emslie needed a police escort out of the stadium.

The dirtiest Oriole of them all, John McGraw, was known for physically restraining runners at his third-base post. His underhanded play led to a moment of comic relief during an 1894 game against Louisville. Pete Browning was tagging up on a sacrifice fly when he felt McGraw grab him by the belt. Browning alertly unbuckled it and slid safely into home. As he reached the plate, he turned and pointed mockingly to third, where McGraw was standing awkwardly with the belt still in his hand.

Baltimore players were so high strung they often argued amongst themselves, admonishing one another for costly errors or mental lapses. After being needled by McGraw for a defensive gaffe, the quiet one, Willie Keeler, fought McGraw naked in the showers while Jack Doyle stood guard. Information regarding the victor has been lost to posterity. Though widely given credit for their success in the 1890s, Ned Hanlon was often ignored by players in game situations. According to Hall of Famer Sam Crawford, "They paid no more attention to him than the batboy." Crawford alleged that Hanlon would sit on the bench in tense situations wringing his hands and barking out orders. Players frequently told him to shut up.

In the spring of 1894, the Orioles descended upon Boston like a plague, leaving devastation in their wake. During the third inning of a May 15 contest, a vicious fight broke out between John McGraw and Tommy "Foghorn" Tucker, who was known for antagonizing opponents. A careless fan dropped a lit cigarette during the scrape, igniting the right field bleachers. The fire destroyed the stadium and spread to adjacent blocks, damaging more than 150 buildings and leaving nearly 2,000 homeless.

The dominance of the Orioles finally ended in 1899, when they finished in fourth place, 15 games out of the running. Unable to effectively govern its 12 teams, the National League eliminated four clubs. The Orioles were among them. They would reappear in the AL during the 1901 slate before moving to New York and becoming the Highlanders (later known as the Yankees).

Ty Cobb

Nearly everyone who saw Ty Cobb play had something to say about him. Ernest Hemingway called him "an absolute shit." Babe Ruth commented that he was "a prick." Even the mild-mannered Lou Gehrig was inspired to remark that Cobb was "about as welcome in American League ballparks as a rattlesnake." Though Cobb is undeniably among the greatest players the game has ever produced, it's hard to give a ringing endorsement to someone so nasty.

Cobb's anger was rarely kept in check on or off the field. Both of his wives charged him with extreme cruelty during divorce proceedings. He treated domestic helpers—cooks, nurses, and handymen—to verbal abuse on a regular basis, firing them on a whim. On the diamond, he played like a man possessed, going into bases with spikes flying and brawling with anyone who dared oppose him. He seemed to enjoy the havoc he created while in uniform, referring to bats as weapons and warning the "mollycoddles" to stay out of baseball.

Long after his retirement, the inner fury that had driven him to succeed was still evident. At an old-timer's luncheon, former catcher Jay Clarke made the mistake of confiding to Cobb that he had employed a deceptive tactic to get umpires to call Cobb out at home on several occasions. Upon hearing this, Cobb immediately flew into a rage, grabbing Clarke by the throat and shouting profanity.

The source of Cobb's wrath can be largely traced to his teenage years. Cobb grew up in Royston, Georgia. His mother was from a prominent Southern family. His father was an esteemed schoolteacher who hounded him to keep his mind on his studies. Against his father's wishes, Cobb gravitated to baseball. By the age of 14, he was playing on the Royston town team.

Encouraged by one of his teammates, Cobb requested tryouts from several clubs in the newly formed South Atlantic League. After looking him over, the Augusta Tourists offered him a salary of $50 per month. He was released after only two games, but a semi-pro outfit in Anniston, Alabama, offered him a roster spot. Cobb called his father for advice and got it. "Don't come home a failure," said W. H. Cobb to his teenage son.

In Anniston, Cobb played well enough to be recalled by the Augusta team. While participating in a pair of exhibition games against the Tigers, he got noticed for his aggressive style of play. He was summoned to Detroit in August of 1905, but his moment in the sun was spoiled by a family tragedy. Suspecting his wife of infidelity, W. H. Cobb had left the house one evening and announced he would not be back that night. At some point after midnight, he climbed up onto the porch roof with a pistol and was shot by Amanda Cobb. She claimed to have mistaken him for a burglar, but evidence did not support that fact. After a coroner's inquest, she was arrested for manslaughter and later acquitted.

The news was devastating to Cobb, and his play suffered on account of it. By his own admission, he had "worshipped" his father. Commenting on his promotion to the Tigers, Cobb later said: "In my grief, it didn't matter much. . . . I only thought, Father won't know it." He played in 41 big-league games during the '05 slate and compiled the lowest batting average of his career at .240.

As his mother's trial commenced the following year, Cobb was hazed by teammates. He found his bats vandalized and hats destroyed. One of the central antagonists was left fielder Matty McIntyre, who would sometimes move aggressively toward balls hit between Cobb and himself and then abruptly stop and let them drop, making the young center fielder look culpable. Cobb got the full brunt of it one afternoon, when he was assaulted by pitcher Ed Siever in the team's hotel and accused of losing the game for the Tigers. Cobb knocked Siever down and continued punching him until he was physically restrained. The hazing experience of '06 had an extremely negative impact on Cobb. He became bitter and mistrustful of others, a loner. At the same time, he became a fierce competitor.

Statistically speaking, Cobb was in a class by himself. During his storied career, he won 11 batting titles. His 4,189 hits were a major-league record that stood for nearly 60 years. His lifetime .366 batting average remains the highest of all time. Additionally, he won an MVP Award in 1911 and a Triple Crown in 1909 while leading the Tigers to three consecutive World Series appearances (1907–09).

Numbers aside, Cobb's baseball career was a study in how to lose friends and alienate people. In 1909, he was caught stealing during an intentional walk to teammate Sam Crawford. He slid hard into the bag and spiked the A's star third baseman, Frank Baker, reportedly opening a gash in Baker's arm. Though some insisted that Cobb was within his rights, A's manager Connie Mack did not agree. After the game, he issued a complaint to AL president Ban Johnson about Cobb's overaggressive style of play. Cobb received a warning from Johnson and death threats from fans the next time the Tigers visited Philadelphia.

In 1909, a banner year for controversy, Cobb got into a fight with a hotel night watchman named George Stanfield. A warrant was issued for Cobb's arrest, and he avoided a charge of attempted murder by skipping town. Stanfield filed a civil suit, which was settled out of court. The criminal charge was resolved when Cobb pled guilty to a lesser offense in court.

Cobb's tremendous unpopularity came back to bite him in 1910, when members of the St. Louis Browns plotted to rob him of a batting crown. Believing he held a secure lead over Napoléon Lajoie of Cleveland, Cobb sat out the last game of the season. Chalmers Automotive, a Detroit-based company, had offered a new car to the winner, making the title especially appealing that year. With his team scheduled to face the Naps (later known as the Indians) at home in a doubleheader, Browns' manager Jack O'Connor saw an opportunity to get back at baseball's reigning schoolyard bully. He instructed rookie third-sacker Red Corriden to play back near the edge of the outfield grass every time Lajoie came to bat. Taking advantage of this charitable gesture, Lajoie beat out several bunts, boosting his average considerably. Browns' pitching coach Harry Howell reportedly attempted to bribe the official scorer to give Lajoie an extra hit, but the offer was refused. It appeared to be of no consequence when newspapers prematurely declared Lajoie the batting champion by less than a percentage point over Cobb.

Smelling a rat, AL president Ban Johnson detained O'Connor and Corriden for questioning. Corriden was absolved, but Howell and O'Connor were banished. When the *Sporting News* published the official season averages, Cobb was declared the winner by a small margin. The Chalmers company gave cars to both contenders, and Lajoie later joked: "The automobile I got ran a lot better than the one they gave Ty."

In 1912, Cobb sealed his reputation as an ogre when he went into the stands and attacked a crippled fan in New York. After taking his center-field post during a May contest at Hilltop Park, the hot-tempered fly chaser was subjected to a continuous flow of personal insults from a disabled man named Claude Luecker. Several innings into the game, "the Georgia Peach" warned umpire Silk O'Loughlin that there would be trouble if the man was not removed from the grounds. When Luecker's malicious barbs continued, Cobb completely lost control. Climbing 12 rows into the stands, the reigning AL batting champ viciously assaulted his antagonist, who had only three fingers as a result of an unfortunate industrial accident. Policemen pried Cobb off the helpless fan, and he was later suspended indefinitely. "A ballplayer should not be expected to take everything," he told reporters, "as we have some self-respect and we cannot endure more than human nature will stand for."

When Tiger players went on strike in support of the club's brightest star, manager Hughie Jennings was forced to send a unit composed mainly of college players into action against the Philadelphia Athletics. The result was a 24–2 massacre. Regular players were reinstated soon afterward as Cobb's suspension was eventually reduced to 10 days.

Though Cobb was universally despised by opponents and teammates, it was a popular attitude among Southerners to perceive him as defender of the South's honor against the "damn Yankees" of the North. Reflecting on his career later in life, Cobb remarked: "I had to fight my entire life to survive. They were all against me. But I beat the bastards and left them in a ditch."

Cobb beat Buck Herzog of the Giants in 1917 after an on-field altercation during a spring training game led to a challenge from Herzog to settle their dispute in Cobb's hotel room. Herzog showed up with teammate Heinie Zimmerman while Cobb recruited eight Detroit players for support. Herzog reportedly knocked Cobb down, but Cobb climbed to his feet and pummeled the second baseman into submission. After the bout, Cobb refused to participate in the remaining exhibition games against the Giants.

It would not be the last time Cobb refused to play. According to teammate Davy Jones, "the Georgia Peach" was in a slump one season and facing Ray Collins of Boston—a pitcher he had never hit particularly well. Stationed at first base, Jones watched intently for a hit-and-run sign from Cobb that never came. After the first pitch, Cobb yelled loudly down to first base that Jones had missed his phantom signal. When the next pitch came in for strike two, Cobb skulked to the dugout, where he sat down and declined to play on the grounds that Jones was not responding to his signs. "All he wanted, of course, was to get out of that game because he couldn't hit that pitcher," Jones told historian Lawrence Ritter. Still sulking the next day, Cobb was ordered by owner Frank Navin to take the field.

In 1921, Cobb got a chance to call the shots when he accepted the position of player/manager for the Tigers. The team never seriously contended during his time in charge, but he was credited with the development of several players, most notably Hall of Famer Harry Heilmann. After a respectable 79–75 finish in 1926, Cobb stepped down as manager. The cause of his abrupt decision soon became public when pitcher Hubert "Dutch" Leonard accused both Cobb and Tris Speaker of conspiring with Cleveland outfielder Joe Wood to fix a 1919 game. Leonard provided compelling evidence, including a letter written by Wood during the season in question. Cobb was cited in the document as being involved, but Wood had made it clear that he had not placed a bet. Both Speaker and Cobb were absolved of any misconduct when Leonard refused to come to Chicago and face the two in court.

Retiring for good after the 1928 campaign, Cobb lived in relative splendor thanks to investments he had made in various commodities, which included cotton and Coca-Cola. When sports writer Al Stump was recruited to assist Cobb in writing his autobiography in 1960, the former outfielder was splitting time between two stately homes in Atherton, California, and Lake Tahoe, Nevada. Estranged from his children, he lived without electric lights and telephone service in both. Stump had agreed to take the assignment despite the many cautionary tales circulating about Cobb's foul temper—how he had booby-trapped his California home with high voltage wires and torn apart a local butcher shop one day after he purchased some fish he was dissatisfied with.

While Stump was working on the memoirs, Cobb was unsteady on his feet and had taken to self-medicating with alcohol and prescription pills. He refused the hospital. The failing baseball legend began each day with several gin and orange juices before switching to scotch. At night, he consumed cognac, champagne, or "Cobb cocktails," a mixture of Southern Comfort, water, and honey.

He frequently objected to what Stump had written even if he had dictated the material himself. Because he carried more clout with the editor, his alterations to the work were readily accepted. Much of what appeared in *My Life in Baseball: The True Record* had been altered to the point of inaccuracy. One of Cobb's most chilling revelations to Stump was an account of how he had killed a man in Detroit early one morning after being jumped in an alley by three thugs (a story that was likely exaggerated). Cobb was allegedly carrying a gun, but it wouldn't fire, and he was knifed in the back by one of the men.

In the spring of 1961, Cobb made his final rounds accompanied by Stump. A large portion of their adventure appeared in the movie *Cobb*, starring Tommy Lee Jones. Together, Cobb and the writer visited casinos, bars, and spring training camps. Cobb threw out the first ball at the Angels/Twins season opener that year. As players moved in close to catch what they assumed would be a feeble toss, Cobb deliberately whipped the ball over their heads. Toward the very end, Cobb became somewhat remorseful, commenting that he had perhaps been a bit too aggressive during his playing days. He stated for the record that if he had his life to live over again, he would have done things differently. "If I had, I believe I would have had more friends," he said wistfully.

APPENDIX A

Pitching Statistics of Featured Players

	W	L	ERA	CG	ShO	SV	IP	H	BB	SO
Don Wilson	104	92	3.15	78	20	2	1748.1	1479	64	1283
Donnie Moore	43	40	3.67	0	0	89	654.2	698	186	416
Juan Marichal	243	142	2.89	244	52	2	3507	3153	709	2303
Pedro Martínez	219	100	2.93	46	17	3	2827.1	2221	760	3154
Ben Christensen*	12	19	4.64	1	0	0	290.2	285	133	241
Lefty Williams	82	48	3.13	80	10	5	1186	1121	347	515
Eddie Cicotte	209	148	2.38	249	35	25	3223.1	2897	827	1374
Jim Bouton	62	63	3.57	57	11	6	1238.2	1131	435	720
Dolf Luque	194	179	3.24	206	26	28	3220.1	3231	918	1130
Early Wynn	300	244	3.54	66	49	15	4564	4291	1775	2334
Dizzy Dean	150	83	3.02	154	26	30	1967.1	1919	453	1163
Carl Mays	208	126	2.92	231	29	31	3021.1	2912	734	862
Johnny Allen	142	75	3.75	109	17	18	1950.1	1849	738	1070
Lefty Grove	300	141	3.06	298	35	55	3940.2	3849	1187	2266
John Rocker	13	22	3.42	0	0	88	255.1	200	164	332
Jack Chesbro	198	132	2.68	260	35	5	2896.2	2647	690	1265
Burleigh Grimes	270	212	3.53	314	35	18	4180	4412	1295	1512

(*) Indicates Minor League Statistics

APPENDIX B

Managerial Records

	Won	Lost	Win Pct.	Titles
George Stallings	879	898	.495	1 Pennant / 1 W. Series
Ossie Vitt	262	198	.570	None
Eddie Stanky	467	435	.518	None
Billy Martin	1253	1013	.553	2 Pennants / 1 W. Series
John McGraw	2763	1948	.586	10 Pennants / 3 W. Series
Leo Durocher	2008	1709	.540	3 Pennants / 1 W. Series
Ned Hanlon	1313	1164	.530	5 Pennants / 2 Temple Cups
Lee Elia	127	158	.446	None

APPENDIX C

~

Batting Statistics of Featured Players

	BA	AB	R	H	2B	3B	HR	RBI	SB
Marty Bergen	.265	1278	180	339	44	15	10	176	24
Johnny Mostil	.301	3507	618	1054	209	82	23	376	176
Eddie Waitkus	.285	4254	528	1214	215	44	24	373	28
Chick Stahl	.305	5069	858	1546	219	118	36	622	189
Len Koenecke	.297	922	155	274	49	9	22	114	11
Roberto Alomar	.300	9073	1508	2724	504	80	210	1134	474
César Cedeño	.285	7310	1084	2087	436	60	199	976	550
Randall Simon	.283	1609	172	455	71	3	49	237	2
Jose Canseco	.266	7057	1186	1877	340	14	462	1407	200
Joe Jackson	.356	4981	873	1772	307	168	54	785	202
Buck Weaver	.272	4809	623	1308	198	69	21	420	173
Chick Gandil	.277	4245	449	1176	173	78	11	557	151
Swede Risberg	.243	1619	196	394	72	27	6	175	52
Happy Felsch	.293	2812	385	825	135	64	38	446	88
Fred McMullin	.256	914	120	234	21	9	1	70	31
Hal Chase	.291	7417	980	2158	322	124	57	941	363
Pete Rose	.303	14053	2165	4256	746	135	160	1314	198
Heinie Zimmerman	.295	5304	695	1566	275	105	58	796	175

Kevin Mitchell	.284	4134	630	1173	224	25	234	760	30
Dave Kingman	.236	6677	901	1575	240	25	442	1210	85
Vince Coleman	.264	5406	849	1425	176	89	28	346	752
Carl Everett	.271	4809	707	1304	258	26	202	792	107
Milton Bradley	.271	3605	541	976	202	17	125	481	88
Ernie Lombardi	.306	5855	601	1792	277	27	190	990	8
Bill Buckner	.289	9397	1077	2715	498	49	174	1208	183
Mickey Owen	.255	3649	338	929	163	21	41	378	36
Roger Peckinpaugh	.259	7233	1006	1876	256	75	48	739	205
Fred Merkle	.273	5782	720	1580	290	81	61	733	272
Joe Medwick	.324	7635	1198	2471	540	113	205	1383	42
Albert Belle	.295	5853	974	1726	389	21	381	1239	88
John McGraw	.334	3924	1024	1309	121	70	13	462	436
Hughie Jennings	.312	4895	992	1526	232	88	18	840	359
Willie Keeler	.341	8591	1719	2932	241	145	33	810	495
Dan Brouthers	.342	6711	1523	2296	460	205	106	1296	256
Joe Kelley	.317	7066	1421	2220	358	194	65	1194	443
Wilbert Robinson	.275	5075	637	1388	212	51	18	722	186
Ty Cobb	.366	11434	2246	4189	724	295	117	1938	897

Bibliography

Chapter 1

Baseball-reference.com.

Baseballinwartime.com.

Thedeadballera.com.

"Who Was the Greatest Catcher?" *Pittsburgh Press*, February 6, 1929.

"Bergen's Tragic End." *Morning Herald*, January 20, 1900.

"Cheerful Chicago." *Sporting Life*, July 2, 1898.

McKenna, Brian. "Marty Bergen." SABR Baseball Biography Project. SABR: Society for American Baseball Research. sabr.org/bioproj/person/c19ac6cc.

James, Bill. *The New Bill James Historical Baseball Abstract*. New York: Free Press, 2003.

McKenna, Brian. "Johnny Mostil, A Troubling Time." Glimpses into Baseball History (blog). baseballhistoryblog.com.

"The Strange Case of Johnny Mostil." Misc. Baseball (blog). miscbaseball.wordpress.com.

Margalus, Jim. "Johnny Mostil: From the Hall of Fame Library Files." White Sox History. South Side Sox, a Chicago White Sox Community. southsidesox.com.

"Johnny Mostil Attempts Suicide." *New York Times*, March 9, 1927.

Goldman, Steve. "DPOTD: Ever Make Love to a Hall of Famer's Wife?" You Can Blog It Up, Baseball Prospectus, June 14, 2010. baseballprospectus.com.

Corbett, Warren. "Ted Lyons." SABR Baseball Biography Project. SABR: Society for American Baseball Research. sabr.org/bioproj/person/b3442150.

Obituaries, *Sporting News*, December 26, 1970.

Associated Press. "Mostil Slashes at Throat and Wrists in Suicide Effort." March 9, 1927.

Weeks, Jon. "Johnny Mostil." SABR Baseball Biography Project. SABR: Society for American Baseball Research. sabr.org/bioproj/person/9650ff1e.

Francis, Philip C. "The Eddie Waitkus Affair." Chatter from the Dugout (blog), September 15, 2005. chatterfromthedugout.com.

United Press International. "Waitkus, Philly Star, Shot by Girl." June 15, 1949.

United Press International. "Waitkus Case Recalls Shooting of Jurges." June 15, 1949.

Associated Press. "Girl Who Shot Eddie Waitkus Ruled Insane." June 30, 1949.

Associated Press. "Eddie Waitkus Termed Good." June 20, 1949.

Associated Press. "Waitkus Assailant Now Sane." March 26, 1952.

United Press International. "Waitkus Refused Compensation Pay." May 16, 1952.

United Press International. "Chicago Girl Warned Mother of Plans." June 15, 1949.

Associated Press. "Wilson of Astros Is Found Dead." January 6, 1975.

Pietruscza, David, et al. Baseball: The Biographical Encyclopedia. Sport Media Publishing, 2003.

"Houston Astros Don Wilson and His Possible Suicide in 1975." Misc. Baseball (blog). miscbaseball.wordpress.com.

Lynch, Mike. "The Mysterious and Tragic Death of Don Wilson." Seamheads.com, October 12, 2010. seamheads.com/2010/10/12/the-mysterious-and-tragic-death-of-don-wilson/.

Auger, Dennis. "Chick Stahl." SABR Baseball Biography Project. SABR: Society for American Baseball Research. sabr.org/bioproj/person/e96a130c.

"I've Done What Chick Stahl Did." New York Times, March 29, 1907.

"Slain Woman's Jewelry Gone." The Day, November 16, 1908.

"Chick Stahl, a Suicide, Takes Carbolic Acid at West Baden." New York Times, March 28, 1907.

"Suicide Follows Stahl's." The Sun, March 31, 1907.

"Mrs. Chick Stahl Found Dead." The Sun, November 17, 1908.

Associated Press. "Koenecke, Ball Player, Is Killed in Plane as He Attacks Crew." September 17, 1935.

Associated Press. "Koenecke's Pilot Is Held as Slayer." September 17, 1935.

Almond, Elliot, and Mike Penner. "Donnie Moore Dies in Apparent Suicide: Home Run in 1986 Playoffs Haunted Moore, Agent Says." Los Angeles Times, July 19, 1989.

Associated Press. "Ex-Angel Pitcher Moore Shoots Wife, Commits Suicide." July 19, 1989.

Hofstetter, Steve. "Just a Game? The Tragic Story of Donnie Moore." Steve Hofstetter's official website, April 28, 2002. stevehofstetter.com/unpublished.cfm?ID=52.

Baker, Kevin. "The Myth of the Home Run That Drove an Angels Pitcher to Suicide." Atlantic, October 27, 2011. theatlantic.com.

Holoman, Diana. "Retracing the Sad Saga of a Lubbock Baseball Legend." Fox 34 News, December 16, 2011. myfoxlubbock.com.

Chapter 2

Baseball-reference.com.

Aldfoundation.org.

Associated Press. "Cubs Manager Apologizes for Blasting Fans." April 30, 1983.

Edes, Gordon. "The Bleeps Hit the Fans as Cubs Lose." Associated Press, April 30, 1983.

"25 Years Later, Elia Rant Still Legendary." The New Editor (blog), March 21, 2008. theneweditor.com.

"Cubs' Lee Elia's Rant Remembered 28 Years Later." CBS Chicago, April 29, 2011. chicago.cbslocal.com.

Drehs, Wayne. "Fans Won't Let Elia Forget Meltdown." *ESPN*, April 29, 2008. espn. go.com.

Wulf, Steve. "The Spit Hits the Fan." *Time*, June 24, 2001.

Isaac, A. "Famous Spitting Incidents." Guyism, November 16, 2010. guyism.com.

Nightengale, Bob. "Roberto Alomar, Bert Blyleven Voted into the Hall of Fame." *USA Today*, January 5, 2011. usatoday.com.

Augustine, Bernie. "Did Spitting Incident Keep Alomar Out of Hall of Fame on First Try?" SILive.com, January 6, 2010. silive.com.

Wilson, John. "Cesar Cedeno . . . the Next Superstar?" *Sporting News*, August 19, 1972.

"The Drama of Cesar Cedeno's Baseball Career." Centerfield maz (blog), February 26, 2009. centerfieldmaz.com.

"Sports Criminals: Cesar Cedeno." PiratesWFC (blog), April 16, 2010. pirateswfc. blogspot.com.

United Press International. "Cedeno Attacks Fan." September 9, 1981.

United Press International. "Dodgers Smith Fined, Benched." September 29, 1981.

Neft, David S., Richard M. Cohen, and Michael L. Neft. *The Sports Encyclopedia: Baseball 2000*. New York: St. Martin's, 2000.

James, Bill. *The New Bill James Historical Baseball Abstract*. New York: Free Press, 2003.

"Juan Marichal." Latino Legends in Sports. latinosportslegends.com.

"The Fight between Juan Marichal and John Roseboro." Misc. Baseball (blog). misc baseball.wordpress.com.

Pietrusza, David, et al. *Baseball: The Biographical Encyclopedia*. Sport Media Publishing, 2003.

Koppett, Leonard. "Marichal Clubs Roseboro with a Bat." *New York Times*, August 22, 1965.

"Simon Says: Infielder Apologizes, Fined for Sausage Race Attack." *Sports Illustrated*, July 10, 2003. sportsillustrated.cnn.com.

"Doing the Time: Simon Suspended 3 Games for Sausage Incident." *Sports Illustrated*, July 11, 2003. sportsillustrated.cnn.com.

"Simon Won't Be Charged for Hitting Sausage with Bat." CBS SportsLine.com, July 10, 2003. cbssports.com/mlb/story/6473428.

"Head Games: Frustrated Martinez Succumbs to Yankee Domination after Latest Loss." *Sports Illustrated*, September 28, 2004. sportsillustrated.cnn.com.

Blum, Ron. "Martinez, Ramirez, Zimmer and Garcia Fined for Game 3 Flap." *USA Today*, October 12, 2003.

Doxsie, Don. "A Decade after Blinding Pitch, Anthony Molina Says He Misses Competition." *Quad-City Times*, April 22, 2009.

Callis, Jim. "Molina Settles with Christensen." *Baseball America*, February 5, 2002. baseballamerica.com.

Bialik, Carl. "Don't You Dare Time My Pitches." *Yale Herald*, September 3, 1999. yaleherald.com.

Chapter 3

Baseball-reference.com.

Baseball-almanac.com.

Thedeadballera.com.

Ballparksofbaseball.com.

Jimbouton.com.

Baseballlibrary.com.

Chaseplace.iwarp.com.

Cmgww.com/baseball/wynn/quotes.html.

Encyclopediaofarkansas.net.

Baseballhall.org.

Baseball.wikia.com.

Verdi, Bob. "Inaction Is MLB's Reaction to 'Juiced.'" *Chicago Tribune*, February 27, 2005.

Motako, Rich. "Canseco Swaps Publishers for His Sequel to 'Juiced.'" *New York Times*, January 11, 2008.

Christian, Red. "Jose Canseco Was Busted for Same Drug That Led to Manny Ramirez's Ban." *New York Daily News*, May 7, 2009.

"Jose Canseco: 'This Book Is Devastating.'" *Today*, February 23, 2005. today.msnbc.msn.com.

Canseco, Jose. *Juiced: Wild Times, Rampant 'Roids, Smash Hits, and How Baseball Got Big*. New York: William Morrow, 2005.

Canseco, Jose. *Vindicated: Big Names, Big Liars, and the Battle to Save Baseball*. New York: Gallery Books, 2008.

Fainaru-Wada, Mark, and Lance Williams. *Game of Shadows*. New York: Gotham, 2007.

Goldfarb, Irv. "Charlie Comiskey." SABR Baseball Biography Project. SABR: Society for American Baseball Research. sabr.org/bioproj/person/8fbc6b31.

Sagert, Kelly Boyer, and Rod Nelson. "Swede Risberg." SABR Baseball Biography Project. SABR: Society for American Baseball Research. sabr.org/bioproj/person/fde3d63f.

Ginsburg, Daniel. "Chick Gandil." SABR Baseball Biography Project. SABR: Society for American Baseball Research. sabr.org/bioproj/person/945ce343.

Lowitt, Bruce. "Black Sox Scandal: Chicago Throws 1919 World Series." *St. Petersburg Times*, December 22, 1999.

Asinof, Eliot. *Eight Men Out: The Black Sox and the 1919 World Series*. New York: Henry Holt, 1963.

Pietrusza, David. *Rothstein: The Life, Times, and Murder of the Criminal Genius Who Fixed the 1919 World Series*. New York: Carroll and Graf, 2003.

Bouton, Jim. *Ball Four: The Final Pitch*. Bulldog, 2001.

Olbermann, Keith. "All Is Finally Forgiven." *Sports Illustrated*, August 3, 1998.

Armour, Mark. "Jim Bouton." SABR Baseball Biography Project. SABR: Society for American Baseball Research. sabr.org/bioproj/person/75723b1f.

Pietrusza, David, et al. *Baseball: The Biographical Encyclopedia*. Sport Media Publishing, 2003.

Kohout, Martin. "Hal Chase." SABR Baseball Biography Project. SABR: Society for American Baseball Research. sabr.org/bioproj/person/aab1d59b.

Lobner, Kyle. "Hal Chase: Prince Hal." Baseball Almanac. baseball-almanac.com.

Deadball Era Committee of the Society for American Baseball Research. *Deadball Stars of the American League*. Edited by David Jones. Dulles, VA: Potomac Books, 2006.

James, Bill. *The New Bill James Historical Baseball Abstract*. New York: Free Press, 2003.

Rose, Pete, and Rick Hill. *My Prison without Bars*. Emmaus, PA: Rodale Books, 2004.

Sokolove, Michael. *Hustle: The Myth, Life, and Lies of Pete Rose*. New York: Simon and Schuster, 2005.

Kaplan, Robert. "Review: My Prison without Bars." bookreporter.com, January 8, 2004.

"Rose Admits to Betting on Reds 'Every Night.'" *ESPN*, March 16, 2007. espn.go.com.

Jones, David. "Heinie Zimmerman." SABR Baseball Biography Project. SABR: Society for American Baseball Research. sabr.org/bioproj/person/e73e465a.

Zingler, David. "Banished: Heinie Zimmerman." Simply Baseball Notebook, etc. (blog). z.lee28.tripod.com/therest/heiniezimmerman.html.

Reeves, Grant T. "Clubhouse Gossip." *Baseball Magazine* 19, no. 4 (1917).

Lewis, Jerry D. "Hush Money Kept Heinie Zimmerman's Mouth—and at Times His Bat—Quiet." *Sports Illustrated*, September 24, 1984.

Chapter 4

Neft, David S., Richard M. Cohen, and Michael L. Neft. *The Sports Encyclopedia: Baseball 2000*. New York: St. Martin's, 2000.

"Adolfo 'Dolf' Luque: The Pride of Havana." Mop-Up Duty, November 3, 2010. mopupduty.com.

Bjarkman, Peter C. "Dolf Luque." SABR Baseball Biography Project. SABR: Society for American Baseball Research. sabr.org/bioproj/person/29c1fec2.

Newspaper Enterprise Association. "Early Wynn Turned into Bitter Man." April 15, 1971.

Associated Press. "Hall of Famers Surprised by Election." January 20, 1972.

Freedman, Lew. *Early Wynn, the Go-Go White Sox and the 1959 World Series*. Jefferson, NC: McFarland, 2009.

Fleitz, David. "Early Wynn." SABR Baseball Biography Project. SABR: Society for American Baseball Research. sabr.org/bioproj/person/6d0d8788.

Nash, Bruce, and Allan Zullo. *The Baseball Hall of Shame*. New York: Pocket Books, 1985.

Leonard, Mary Delach. "Who Owns This Field of Dreams?" *St. Louis Beacon*, March 30, 2011. stlbeacon.org.

Feldmann, Doug. *Dizzy and the Gas House Gang: The 1934 St. Louis Cardinals and Depression-Era Baseball*. Jefferson, NC: McFarland, 2000.

Smith, Curt. *America's Dizzy Dean*. St. Louis: Chalice Press, 1978.

"'Dizzy' Dean." The Encyclopedia of Arkansas History and Culture. encyclopediaofarkansas.net.

James, Bill. *The New Bill James Historical Baseball Abstract*. New York: Free Press, 2003.

Neft David S., Richard M. Cohen, and Michael L. Neft. *The Sports Encyclopedia: Baseball 2000*. New York: St. Martin's, 2000.

Berby, Richard. "Mays' Beaning of Chapman Recounted." *Baseball Research Journal* (1984). sabr.org/content/baseball-research-journal-archives.

Wood, Allan. "Carl Mays." SABR Baseball Biography Project. SABR: Society for American Baseball Research. sabr.org/bioproj/person/99ca7c89.

Sowell, Mike. *The Pitch That Killed*. New York: Macmillan, 1989.

Capel, Wint. *Fiery Fastballer: The Life of Johnny Allen, World Series Pitcher*. Lincoln, NE: iUniverse, 2001.

Associated Press. "Cleveland Club Asks Protection for Allen." May 13, 1936.

Leib, Fred. "Johnny Allen Hated to Lose." *St. Petersburg Times*, May 4, 1964.

Boyle, Havey J. "Allen's Attack on Umpire Barr Causes One of Worst Brawls Ever." *Pittsburgh Post Gazette*, May 28, 1943.

United Press International. "Allen, Former Major League Pitcher Dies." March 30, 1959.

Associated Press. "Johnny Allen Finally Loses the Big Game." March 29, 1959.

Goldman, Steve. "Gamesmanship, Dammit." You Could Look It Up. Baseball Prospectus, June 2, 2004. baseballprospectus.com.

Popelka, Greg. "Tribe Game Vault: 6/7/38: The Great Johnny Allen Torn Shirt Controversy." The Cleveland Fan, June 20, 2012. theclevelandfan.com.

"Johnny Allen, Who Hated Umps, Now Will Try Their Job Himself." *Milwaukee Journal*, March 17, 1949.

Lieb, Frederick G. "Johnny Allen: Rhubarber to Ump." *Sporting News*, December 31, 1952.

Weeks, Jon. "Johnny Allen." SABR Baseball Biography Project. SABR: Society for American Baseball Research. sabr.org/bioproj/person/4bb1afb9.

Smith, Red. The "New York Times" Book of Sports Legends. Edited by Joseph Vecchione. New York: Fireside, 1991.

Kaplan, Jim. Lefty Grove: American Original. Cleveland: Society for American Baseball Research, 2000.

Smith, Red. The "New York Times" Book of Sports Legends. Edited by Joseph Vecchione. New York: Fireside, 1991.

Chapter 5

Baseballlibrary.com.

Baseball-reference.com.

Baseball-almanac.com.

Johnrocker.net.

Davekingmanfan.com.

Dodgerblues.com.

Pearlman, Jeff. The Bad Guys Won! New York: HarperCollins, 2004.

Gooden, Dwight, and Bob Klapisch. Heat: My Life On and Off the Diamond. New York: William Morrow, 1999.

"Kevin Mitchell—at Home in the Hood—New Mariner Escaped the Ghetto, Not Questions about Him and His Friends." Seattle Times, February 16, 1992.

Associated Press. "Mitchell's Friend Arrested for Murder." September 18, 1991.

"7 in Sacramento Region Top Delinquent Tax List; Pamela Anderson and Former Baseball Player Kevin Mitchell Also Owe State." Sacramento Business Journal, April 12, 2010.

Madden, Bill, Michael Smith, and Leo Standora. "Rocker's Out! Barred till May 1 for His Racial Slurs." New York Daily News, February 1, 2000.

"The Rocker Files: A Chronology of John Rocker's Last Three Months." Sports Illustrated, March 2000. sportsillustrated.cnn.com.

Pearlman, Jeff. "John Rocker." Jeffpearlman.com (blog), February 6, 2012.

Rocker, John, and J. Marshall Craig. Rocker: Scars and Strikes. RMC Publishing, 2011.

Pearlman, Jeff. "At Full Blast." Sports Illustrated, December 23, 1999. sportsillustrated.cnn.com.

Associated Press. "Rocker Sorry for Remarks." August 6, 2002.

Silva, Mike. "John Rocker on New Book, the Mets, Bud Selig, Steroids, and Politics." Mike Silva's New York Baseball Digest, December 12, 2011. nybaseballdigest.com.

Callan, Mathew. "Me Elsewhere: John Rocker and Johan Santana Together at Last." Scratchbomb.com (blog), June 6, 2012.

Anderson, Dave. "Kingman, Schmidt Give Baseball Shot." New York Times, April 25, 1976.

Associated Press. "Kingman Fined $3,500." June 25, 1986.

Hummer, Steve. "Anything Is Possible except Met Collapse." *Sun Sentinel*, July 16, 1986.

Treder, Steve. "Where Did Kong Go Wrong?" The Hardball Times, April 5, 2005. thehardballtimes.com.

Associated Press. "Coleman Charged with Tossing Fireworks." August 4, 1993.

Sexton, Joe. "Coleman Reads Apology Script." *New York Times* News Service, July 30, 1993.

Sexton, Joe. "Baseball: Coleman's Tarnished Met Career Is Finished." *New York Times*, August 27, 1993.

Associated Press. "Stains Linking Gooden to Dress May Not Be Enough for Rape Case." April 4, 1992.

Schmuck, Peter. "Mets Sign Coleman to Four-Year Pact." *Baltimore Sun*, December 6, 1990.

Donaghy, Jim. "Mets Can't Escape World of Reality." Associated Press, March 19, 1992.

Associated Press. "Coleman Enters Plea Agreement." November 5, 1993.

Associated Press. "Vince Coleman Has Career of Conflicts." July 27, 1993.

Hummel, Rick. "Press Club: Papers' Punches Keep Mets Reeling Herr Says." *St. Louis Dispatch*, August 11, 1991.

Luft, Jacob. "The World according to Carl Everett." *Sports Illustrated*, June 16, 2005. sportsillustrated.cnn.com.

Silva, Drew. "Carl Everett Arrested on Domestic Violence Charges." Hardball Talk, September 8, 2011. hardballtalk.nbcsports.com.

Borelli, Steve. "Carl Everett Arrested; Accused of Pointing Gun at Wife." *USA Today*, April 26, 2011. usatoday.com.

Verducci, Tom. "Mighty Mouth." *Sports Illustrated*, June 19, 2000. sportsillustrated. cnn.com.

Swarns, Rachel. "Everett Girl Said to Be against Move Home." *New York Times*, August 12, 1997.

Nightengale, Bob. "Boston's Bad Boy." *USA Today Baseball Weekly*, February 28, 2001.

"Everett Rips Gays, Fans, Wrigley." NBC Sports, June 25, 2005. nbcsports.msnbc. com.

Reader, Bill. "Carl Everett's Highlights and Lowlights." *Seattle Times*, December 15, 2005.

Taylor, Brett. "The End of the Milton Bradley Era: A Portrait of the Player as a Young Man." Bleacher Nation, December 21, 2009. bleachernation.com.

Yellon, Al. "The Lesson of Milton Bradley." *Chicago Cubs News*, May 9, 2011.

Brewer, Jerry. "No Hits, No Mulligans: Why Milton Bradley's Career Is Over." *Seattle Times*, May 9, 2011.

Associated Press. "Bradley Returns after Two Weeks Away." May 20, 2010.

Baker, Geoff. "Milton Bradley to Mariners: 'Can You Help Me?'" *Seattle Times*, May 5, 2010.

Remington, Alex. "Milton Bradley and the Race Card." FanGraphs, May 12, 2011. fangraphs.com.

"Bradley Injured after Getting Tossed." MLB.com, September 23, 2007.

Associated Press. "Milton Bradley Arrested at a Home in Los Angeles." September 28, 2011.

"Latest Incident Is Final Straw." *ESPN*, April 3, 2004. espn.go.com.

Chapter 6

Baseball-reference.com.

Baseball-almanac.com.

Baseballinwartime.com.

Retrosheet.org.

Thedeadballera.com.

McElreavy, Wayne. "Jack Chesbro." SABR Baseball Biography Project. SABR: Society for American Baseball Research. sabr.org/bioproj/person/1475a701.

Associated Press. "Jack Chesbro, Pioneer of Spitball Hurlers and Ace of Old Highlanders Dies of Heart Attack." November 7, 1931.

"Chesbro Chief." *Sporting Life*, January 7, 1905.

Koelsch, W. F. "Metropolitan Mention." *Sporting Life*, February 11, 1905.

Neft, David S., Richard M. Cohen, and Michael L. Neft. *The Sports Encyclopedia: Baseball 2000*. New York: St. Martin's, 2000.

Pietrusza, David, et al. *Baseball: The Biographical Encyclopedia*. Sport Media Publishing, 2003.

United Press International. "Ernie Lombardi Honored in Death." March 11, 1986.

Bingham, Walter. "Those Were the Days . . . Seriously." *Cape Cod Times*, October 20, 2011.

Goldman, Steve. "The Unintended Consequences of Defunct Catchers." You Could Look It Up. Baseball Prospectus, July 22, 2008. baseballprospectus.com.

James, Bill. *The New Bill James Historical Baseball Abstract*. New York: Free Press, 2003.

Massey, Ken. "25 Facts about Ernie Lombardi." Red Reporter, a Cincinnati Reds Community, July 22, 2001. redreporter.com.

"The Game I'll Never Forget: Bill Buckner as Told to George Vass." *Baseball Digest*, April 1981.

Associated Press. "Buckner Sent to Red Sox." May 26, 1984.

Associated Press. "Buckner Throws Out First Pitch as Red Sox Hand Out Bling." April 9, 2008.

Brooks, Anthony. "Bill Buckner Is Back in New England and Back in Baseball." Radio Boston, July 11, 2011. radioboston.wbur.org.

Jezierny, Nick. "Demons Haunt Buckner the Scapegoat." *The Telegraph*, October 31, 2004.

Associated Press. "Buckner's Series Error Costs Actor Sheen $93,500." August 5, 1992.

Goldstein, Richard. "Mickey Owen Dies at 89, Allowed Fateful Passed Ball." *New York Times*, July 15, 2005.

Deadball Era Committee of the Society for American Baseball Research. *Deadball Stars of the American League*. Edited by David Jones. Dulles, VA: Potomac Books, 2006.

Gordon, Peter. "Roger Peckinpaugh." SABR Baseball Biography Project. SABR: Society for American Baseball Research. sabr.org/bioproj/person/829dbefb.

Leventhal, Josh. *The World Series: An Illustrated Encyclopedia of the Fall Classic*. New York: Black Dog and Leventhal, 2001.

Anderson, David. *More Than Merkle*. Lincoln: University of Nebraska Press, 2000.

Deadball Era Committee of the Society for American Baseball Research. *Deadball Stars of the National League*. Edited by Tom Simon. Washington, DC: Brassey's, 2004.

Cameron, Mike. *Public Bonehead, Private Hero: The Real Legacy of Baseball's Fred Merkle*. Crystal Lake, IL: Sporting Chance, 2010.

Chapter 7

Baseballlibrary.com.

Baseball-reference.com.

Baseball-almanac.com.

Thedeadballera.com.

Oaklandoaks.tripod.com.

Pietrusza, David, et al. *Baseball: The Biographical Encyclopedia*. Sport Media Publishing, 2003.

Cataneo, David. *Peanuts and Crackerjack: A Treasury of Baseball Legends and Lore*. Nashville, TN: Rutledge Hill, 1991.

Menke, Frank G. "Stallings Not Backward in Censuring Players." *Clearfield Progress*, October 3, 1914.

Kohout, Martin. "George Stallings." SABR Baseball Biography Project. SABR: Society for American Baseball Research. sabr.org/bioproj/person/1caa4821.

Francis, Philip P. "The Cleveland Crybabies: Some Called Him a Nasty Little Man." Chatter from the Dugout (blog). chatterfromthedugout.com.

Johnson, Bill. "Hal Trosky." SABR Baseball Biography Project. SABR: Society for American Baseball Research. sabr.org/bioproj/person/9a6065ce.

Holmes, Dan. "Oscar Stanage: The Detroit Tigers Catcher Who Stood Up to Ty Cobb." Detroit Athletic Co. (blog), August 7, 2011. detroitathletic.com.

"The Ghost of Ossie Vitt: A One-Poem Chapbook." Poet Red Shuttleworth (blog), May 27, 2012. poetredshuttleworth.blogspot.com.

Feldman, Jay. "Of Mice and Mitts, and of a Rule That Helped to Clean Up Baseball." *Sports Illustrated*, Feb 20, 1984.

"Stanky and the Record Book." Old Time Writer (blog). oldtimewriter.com.

Durso, Joseph. "Eddie Stanky, 83, Spark Plug on 3 Pennant-Winning Teams." *New York Times*, June 7, 1999.

Liptak, Mark. "Ron Hansen Speaks!" and "J. C. Martin Speaks!" Interviews conducted by Mark Liptak. White Sox Interactive. whitesoxinteractive.com.

Spatz, Lyle. *The Team That Forever Changed Baseball and America: The 1947 Brooklyn Dodgers*. Lincoln: University of Nebraska Press, 2012.

Hartzell, Bob. "George Steinbrenner." Another Look. Baseball Prospectus, July 20, 2010. baseballprospectus.com.

Pepe, Phil. *The Ballad of Billy and George*. Guilford, CT: Lyons, 2008.

Golenbock, Peter. *George: The Poor Little Rich Boy Who Built the Yankee Empire*. Hoboken, NJ: John Wiley, 2009.

Webley, Kayla. "Hiring and Firing Billy Martin." *Time*, July 30, 2010. time.com.

Alexander, Charles C. *John McGraw*. Lincoln: University of Nebraska Press, 1995.

Deadball Era Committee of the Society for American Baseball Research. *Deadball Stars of the National League*. Edited by Tom Simon. Washington, DC: Brassey's, 2004.

Jensen, Don. "John McGraw." SABR Baseball Biography Project. SABR: Society for American Baseball Research. sabr.org/bioproj/person/fef5035f.

Shaplen, Rob. "The Nine Lives of Leo Durocher." *Sports Illustrated*, June 6, 1955.

Durocher, Leo. *Nice Guys Finish Last*. With Ed Linn. New York: Simon and Schuster, 1975.

Chapter 8

Ballparksofbaseball.com.

Baseball-reference.com.

Baseball-almanac.com.

Retrosheet.org.

Thedeadballera.com.

Baseballlibrary.com.

Brainyquote.com.

Seinfeldscripts.com.

Youtube.com.

Pietrusza, David, et al. *Baseball: The Biographical Encyclopedia*. Sport Media Publishing, 2003.

Neft, David S., Richard M. Cohen, and Michael L. Neft. *The Sports Encyclopedia: Baseball 2000*. New York: St. Martin's, 2000.

Leventhal, Josh. *Take Me Out to the Ballpark*. New York: Black Dog and Leventhal, 2000.

Associated Press. "Frick out of Picture." September 23, 1941.

Associated Press. "Frick Kills Rumors regarding Phillies." October 18, 1941.

Associated Press. "Gerry Nugent Started as 'Grandstand Manger' Now One of Shrewdest Traders in Baseball World." July 11, 1940.

"Phillies Owner William Cox Suspended for Life." Philly Sports History, March 20, 2012. phillysportshistory.com.

Thomas, Robert McG. "William D. Cox, 79, Team Owner Who Was Banned from Baseball." *New York Times*, March 30, 1989.

Holtzman, Jerome. "Turn Back the Clock . . . 1943: Owner William Cox, the Last Man Banned before Pere Rose." *Baseball Digest*, August 2004.

Corbett, Warren. "Marge Schott." SABR Baseball Biography Project. SABR: Society for American Baseball Research. sabr.org/bioproj/person/09e49f1e.

Associated Press. "The Schott Chronology." February 4, 1993.

Associated Press. "Schott Ruling Comes Too Late Critics Say." February 4, 1993.

Smith, Claire. "Baseball Bans Cincinnati Owner for a Year over Racial Remarks." *New York Times*, February 4, 1993.

"Think Everyone Hates Schott? Look Again." *USA Baseball Weekly*, June 6, 1996.

Lieb, Fred. *The Boston Red Sox*. New York: Putnam, 1947.

Levitt, Dan, Mark Armour, and Matthew Levitt. "Harry Frazee and the Red Sox." SABR Baseball Biography Project. SABR: Society for American Baseball Research. sabr.org/bioproj/harry-frazee-and-the-red-sox.

Johnson, Richard, and Glenn Stout. *Red Sox Century*. Exp. ed. New York: Houghton Mifflin, 2005.

Herzog, Brad. "Hard to Believe They Were That Bad." *Sports Illustrated*, April 19, 1999. sportsillustrated.cnn.com.

The Encyclopedia of Cleveland History. ech.cwru.edu.

Weeks, Jonathan. *Cellar Dwellers: The Worst Teams in Baseball History*. Lanham, MD: Scarecrow, 2012.

Hetrick, Thomas. *Misfits! The Cleveland Spiders in 1899*. Jefferson, NC: McFarland, 1991.

Golenbock, Peter. *George: The Poor Little Rich Boy Who Built the Yankee Empire*. Hoboken, NJ: John Wiley, 2009.

"Yankees' Steinbrenner Dies at 80." *ESPN*, July 14, 2010. espn.go.com.

McMillan, Ken. *Tales from the Yankee Dugout*. Champaign, IL: Sports Publishing, 2001.

"George Steinbrenner (1930–2010)." *ESPN*, July 13, 2010. espn.go.com.

Chapter 9

Baseball-almanac.com.

Baseballlibrary.com.

Baseball-reference.com.

Imdb.com.

Goldenrankings.com.

Retrosheet.org.

Ballparksofbaseball.com.

Cote, Joseph. "Accused Murderer Testifies." *Nashua Telegraph*, December 19, 2009.

Associated Press. "Woman Accused of Plowing Car into Group after Argument, Killing One." May 14, 2008.

Associated Press. "Suspect Wants Statement Tossed." October 13, 2009.

Cote, Joseph. "Convicted Murderer's Appeal in Hands of State Supreme Court." *Nashua Telegraph*, September 16, 2011.

Tuohy, Lynne. "New Hampshire Court Upholds Conviction in Sox-Yankees Dispute." Associated Press, November 22, 2011.

Pietrusza, David, et al. *Baseball: The Biographical Encyclopedia*. Sport Media Publishing, 2003.

Mandich, Steve. "Disco Demolition Night: A Midsummer Nightmare." *Roctober*, Winter 2003.

Caple, Jim. "Dropping the Ka-Boom." *ESPN*, July 9, 2004. espn.go.com.

LaPointe, Joe. "The Night Disco Went Up in Smoke." *New York Times*, July 4, 2009.

Veeck, Bill, and Ed Linn. *Veeck as in Wreck*. Chicago: University of Chicago Press, 2001.

LaPointe, Joe. "Boy Who Helped Yankees Is a Hit Again." *New York Times*, April 14, 2006.

Sheinin, Dave. "From Way Out in Right Field." *Washington Post*, May 6, 2010.

"Cutters Add Jeff Maier to Front Office Staff." *Our Sports Central*, August 10, 2006.

United Press International. "Today Is Golden Anniversary of the Girl with the Bat." July 31, 1985.

Leventhal, Josh. *Take Me Out to the Ballpark*. New York: Black Dog and Leventhal, 2000.

Seymour, Harold. *Baseball: The People's Game*. New York: Oxford University Press, 1990.

Levine, Bruce. "Cubs Hoping to Be Goatbusters." *ESPN Chicago*, June 14, 2011. espn.go.com/chicago.

Sullivan, Pat. "Cubs History Lesson for Theo Epstein." *Chicago Tribune*, October 15, 2011.

Bradley, Mickey, and Dan Gordon. *Haunted Baseball*. Guilford, CT: Lyons, 2007.

"Take Me Out: Attack at Comiskey Park." The Smoking Gun, September 1, 2002. thesmokinggun.com.

Associated Press. "Gamboa Disappointed." August 6, 2003.

Associated Press. "Gamboa Attacker Held on $200,000 Bond." September 21, 2002.

Bennett, Dashiell. "William Ligue's Son Still Proud He Beat Up That First Base Coach." Deadspin, July 17, 2009. deadspin.com.

"What the Hell Happened To: William Ligue Jr." Luol's Dong (blog), February 11, 2008. luolsdong.blogspot.com.

Associated Press. "Dybas Pleads Guilty, Gets 6 Months." December 4, 2003.

Associated Press. "Fans Misbehavior Could Be More Costly." April 23, 2003.

Associated Press. "Baseball to Review Security after Fan Violence." April 17, 2003.

Associated Press. "Bill Unanimously Approved." April 30, 2003.

Associated Press. "Man Charged for Attacking AL Umpire." April 17, 2003.

Jackson, Paul. "The Night Beer and Violence Bubbled Over in Cleveland." *ESPN*, June 4, 2008. espn.go.com.

Calcaterra, Craig. "Happy Anniversary Ten Cent Beer Night!" Hardball Talk, June 4, 2012. hardballtalk.nbcsports.com.

"Cleveland Indians' Ten Cent Beer Night: The Worst Idea Ever." Bleacher Report, March 21, 2009. bleacherreport.com.

Bennett, Dashiell. "Relive the Majesty and Terror of 'Ten-Cent Beer Night.'" Deadspin, June 4, 2009. deadspin.com.

Johnson, K. C. "The Invisible Fan." *Chicago Tribune*, September 26, 2011.

Hoekstra, Dave. "Steve Bartman Catches More Hell in *ESPN* Documentary." *Chicago Sun-Times*, September 27, 2011.

Taylor, Phil. "Bartman Wasn't Interested in Cashing In on 15 Minutes of Infamy." *Sports Illustrated*, September 29, 2011. sportsillustrated.cnn.com.

McGrath, Dan. "A Fan, A Goat and Long, Painful Memories." *New York Times*, October 1, 2011.

"Report: Alou Says He Would Not Have Caught Bartman Ball." *ESPN*, June 3, 2008. espn.go.com.

Chapter 10

Baseballlibrary.com.

Baseball-reference.com.

Thedeadballera.com.

Baseball-almanac.com.

Albertbelle.net.

Retrosheet.org.

Pietrusza, David, et al. *Baseball: The Biographical Encyclopedia*. Sport Media Publishing, 2003.

Faber, Charles. "Joe Medwick." SABR Baseball Biography Project. SABR: Society for American Baseball Research. sabr.org/bioproj/person/8fed3607.

Leventhal, Josh. *The World Series: An Illustrated Encyclopedia of the Fall Classic*. New York: Black Dog and Leventhal, 2001.

Durocher, Leo. *Nice Guys Finish Last*. With Ed Linn. Chicago: University of Chicago Press, 1975.

Faber, Charles. "Burleigh Grimes." SABR Baseball Biography Project. SABR: Society for American Baseball Research. sabr.org/bioproj/person/0957655a.

Seamon, Tobias. "The All-Bastard Athletic Club." *The Morning News*, June 10, 2002. themorningnews.org.

"Burleigh Grimes, Ex-Pitcher and Hall of Fame Member." *New York Times*, September 10, 1985.

Carter, Bob. "Belle Battled Fans, Teammates, Self." *ESPN*. espn.go.com.

Sarson, Adam. "What Might Have Been . . . Albert Belle." RealGM, February 20, 2008. realgm.com.

James, Christopher. "For Whom the Belle Tolls: Media Manipulation and the Legacy of Albert Belle." Toronto Baseball Guys (blog), January 17, 2006. torontobaseball guys.blogspot.com.

"Albert Belle Chronology." *Sports Illustrated*. sportsillustrated.cnn.com.

Patrick, Dan. "Belle Has Been the Anti-Puckett." *ESPN*, December 6, 2001. espn. go.com.

"Tim Hurst's Nerve." *Sporting Life*, April 14, 1917.

"The Humor of Baseball." *Sporting Life*, January 31, 1914.

"One of Hurst's Good Ones." *Sporting Life*, April 15, 1905.

"Tim Hurst, Sports Character, Dead." *New York Times*, June 4, 1915.

Solomon, Burt. *Where They Ain't: The Fabled Life and Untimely Death of the Original Baltimore Orioles*. New York: Free Press, 1999.

Lansche, Jerry. *Glory Fades Away*. Dallas: Taylor, 1991.

Rosenberg, Howard M. *Cap Anson 3: Muggsy McGraw and the Tricksters: Baseball's Fun Age of Rule-Bending*. Arlington, VA: Tile Books, 2005.

Stump, Al. *Cobb: A Biography*. Chapel Hill, NC: Algonquin Books, 1996.

Ritter, Lawrence. *The Glory of Their Times*. New York: Macmillan, 1966.

Ginsburg, Daniel. "Ty Cobb." SABR Baseball Biography Project. SABR: Society for American Baseball Research. sabr.org/bioproj/person/7551754a.

Alexander, Charles C. *Ty Cobb*. Sport in American Life. Dallas: Southern Methodist University Press, 2006.

Cobb, Ty. *My Life in Baseball: The True Record*. With Al Stump. Lincoln, NE: Bison Books, 1993.

Associated Press. "Detroit Team Declares Strike." May 18, 1912.

"1910: The Strangest Batting Race." Cleveland.indians.mlb.com.

"The Cobb-Lajoie Race of 1910." Ty Cobb: The Home Page. wso.williams. edu./~jkossuth/cobb/lajoie.htm.

Index

~

About the Author

Photo by Ben Bowen

Jonathan Weeks resides in Malone, New York, and works as a vocational coun-selor, assisting adults with developmental disabilities. *Baseball's Most Notorious Personalities* is his second book on the topic of baseball. Weeks has been known to regale anyone who will listen with stories of his Little League years, insisting that he could have played professionally if not for a horrible allergy to infield dust. The truth of the matter is that he wasn't particularly talented in any aspect of the game.